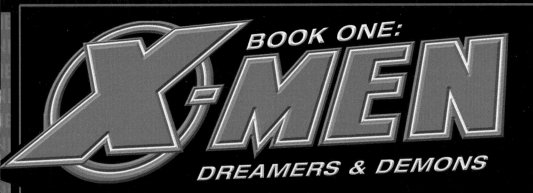

BOOK ONE:
X-MEN
DREAMERS & DEMONS

writer **CHRIS CLAREMONT**
pencils **SEAN CHEN**

inks **SANDU FLOREA**
colors **AVALON'S IAN HANNIN**
letters **DAVE SHARPE**
covers **GREG LAND**

assistant editors
ANDY SCHMIDT, NICOLE WILEY
and **MOLLY LAZER**
editor
TOM BREVOORT

collections editor
JEFF YOUNGQUIST
assistant editor
JENNIFER GRÜNWALD
director of sales
DAVID GABRIEL
production
LORETTA KROL
book designer
JEOF VITA
creative director
TOM MARVELLI

editor in chief
JOE QUESADA
publisher
DAN BUCKLEY

D1464810

#1

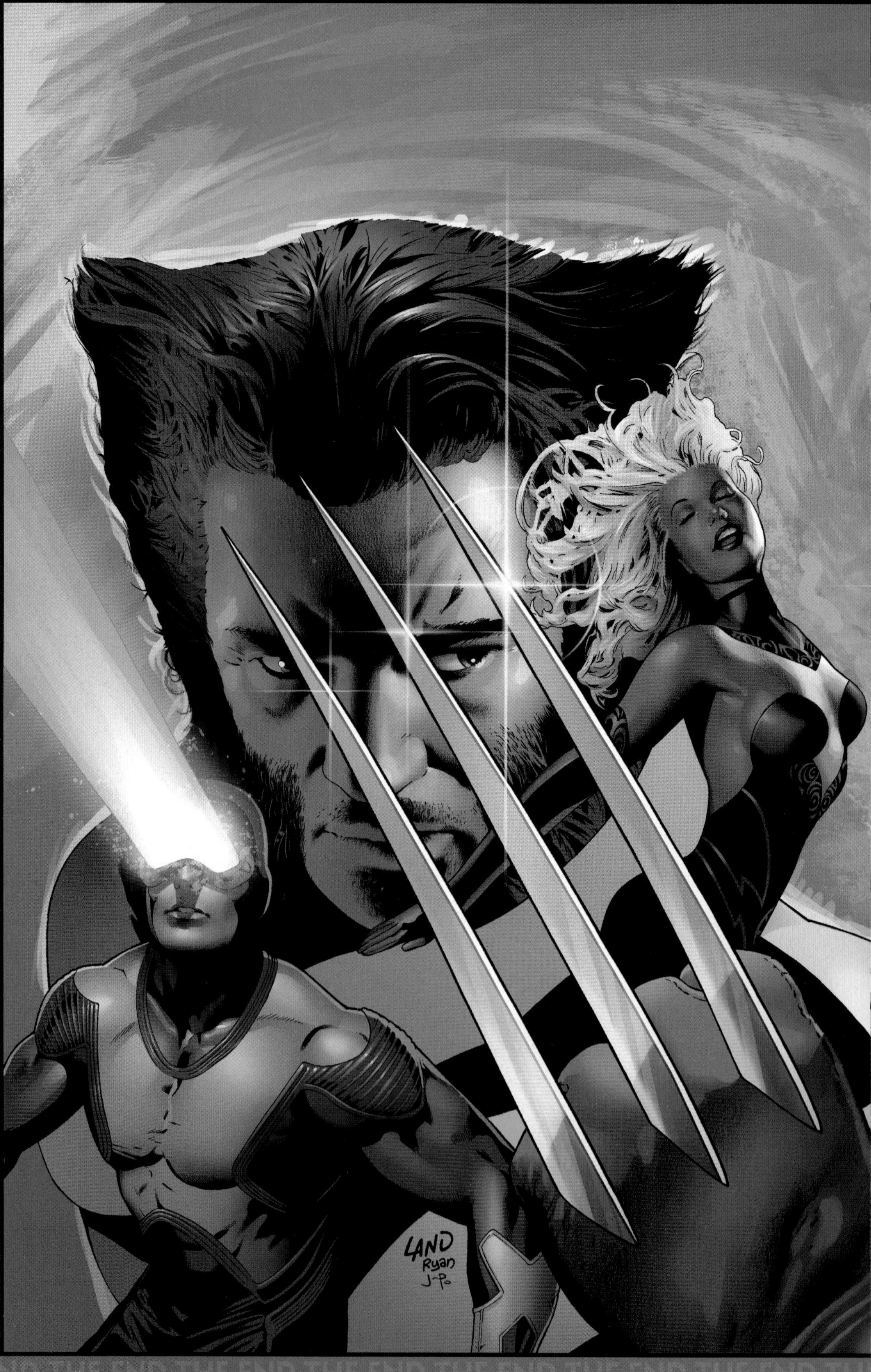
LAND
Ryan
J-Po

THE END THE END THE END THE END THE END THE END

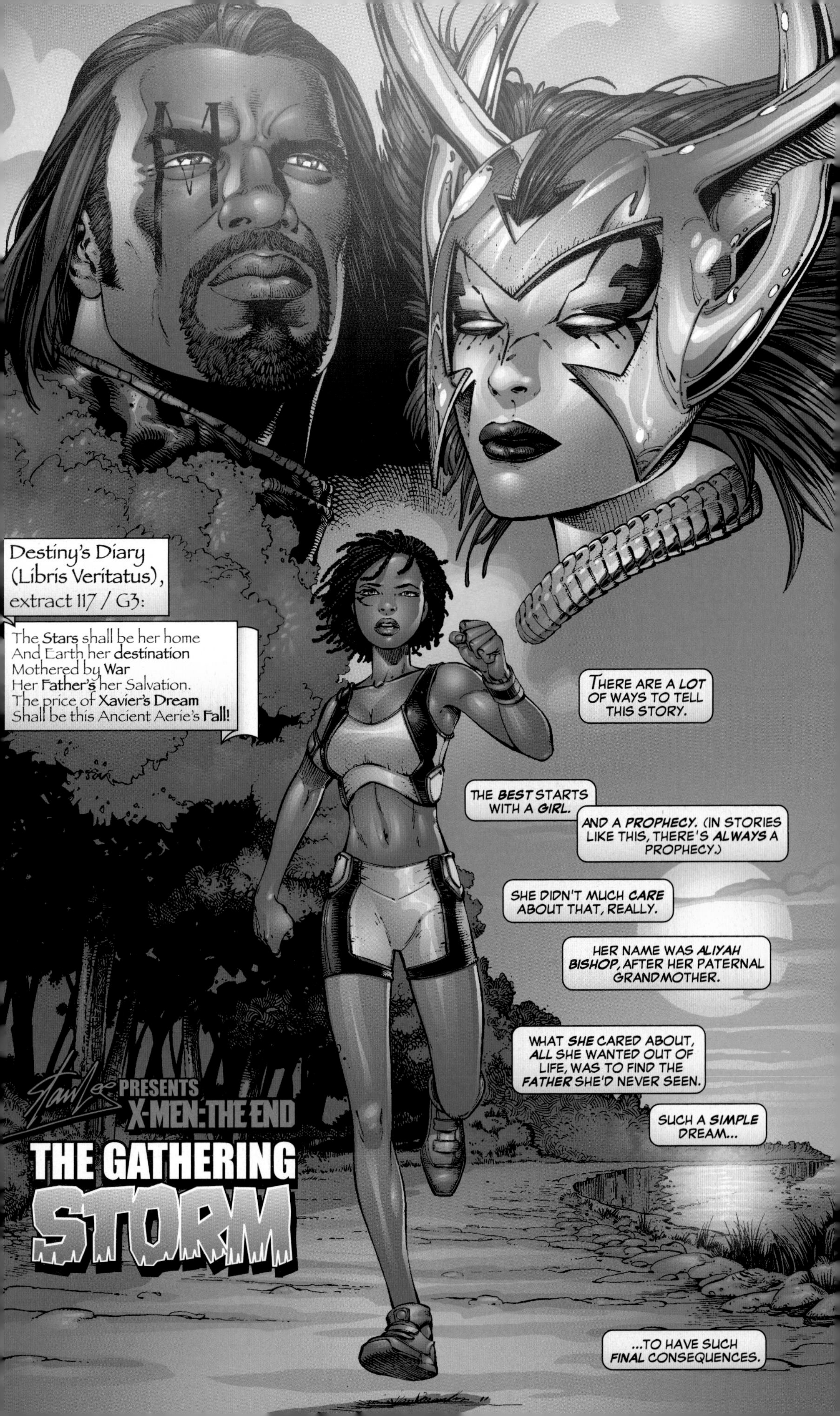

Destiny's Diary (Libris Veritatus), extract 117 / G3:
The Stars shall be her home
And Earth her destination
Mothered by War
Her Father's her Salvation.
The price of Xavier's Dream
Shall be this Ancient Aerie's Fall!
THERE ARE A LOT OF WAYS TO TELL THIS STORY.
THE BEST STARTS WITH A GIRL.
AND A PROPHECY. (IN STORIES LIKE THIS, THERE'S ALWAYS A PROPHECY.)
SHE DIDN'T MUCH CARE ABOUT THAT, REALLY.
HER NAME WAS ALIYAH BISHOP, AFTER HER PATERNAL GRANDMOTHER.
WHAT SHE CARED ABOUT, ALL SHE WANTED OUT OF LIFE, WAS TO FIND THE FATHER SHE'D NEVER SEEN.
SUCH A SIMPLE DREAM...
...TO HAVE SUCH FINAL CONSEQUENCES.
PRESENTS
X-MEN: THE END
THE GATHERING
STORM

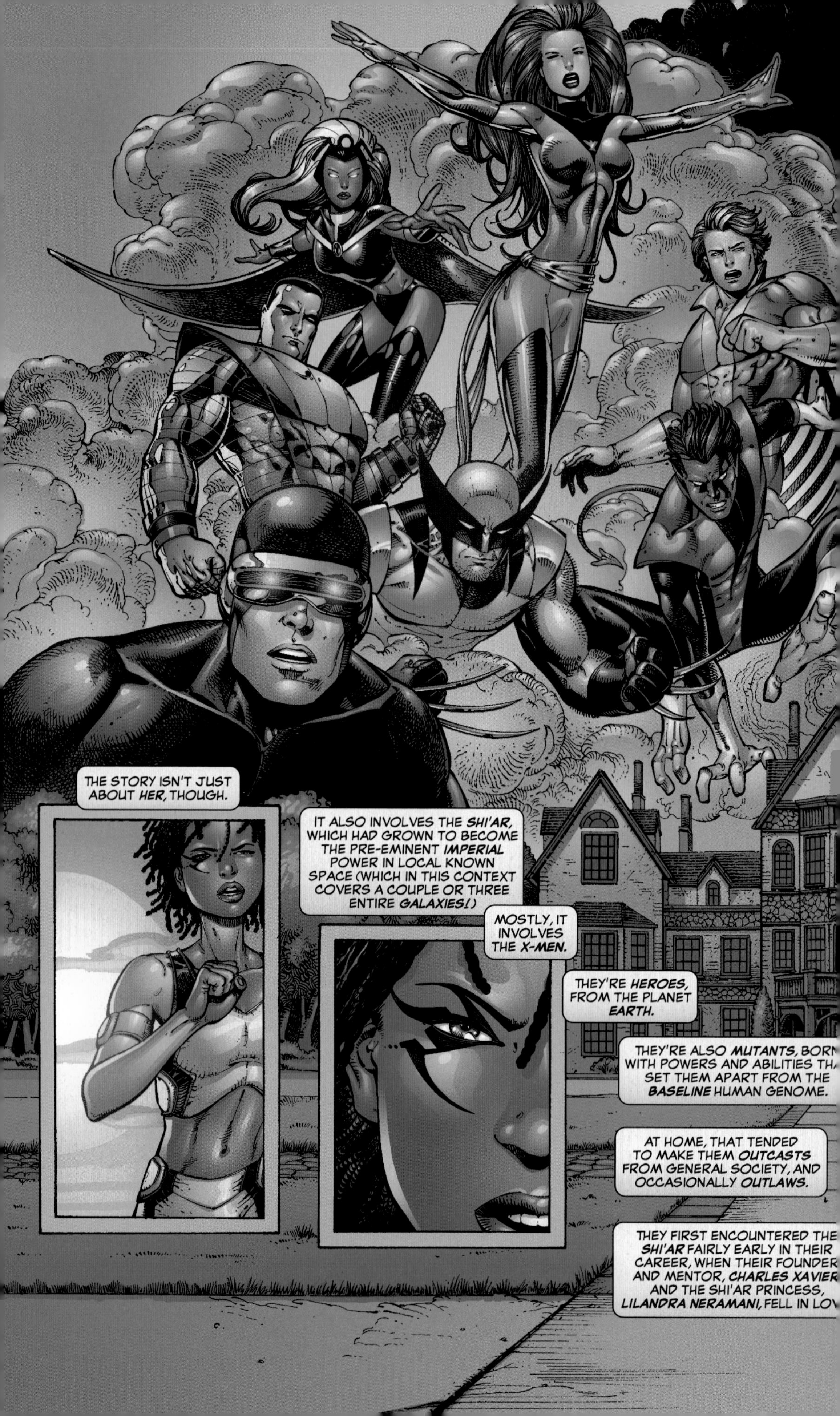
THE STORY ISN'T JUST ABOUT HER, THOUGH.
IT ALSO INVOLVES THE SHI'AR, WHICH HAD GROWN TO BECOME THE PRE-EMINENT IMPERIAL POWER IN LOCAL KNOWN SPACE (WHICH IN THIS CONTEXT COVERS A COUPLE OR THREE ENTIRE GALAXIES!)
MOSTLY, IT INVOLVES THE X-MEN.
THEY'RE HEROES, FROM THE PLANET EARTH.
THEY'RE ALSO MUTANTS, BORN WITH POWERS AND ABILITIES THAT SET THEM APART FROM THE BASELINE HUMAN GENOME.
AT HOME, THAT TENDED TO MAKE THEM OUTCASTS FROM GENERAL SOCIETY, AND OCCASIONALLY OUTLAWS.
THEY FIRST ENCOUNTERED THE SHI'AR FAIRLY EARLY IN THEIR CAREER, WHEN THEIR FOUNDER AND MENTOR, CHARLES XAVIER AND THE SHI'AR PRINCESS, LILANDRA NERAMANI, FELL IN LOV

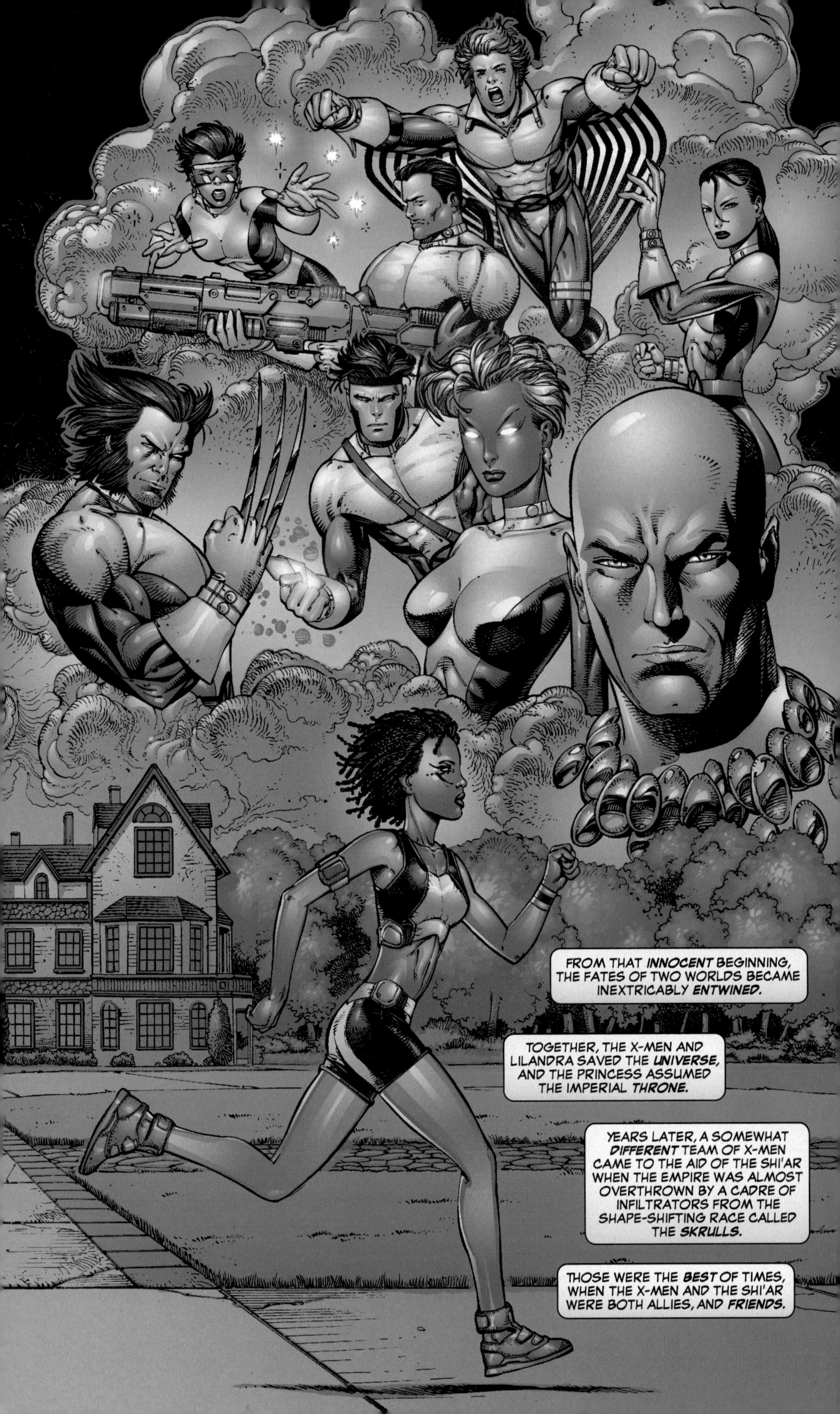
FROM THAT INNOCENT BEGINNING, THE FATES OF TWO WORLDS BECAME INEXTRICABLY ENTWINED.
TOGETHER, THE X-MEN AND LILANDRA SAVED THE UNIVERSE, AND THE PRINCESS ASSUMED THE IMPERIAL THRONE.
YEARS LATER, A SOMEWHAT DIFFERENT TEAM OF X-MEN CAME TO THE AID OF THE SHI'AR WHEN THE EMPIRE WAS ALMOST OVERTHROWN BY A CADRE OF INFILTRATORS FROM THE SHAPE-SHIFTING RACE CALLED THE SKRULLS.
THOSE WERE THE BEST OF TIMES, WHEN THE X-MEN AND THE SHI'AR WERE BOTH ALLIES, AND FRIENDS.

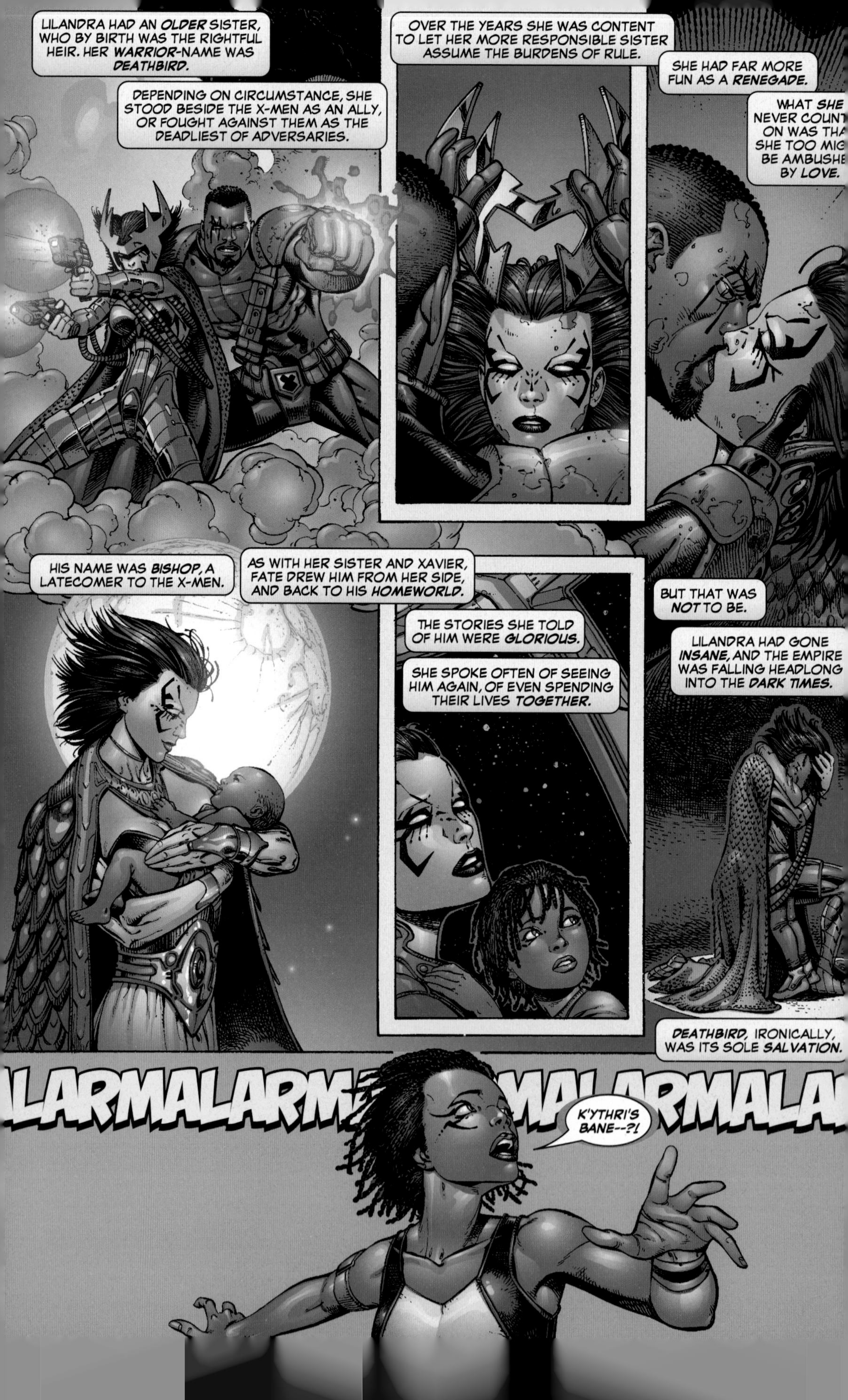
LILANDRA HAD AN OLDER SISTER, WHO BY BIRTH WAS THE RIGHTFUL HEIR. HER WARRIOR-NAME WAS DEATHBIRD.
DEPENDING ON CIRCUMSTANCE, SHE STOOD BESIDE THE X-MEN AS AN ALLY, OR FOUGHT AGAINST THEM AS THE DEADLIEST OF ADVERSARIES.
OVER THE YEARS SHE WAS CONTENT TO LET HER MORE RESPONSIBLE SISTER ASSUME THE BURDENS OF RULE.
SHE HAD FAR MORE FUN AS A RENEGADE.
WHAT SHE NEVER COUNT ON WAS THA SHE TOO MIG BE AMBUSHE BY LOVE.
HIS NAME WAS BISHOP, A LATECOMER TO THE X-MEN.
AS WITH HER SISTER AND XAVIER, FATE DREW HIM FROM HER SIDE, AND BACK TO HIS HOMEWORLD.
THE STORIES SHE TOLD OF HIM WERE GLORIOUS.
SHE SPOKE OFTEN OF SEEING HIM AGAIN, OF EVEN SPENDING THEIR LIVES TOGETHER.
BUT THAT WAS NOT TO BE.
LILANDRA HAD GONE INSANE, AND THE EMPIRE WAS FALLING HEADLONG INTO THE DARK TIMES.
DEATHBIRD, IRONICALLY, WAS ITS SOLE SALVATION.
ALARMALARMA MALARMALA
K'YTHRI'S BANE--?!

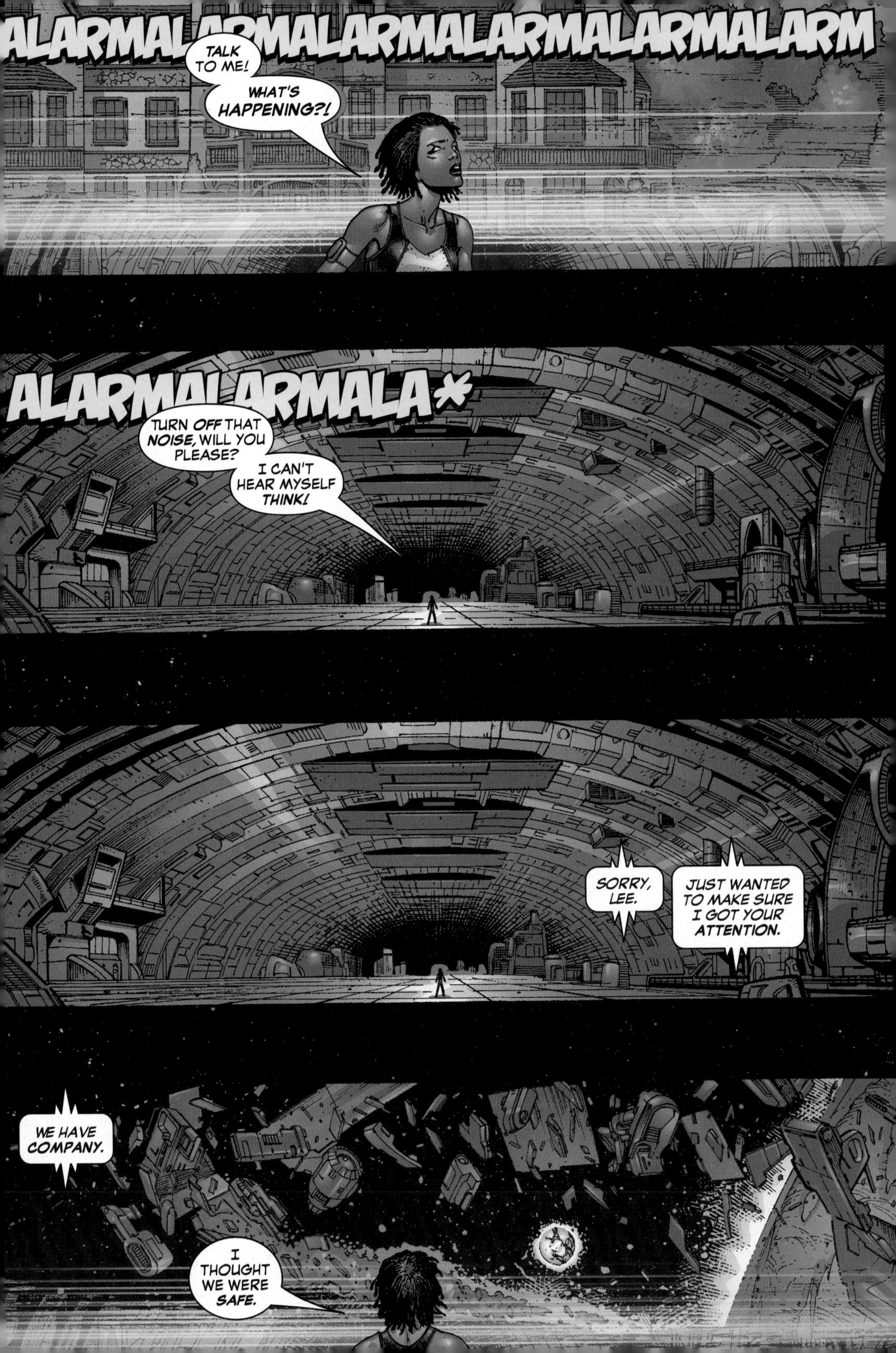
ALARMALARMALARMALARMALARMALARM
TALK TO ME!
WHAT'S HAPPENING?!
ALARMALARMALA*
TURN OFF THAT NOISE, WILL YOU PLEASE?
I CAN'T HEAR MYSELF THINK!
SORRY, LEE.
JUST WANTED TO MAKE SURE I GOT YOUR ATTENTION.
WE HAVE COMPANY.
I THOUGHT WE WERE SAFE.

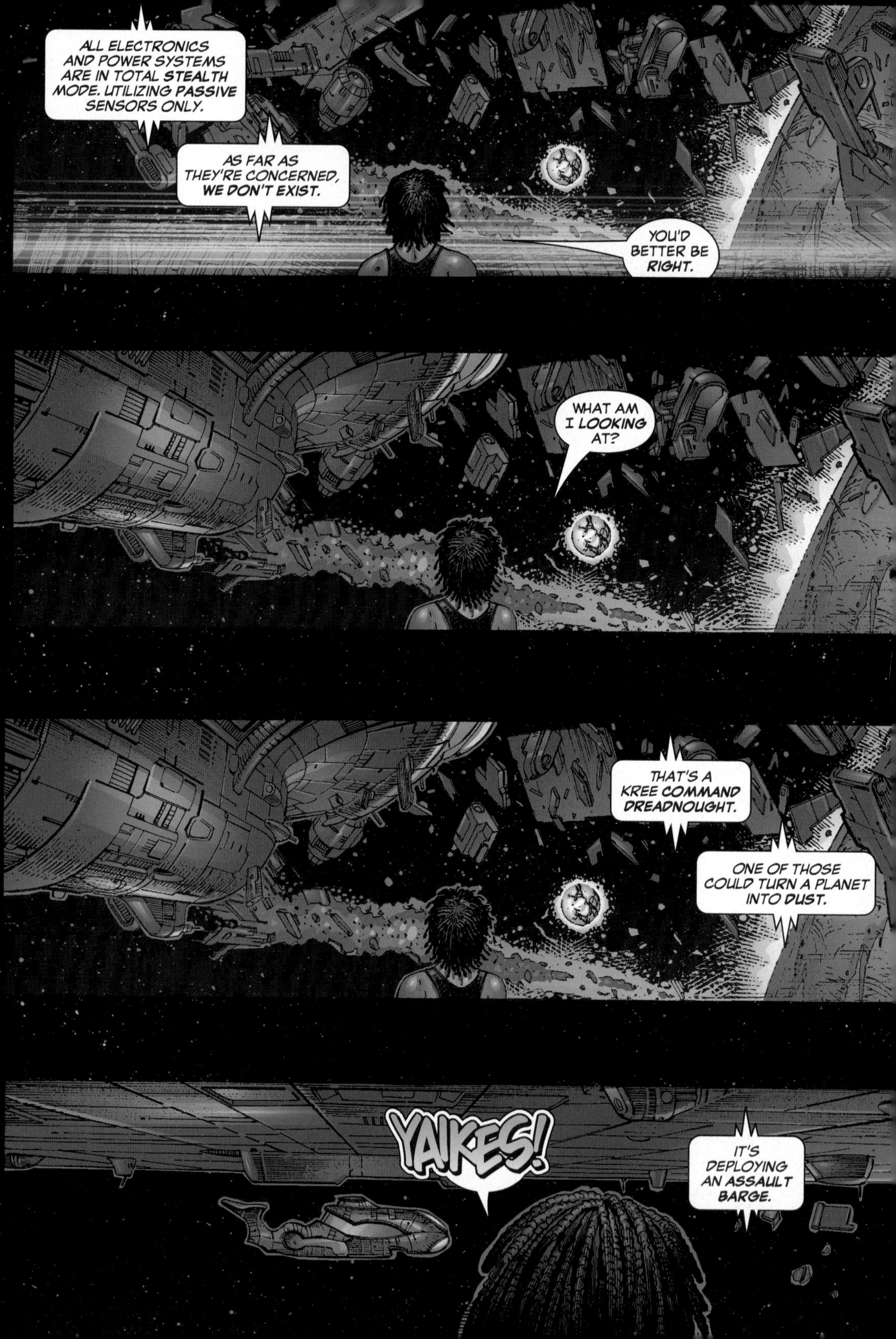
ALL ELECTRONICS AND POWER SYSTEMS ARE IN TOTAL STEALTH MODE. UTILIZING PASSIVE SENSORS ONLY.
AS FAR AS THEY'RE CONCERNED, WE DON'T EXIST.
YOU'D BETTER BE RIGHT.
WHAT AM I LOOKING AT?
THAT'S A KREE COMMAND DREADNOUGHT.
ONE OF THOSE COULD TURN A PLANET INTO DUST.
YAIKES!
IT'S DEPLOYING AN ASSAULT BARGE.

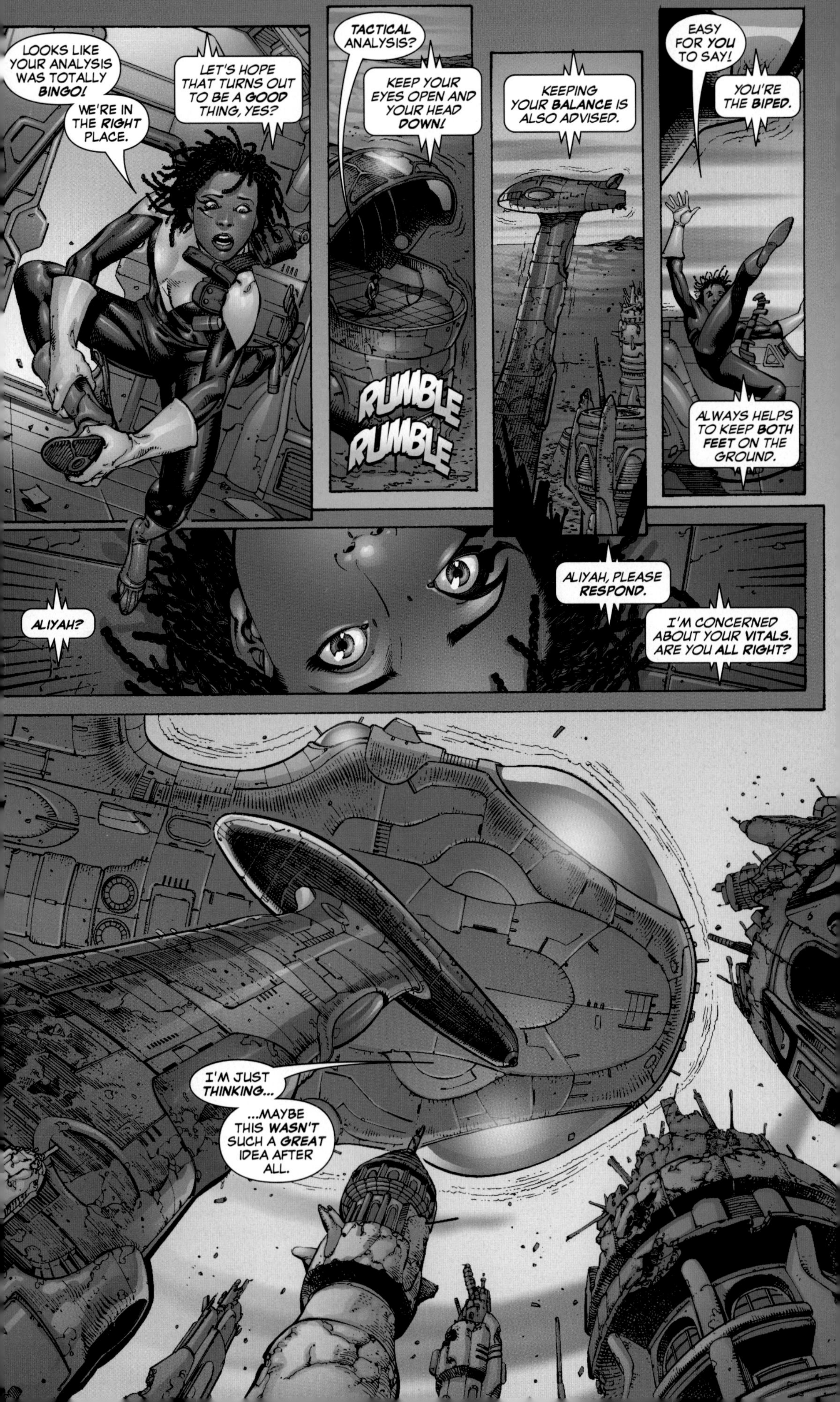
LOOKS LIKE YOUR ANALYSIS WAS TOTALLY BINGO!
WE'RE IN THE RIGHT PLACE.
LET'S HOPE THAT TURNS OUT TO BE A GOOD THING, YES?
TACTICAL ANALYSIS?
KEEP YOUR EYES OPEN AND YOUR HEAD DOWN!
RUMBLE RUMBLE
KEEPING YOUR BALANCE IS ALSO ADVISED.
EASY FOR YOU TO SAY!
YOU'RE THE BIPED.
ALWAYS HELPS TO KEEP BOTH FEET ON THE GROUND.
ALIYAH?
ALIYAH, PLEASE RESPOND.
I'M CONCERNED ABOUT YOUR VITALS. ARE YOU ALL RIGHT?
I'M JUST THINKING...
...MAYBE THIS WASN'T SUCH A GREAT IDEA AFTER ALL.

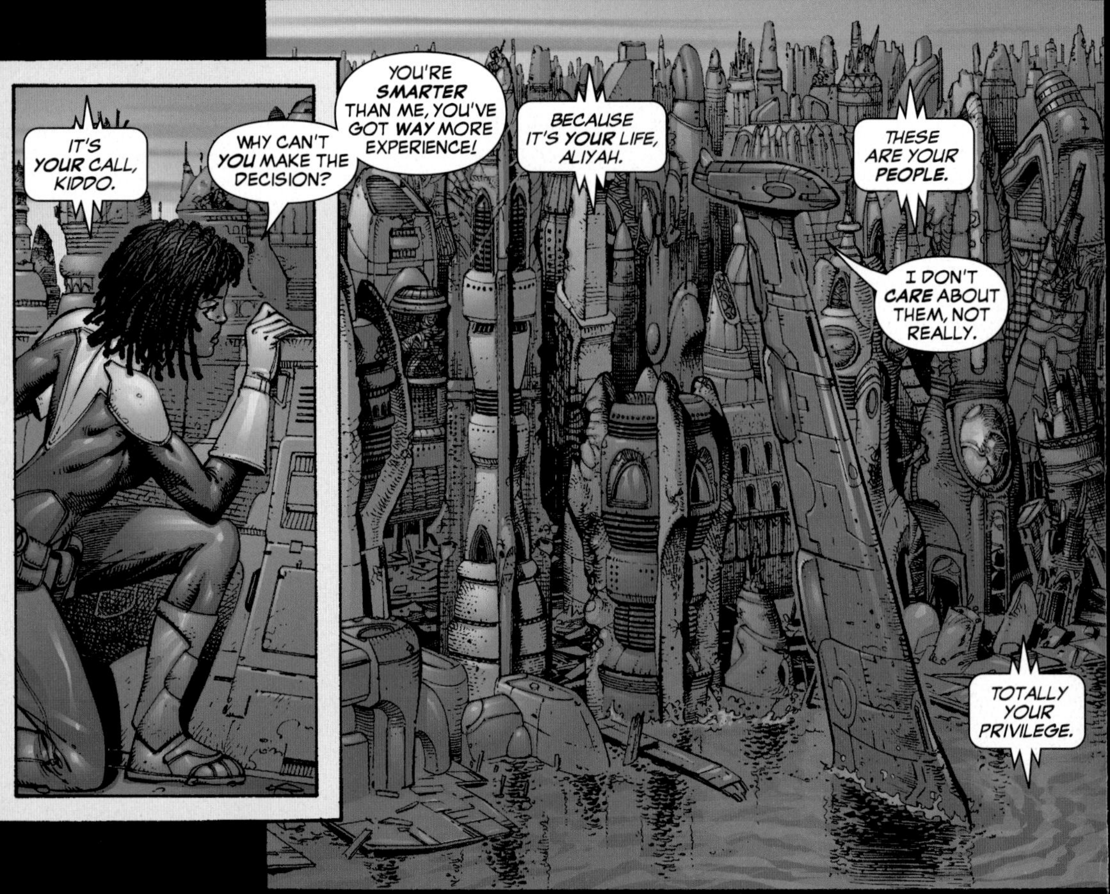
IT'S YOUR CALL, KIDDO.
WHY CAN'T YOU MAKE THE DECISION?
YOU'RE SMARTER THAN ME, YOU'VE GOT WAY MORE EXPERIENCE!
BECAUSE IT'S YOUR LIFE, ALIYAH.
THESE ARE YOUR PEOPLE.
I DON'T CARE ABOUT THEM, NOT REALLY.
TOTALLY YOUR PRIVILEGE.

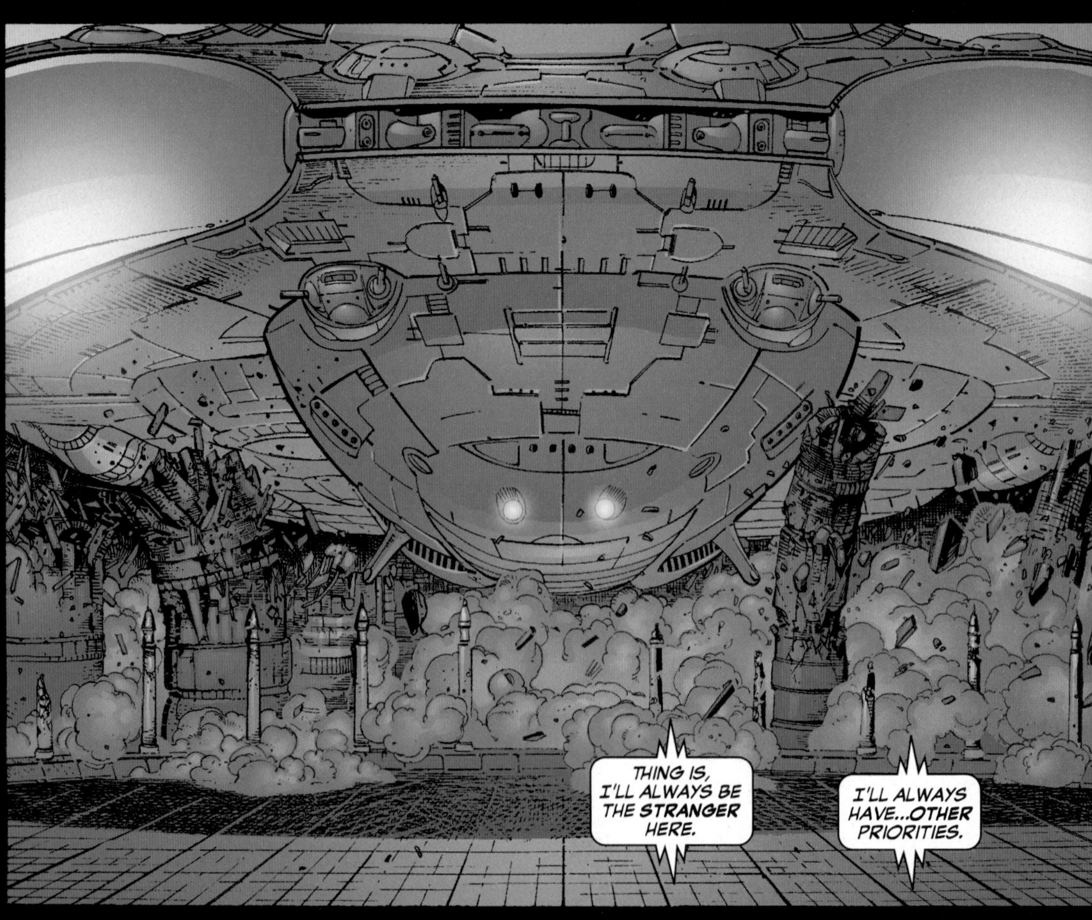
THING IS, I'LL ALWAYS BE THE STRANGER HERE.
I'LL ALWAYS HAVE...OTHER PRIORITIES.

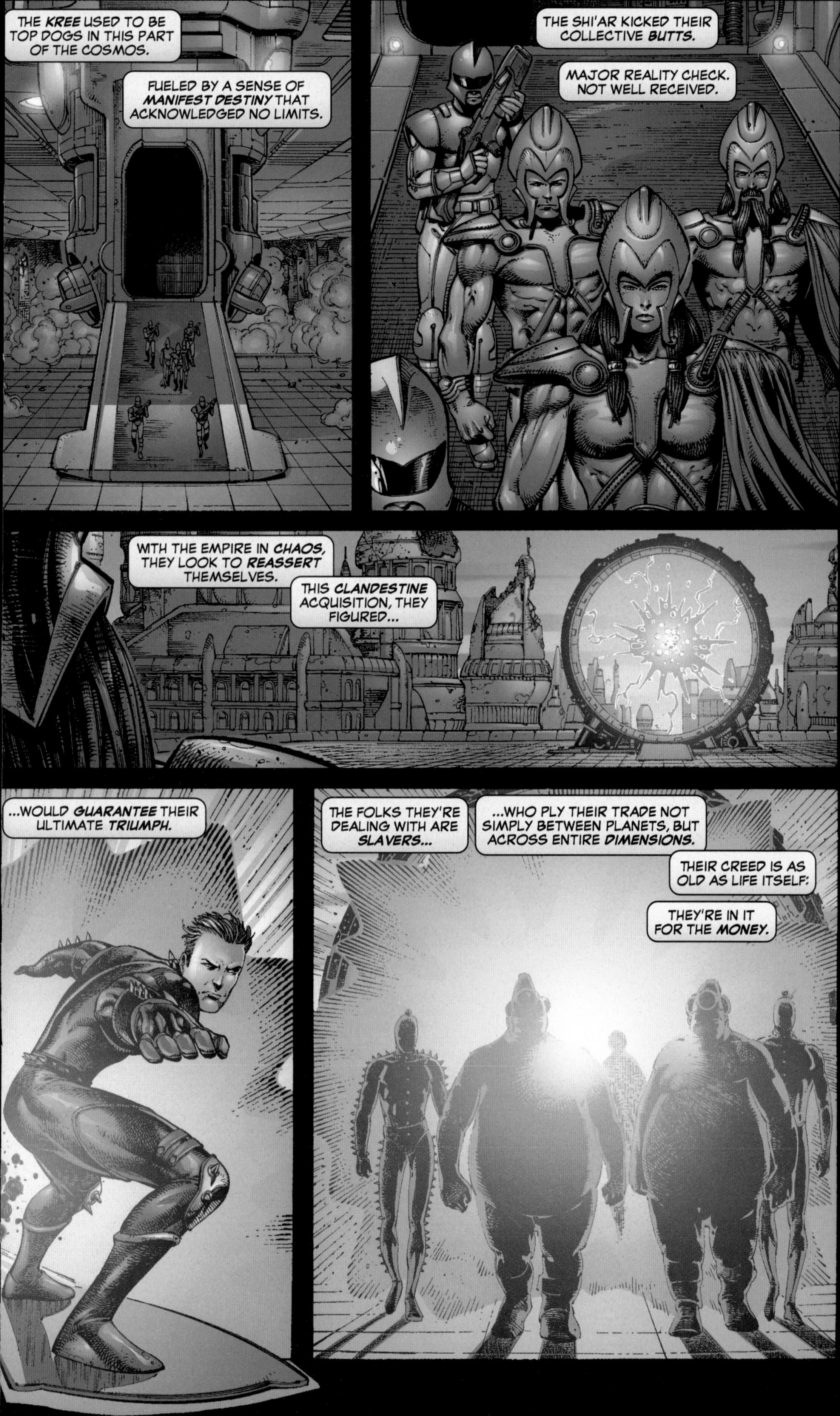
THE KREE USED TO BE TOP DOGS IN THIS PART OF THE COSMOS.
FUELED BY A SENSE OF MANIFEST DESTINY THAT ACKNOWLEDGED NO LIMITS.
THE SHI'AR KICKED THEIR COLLECTIVE BUTTS.
MAJOR REALITY CHECK. NOT WELL RECEIVED.
WITH THE EMPIRE IN CHAOS, THEY LOOK TO REASSERT THEMSELVES.
THIS CLANDESTINE ACQUISITION, THEY FIGURED...
...WOULD GUARANTEE THEIR ULTIMATE TRIUMPH.
THE FOLKS THEY'RE DEALING WITH ARE SLAVERS...
...WHO PLY THEIR TRADE NOT SIMPLY BETWEEN PLANETS, BUT ACROSS ENTIRE DIMENSIONS.
THEIR CREED IS AS OLD AS LIFE ITSELF:
THEY'RE IN IT FOR THE MONEY.

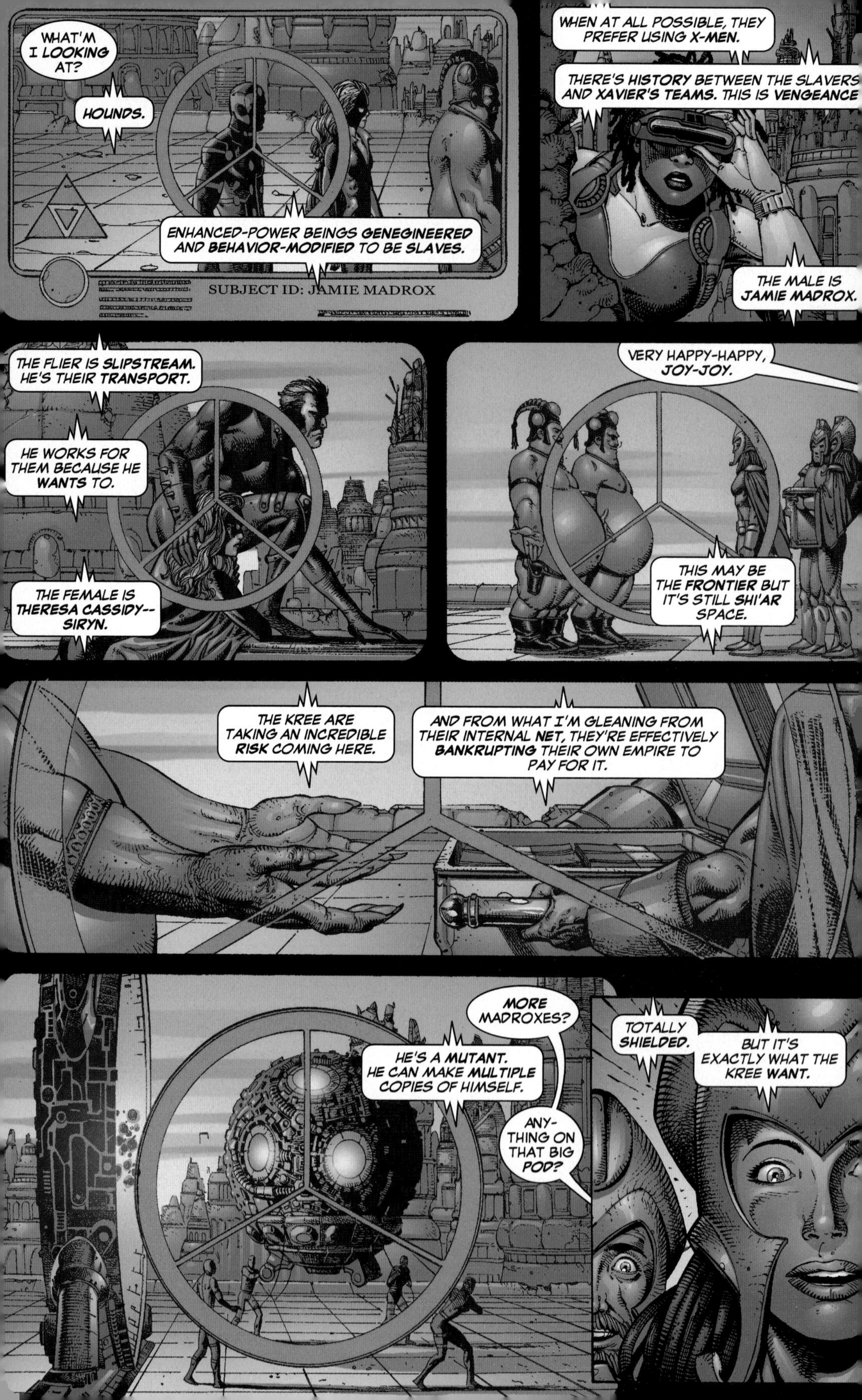
WHAT'M I LOOKING AT?
HOUNDS.
ENHANCED-POWER BEINGS GENEGINEERED AND BEHAVIOR-MODIFIED TO BE SLAVES.
SUBJECT ID: JAMIE MADROX
WHEN AT ALL POSSIBLE, THEY PREFER USING X-MEN.
THERE'S HISTORY BETWEEN THE SLAVERS AND XAVIER'S TEAMS. THIS IS VENGEANCE
THE MALE IS JAMIE MADROX.
THE FLIER IS SLIPSTREAM. HE'S THEIR TRANSPORT.
HE WORKS FOR THEM BECAUSE HE WANTS TO.
THE FEMALE IS THERESA CASSIDY-- SIRYN.
VERY HAPPY-HAPPY, JOY-JOY.
THIS MAY BE THE FRONTIER BUT IT'S STILL SHI'AR SPACE.
THE KREE ARE TAKING AN INCREDIBLE RISK COMING HERE.
AND FROM WHAT I'M GLEANING FROM THEIR INTERNAL NET, THEY'RE EFFECTIVELY BANKRUPTING THEIR OWN EMPIRE TO PAY FOR IT.
MORE MADROXES?
HE'S A MUTANT. HE CAN MAKE MULTIPLE COPIES OF HIMSELF.
ANY-THING ON THAT BIG POD?
TOTALLY SHIELDED.
BUT IT'S EXACTLY WHAT THE KREE WANT.

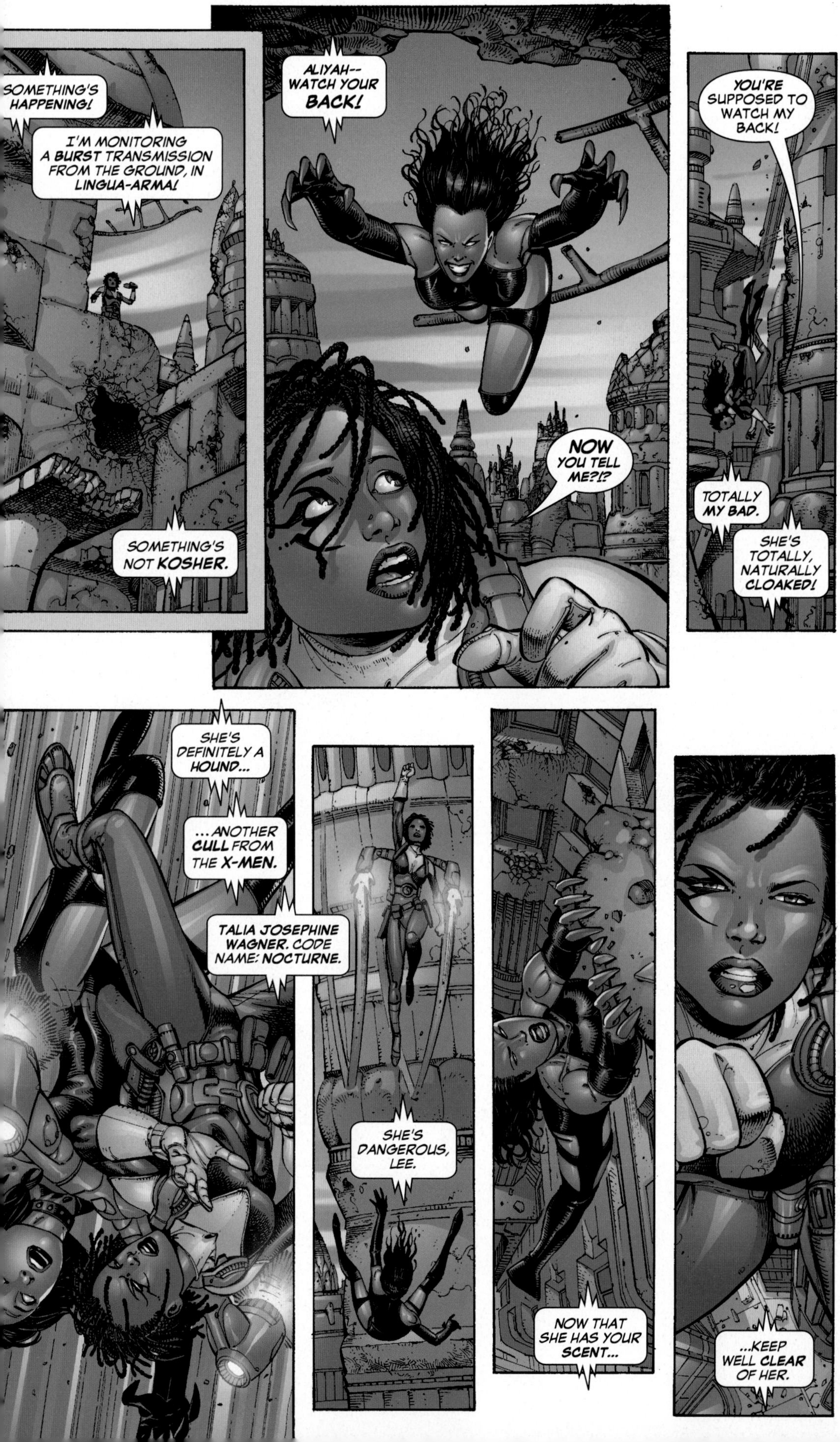
SOMETHING'S HAPPENING!
I'M MONITORING A BURST TRANSMISSION FROM THE GROUND, IN LINGUA-ARMA!
SOMETHING'S NOT KOSHER.
ALIYAH-- WATCH YOUR BACK!
NOW YOU TELL ME?!?
YOU'RE SUPPOSED TO WATCH MY BACK!
TOTALLY MY BAD.
SHE'S TOTALLY, NATURALLY CLOAKED!
SHE'S DEFINITELY A HOUND...
...ANOTHER CULL FROM THE X-MEN.
TALIA JOSEPHINE WAGNER. CODE NAME: NOCTURNE.
SHE'S DANGEROUS, LEE.
NOW THAT SHE HAS YOUR SCENT...
...KEEP WELL CLEAR OF HER.

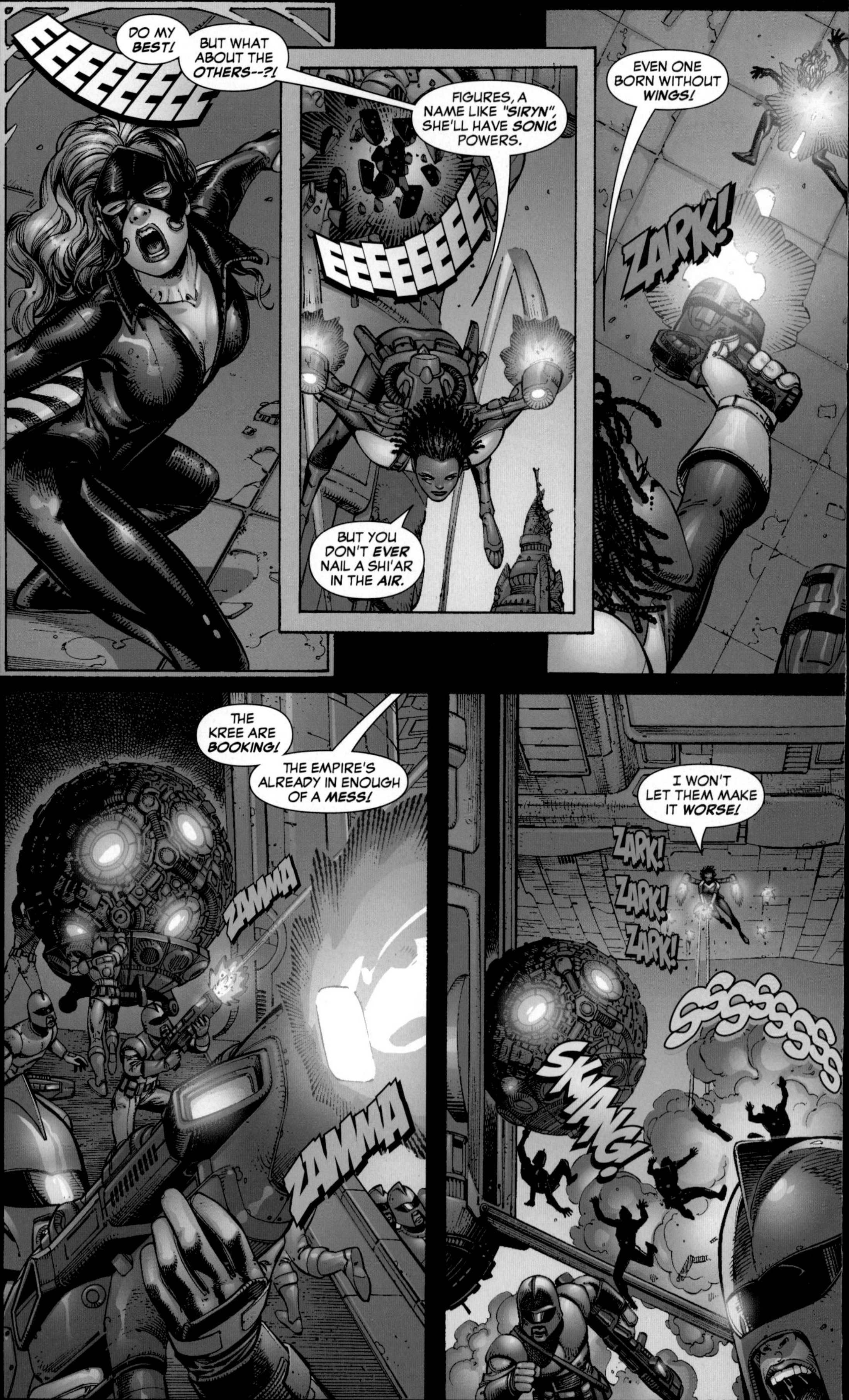
EEEEEEEE
DO MY BEST!
BUT WHAT ABOUT THE OTHERS--?!
FIGURES, A NAME LIKE "SIRYN", SHE'LL HAVE SONIC POWERS.
EEEEEEEE
BUT YOU DON'T EVER NAIL A SHI'AR IN THE AIR.
EVEN ONE BORN WITHOUT WINGS!
ZARK!
THE KREE ARE BOOKING!
THE EMPIRE'S ALREADY IN ENOUGH OF A MESS!
ZAMMA
ZAMMA
I WON'T LET THEM MAKE IT WORSE!
ZARK!
ZARK!
ZARK!
SSSSSSS
SKWANG!

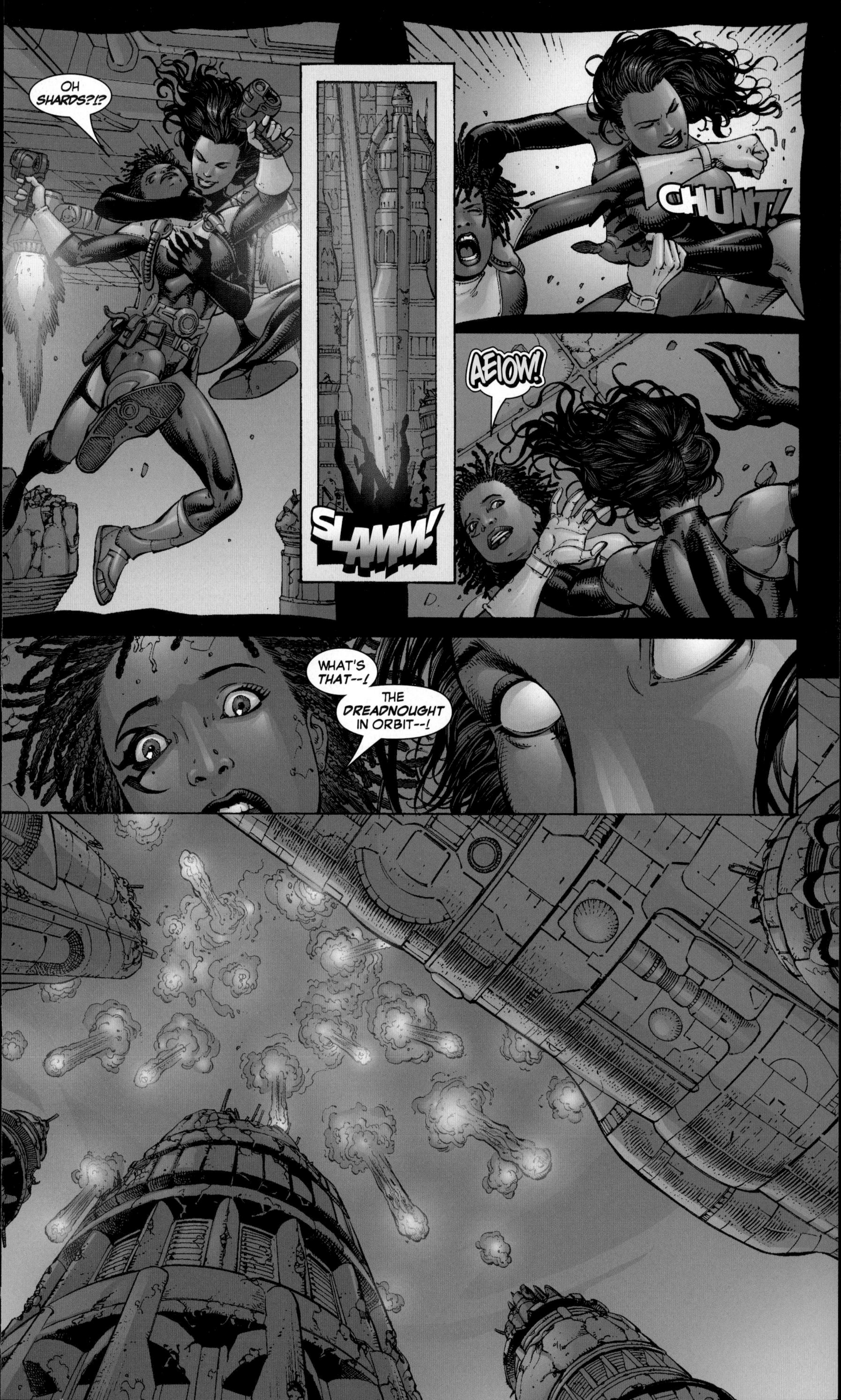
OH SHARDS?!?
SLAMM!
CHUNT!
AEIOW!
WHAT'S THAT--!
THE DREADNOUGHT IN ORBIT--!

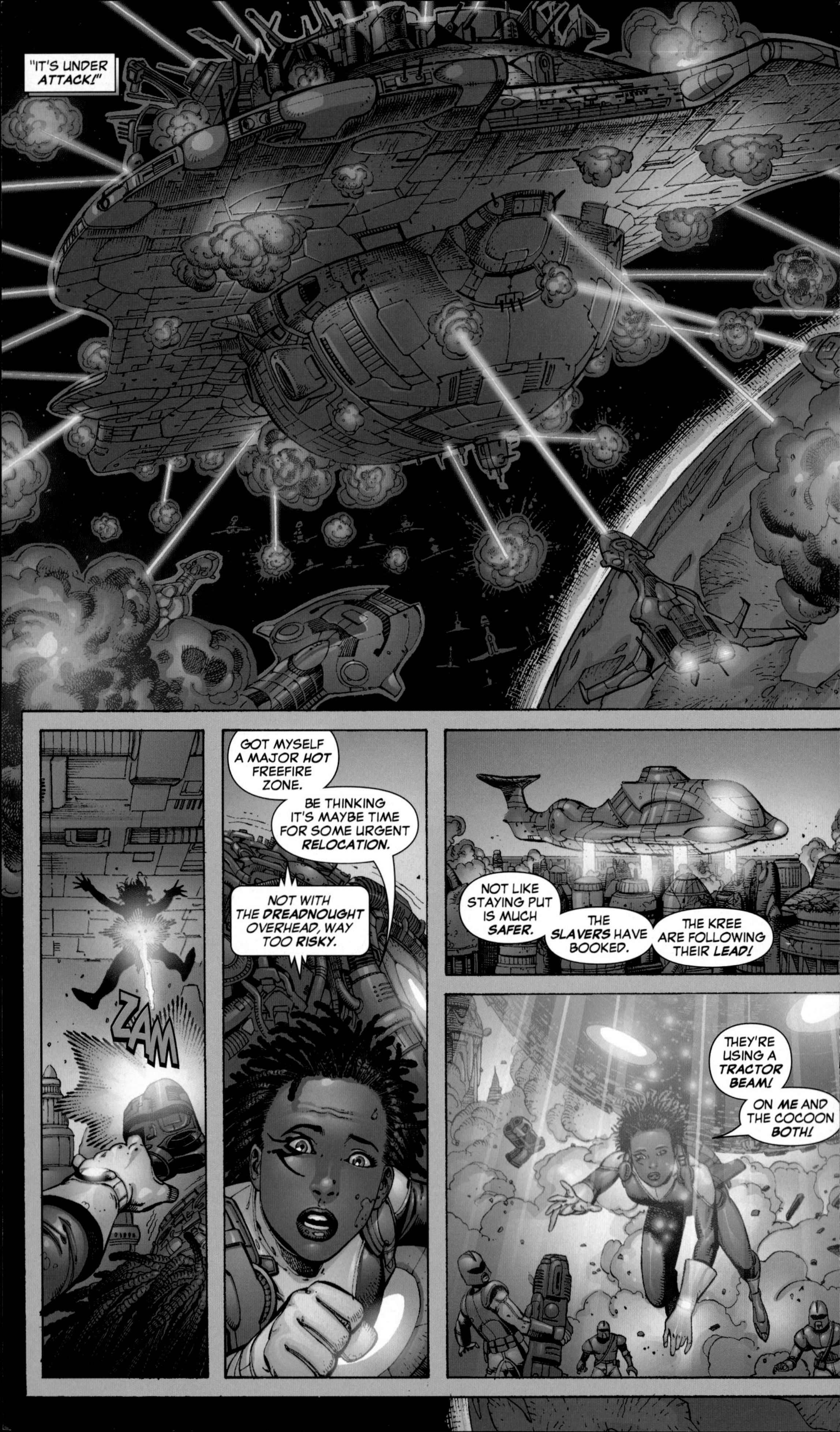
"IT'S UNDER ATTACK!"
ZAM
GOT MYSELF A MAJOR HOT FREEFIRE ZONE.
BE THINKING IT'S MAYBE TIME FOR SOME URGENT RELOCATION.
NOT WITH THE DREADNOUGHT OVERHEAD, WAY TOO RISKY.
NOT LIKE STAYING PUT IS MUCH SAFER.
THE SLAVERS HAVE BOOKED.
THE KREE ARE FOLLOWING THEIR LEAD!
THEY'RE USING A TRACTOR BEAM!
ON ME AND THE COCOON BOTH!

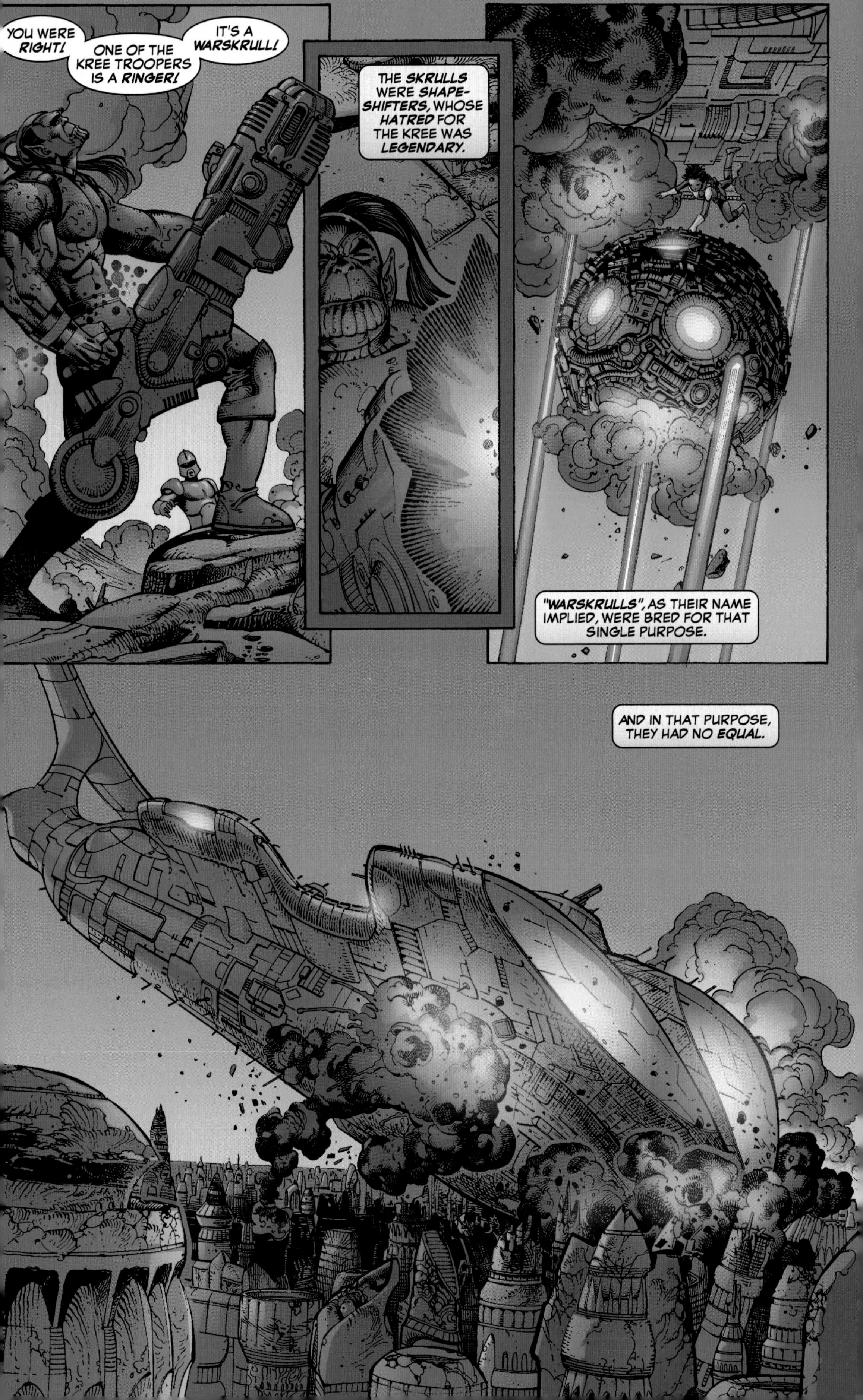
YOU WERE RIGHT!
ONE OF THE KREE TROOPERS IS A RINGER!
IT'S A WARSKRULL!
THE SKRULLS WERE SHAPE-SHIFTERS, WHOSE HATRED FOR THE KREE WAS LEGENDARY.
"WARSKRULLS", AS THEIR NAME IMPLIED, WERE BRED FOR THAT SINGLE PURPOSE.
AND IN THAT PURPOSE, THEY HAD NO EQUAL.

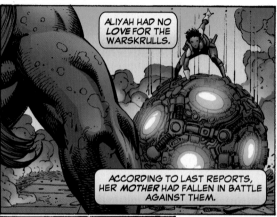

ALIYAH HAD NO LOVE FOR THE WARSKRULLS.

ACCORDING TO LAST REPORTS, HER *MOTHER* HAD FALLEN IN BATTLE AGAINST THEM.

SHE DIDN'T BOTHER WITH HER *WEAPON*. THE SKRULL WAS WEARING ARMOR.

BUT MORE IMPORTANTLY FOR HER, THIS FIGHT WAS WHOLLY *PRIMAL*.

SHE'D GET AN EARFUL ABOUT THIS LATER, FROM HER COMPANION AND *MENTOR*.

(ASSUMING SHE *SURVIVED*.)

WHICH RIGHT NOW, SHE'D BE THE *FIRST* TO ADMIT, LOOKED PRETTY *DOUBTFUL*.

THAT WAS WHEN SHE MADE HER *SECOND* MISTAKE.

SHE DIDN'T THINK IT MATTERED, SHE THOUGHT SHE WAS ON THE EXPRESS-WAY TO REJOIN HER *MOM*.

ARRRGH!

NOT HARDLY.

SKRIIIII!

WHAT--?! WHO--?!?

SHARDS-- THE COCOON!

SO MANY, MANY QUESTIONS.

BUT THE STRANGER'S IN NO SHAPE TO ANSWER.

AND AN INSTANT LATER, THERE ARE A LOT MORE IMPORTANT THINGS TO WORRY ABOUT.

FOOM!

FOOM! FOOM! FOOM! FOOM! FOOM! FOOM!

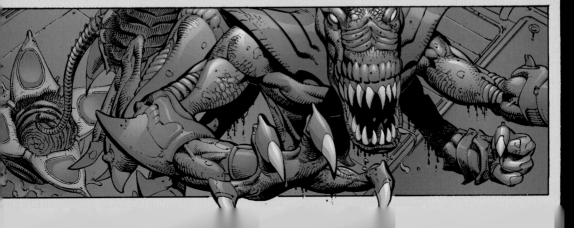

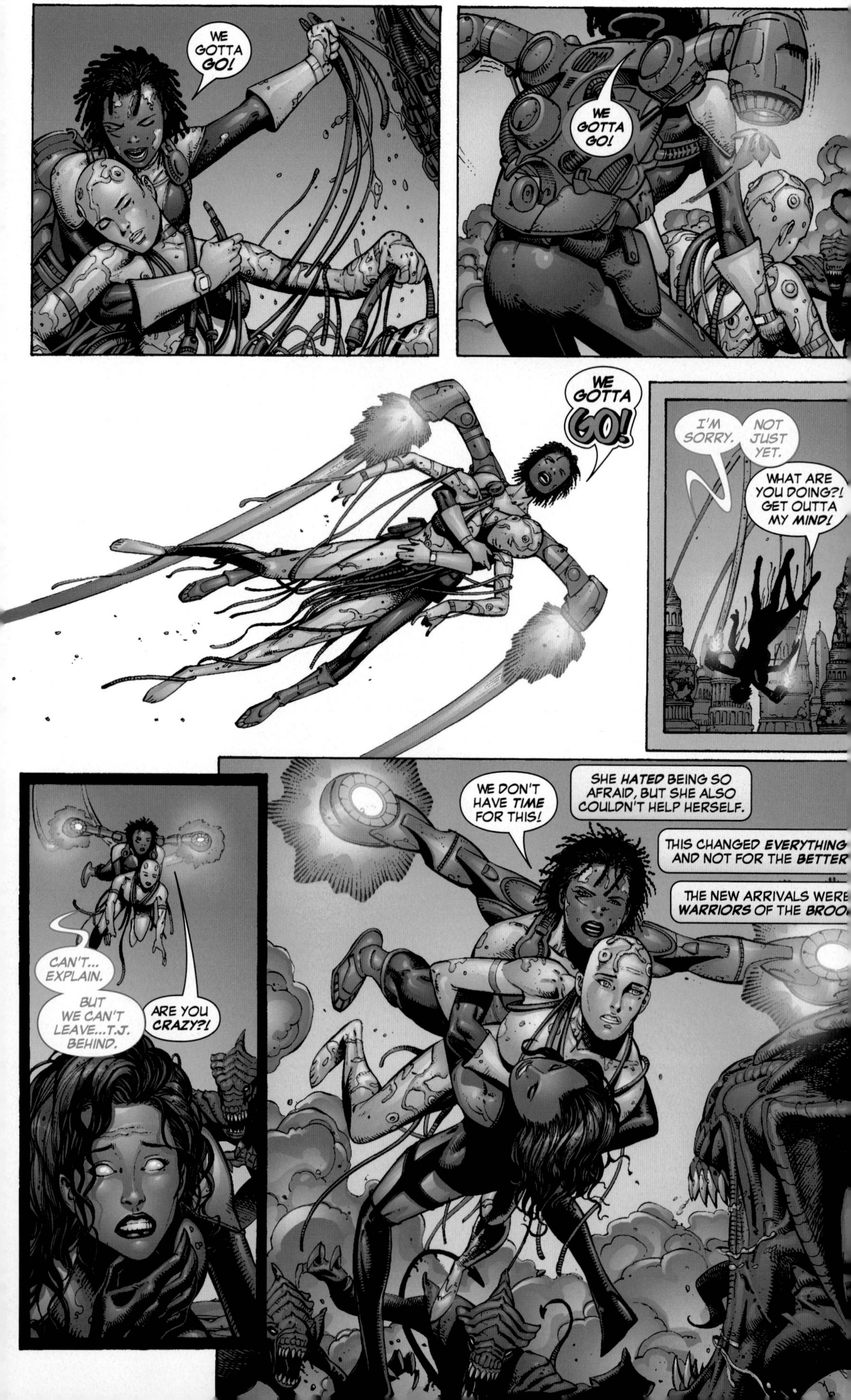
WE GOTTA GO!
WE GOTTA GO!
WE GOTTA GO!
I'M SORRY.
NOT JUST YET.
WHAT ARE YOU DOING?! GET OUTTA MY MIND!
CAN'T... EXPLAIN.
BUT WE CAN'T LEAVE...T.J. BEHIND.
ARE YOU CRAZY?!
WE DON'T HAVE TIME FOR THIS!
SHE HATED BEING SO AFRAID, BUT SHE ALSO COULDN'T HELP HERSELF.
THIS CHANGED EVERYTHING AND NOT FOR THE BETTER
THE NEW ARRIVALS WERE WARRIORS OF THE BROO

THROUGHOUT KNOWN SPACE, THERE WAS *NO* SPECIES MORE *FEARED.*

AND WITH *GOOD* REASON.

YOU DIDN'T *FIGHT* THE BROOD, UNLESS YOU HAD ABSOLUTELY *NO CHOICE...*

...OR YOU HAD A *DEATH* WISH.

THE *SANE* RESPONSE WAS TO *RUN.*

AND *PRAY.*

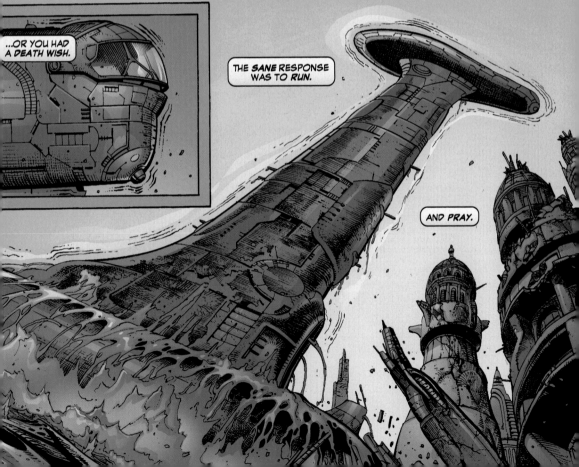

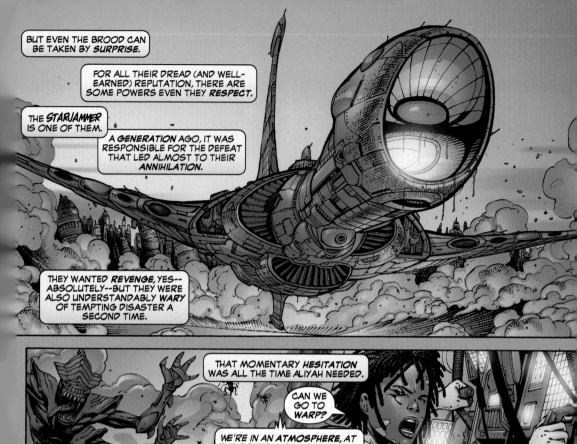

BUT EVEN THE BROOD CAN BE TAKEN BY *SURPRISE.*

FOR ALL THEIR DREAD (AND WELL-EARNED) REPUTATION, THERE ARE SOME POWERS EVEN THEY *RESPECT.*

THE *STARJAMMER* IS ONE OF THEM.

A *GENERATION* AGO, IT WAS RESPONSIBLE FOR THE DEFEAT THAT LED ALMOST TO THEIR *ANNIHILATION.*

THEY WANTED *REVENGE,* YES-- ABSOLUTELY--BUT THEY WERE ALSO UNDERSTANDABLY *WARY* OF TEMPTING DISASTER A SECOND TIME.

THAT MOMENTARY *HESITATION* WAS ALL THE TIME ALIYAH NEEDED.

CAN WE GO TO WARP?

WE'RE IN AN *ATMOSPHERE,* AT THE BOTTOM OF A PLANETARY GRAVITY WELL.

ALIYAH, THE CONSEQUENCES--!

THE *BROOD* ARE HERE, THE PLANET'S ALREADY DEAD.

WILL *WE* SURVIVE?

YES.

GO TO WARP! NOW!!

WARP DRIVES SHIFT A SPACECRAFT FAR *FASTER* THAN THE SPEED OF LIGHT.

THEY INVOLVE MANIPULATION OF PRIMAL STELLAR ENERGIES ON THE *QUANTUM* LEVEL.

YOU'RE NOT SUPPOSED TO EMPLOY THOSE ENERGIES ANYWHERE NEAR A *PLANET.*

AND ESPECIALLY NOT INSIDE AN ATMOSPHERE.

HE *COLLATERAL* DAMAGE ISN'T ONFINED TO THE OBSERVABLE PLANE OF BEING.

IN THE BLINK OF AN EYE, *SUBSPACE* SHOCKWAVES VIOLENTLY DESTABILIZE THE NUCLEAR STRUCTURE OF THIS SYSTEM'S *STAR.*

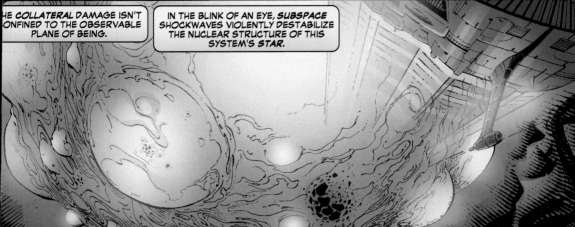

WE'RE CLEAR...

...BUT WE HAVE A PROBLEM.

THE LOCAL STAR'S GOING SUPERNOVA.

WE'RE TOO CLOSE.

WE CAN'T OUTRUN THE SHOCKWAVE.

THE SHIELDS--?

THEY MIGHT HOLD, BUT WE'LL BE CRIPPLED. SITTING DUCKS FOR WHOEVER FINDS US FIRST.

I'M SORRY, I'M SO SORRY.

JUDGMENT CALL, KIDDO. I'D HAVE DONE THE SAME.

DON'T GIVE UP QUITE YET, GUYS.

MAYBE I CAN HELP?

THEY'D HEARD THE *STORIES*.

ABOUT A YOUNG WOMAN, ONE OF THE *FOUNDING* TEAM OF X-MEN, WHO'D BECOME *ONE* WITH ONE OF THE *PRIMAL* FORCES OF EXISTENCE.

HER NAME WAS *JEAN GREY*.

THE *PHOENIX* WAS THE LITERAL MANIFESTATION OF THE *PASSION* OF *CREATION*. THE *SPARK* THAT BROUGHT THE COSMOS INTO BEING, THE *FIRE* THAT WOULD ULTIMATELY *CONSUME* IT.

THE EXPLODING STAR WAS *WATER* TO SOMEONE ALMOST DEAD FROM *THIRST*. SHE DRAINED IT WITH A *JOY* THAT WAS TRANSCENDENT AND FELT HERSELF-- FOR THE FIRST TIME IN AN AGE--*REBORN*.

THE MOMENT DID NOT GO *UNNOTICED*.

THE XAVIER INSTITUTE

SCOTT-- IS EVERYTHING ALL RIGHT?

EMMA...

IT'S... JEAN.

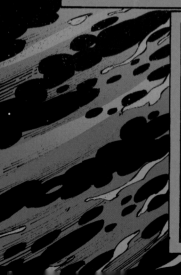

CHICAGO

ELECT CHICAGO'S PRYDE!

MOM?

HAMMER BAY, GENOSHA

PROFESSOR XAVIER?

FORGIVE ME, RAFAEL. SOMETHING'S COME UP, CLASS.

LET'S TAKE A *BREAK*, SHALL WE?

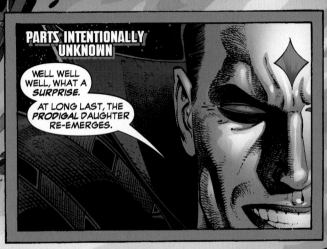

PARTS INTENTIONALLY UNKNOWN

WELL WELL WELL, WHAT A SURPRISE.

AT LONG LAST, THE PRODIGAL DAUGHTER RE-EMERGES.

THE HINDU KUSH

THEY SAID YOU WERE GONE FOR GOOD.

THEY SWORE TO ME, THE THREAT WAS OVER!

DID I BETRAY YOU, DID I BETRAY EVERYTHING I HELD OF VALUE, FOR NOTHING?!?

THE KIMANU HIGHLANDS, EAST AFRICA

LOGAN-- DO YOU SENSE--?

NOTHIN' T' DO WITH US, 'RO.

JEANNIE CAN TAKE CARE OF HERSELF.

RIGHT NOW, ALL I'M CONCERNED ABOUT--IS YOU.

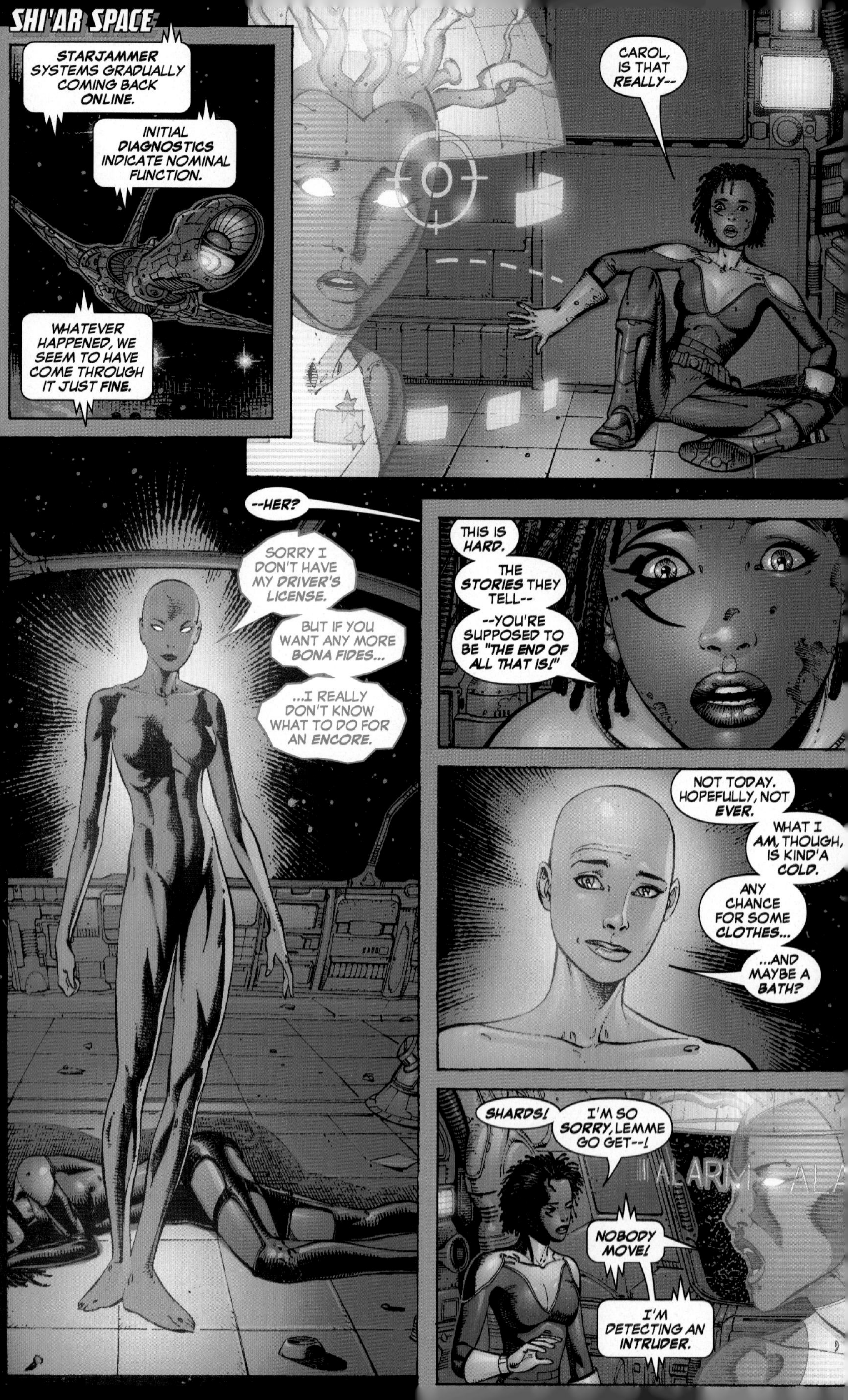
SHI'AR SPACE
STARJAMMER SYSTEMS GRADUALLY COMING BACK ONLINE.
INITIAL DIAGNOSTICS INDICATE NOMINAL FUNCTION.
WHATEVER HAPPENED, WE SEEM TO HAVE COME THROUGH IT JUST FINE.
CAROL, IS THAT REALLY--
--HER?
SORRY I DON'T HAVE MY DRIVER'S LICENSE.
BUT IF YOU WANT ANY MORE BONA FIDES...
...I REALLY DON'T KNOW WHAT TO DO FOR AN ENCORE.
THIS IS HARD.
THE STORIES THEY TELL--
--YOU'RE SUPPOSED TO BE "THE END OF ALL THAT IS!"
NOT TODAY. HOPEFULLY, NOT EVER.
WHAT I AM, THOUGH, IS KIND'A COLD.
ANY CHANCE FOR SOME CLOTHES...
...AND MAYBE A BATH?
SHARDS!
I'M SO SORRY, LEMME GO GET--!
NOBODY MOVE!
I'M DETECTING AN INTRUDER.

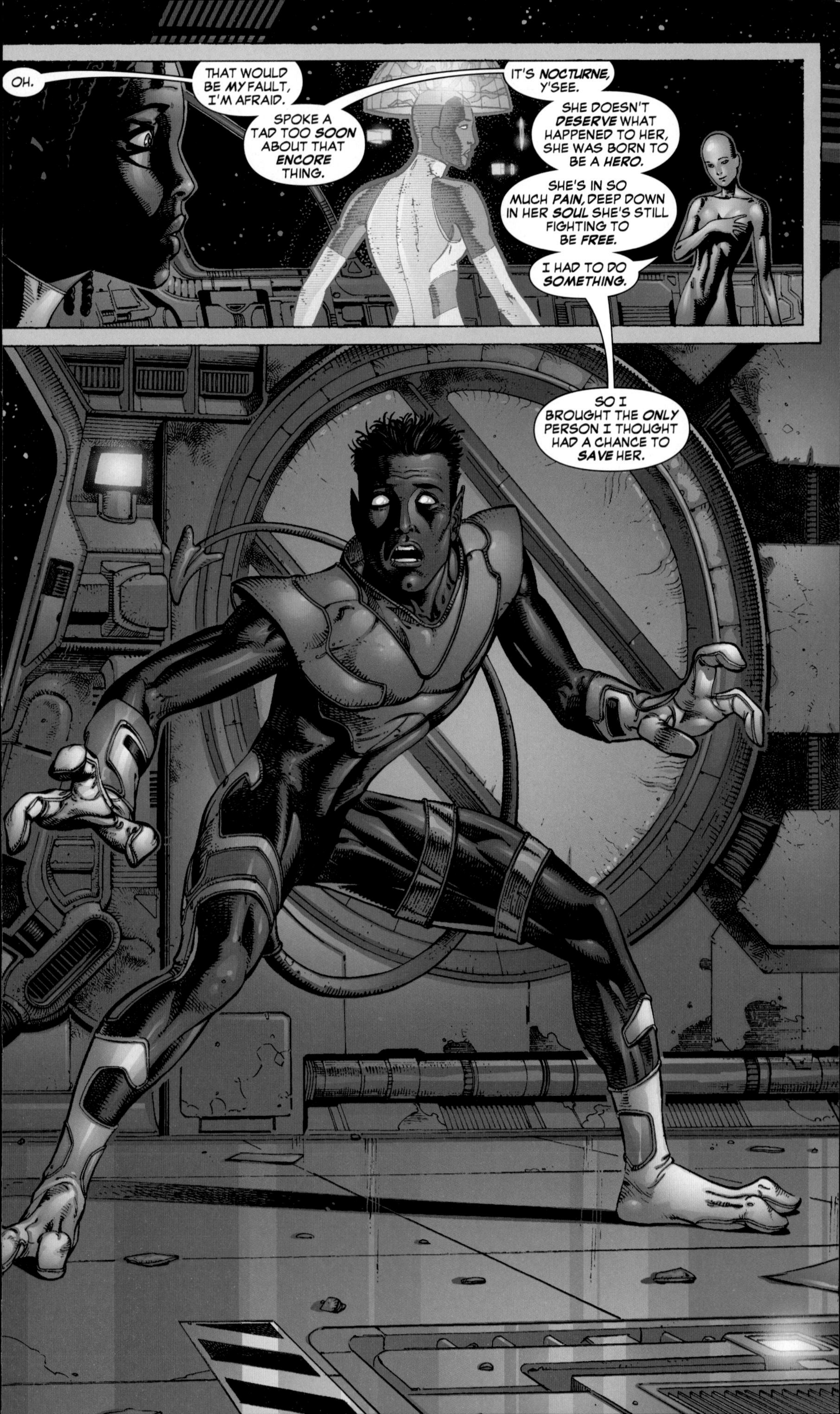
OH.
THAT WOULD BE MY FAULT, I'M AFRAID.
SPOKE A TAD TOO SOON ABOUT THAT ENCORE THING.
IT'S NOCTURNE, Y'SEE.
SHE DOESN'T DESERVE WHAT HAPPENED TO HER, SHE WAS BORN TO BE A HERO.
SHE'S IN SO MUCH PAIN, DEEP DOWN IN HER SOUL SHE'S STILL FIGHTING TO BE FREE.
I HAD TO DO SOMETHING.
SO I BROUGHT THE ONLY PERSON I THOUGHT HAD A CHANCE TO SAVE HER.

#2

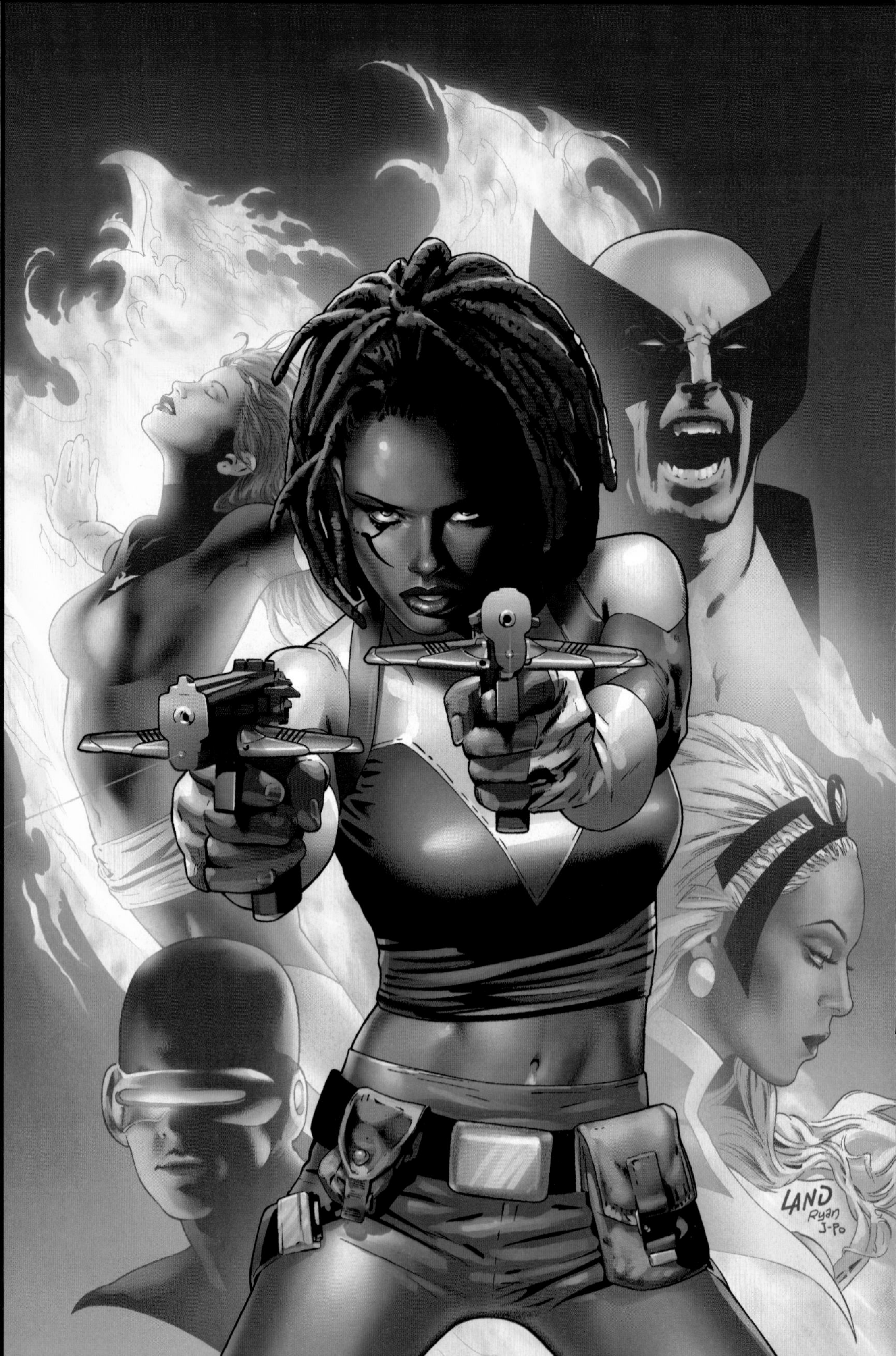
LAND
Ryan
J-Po

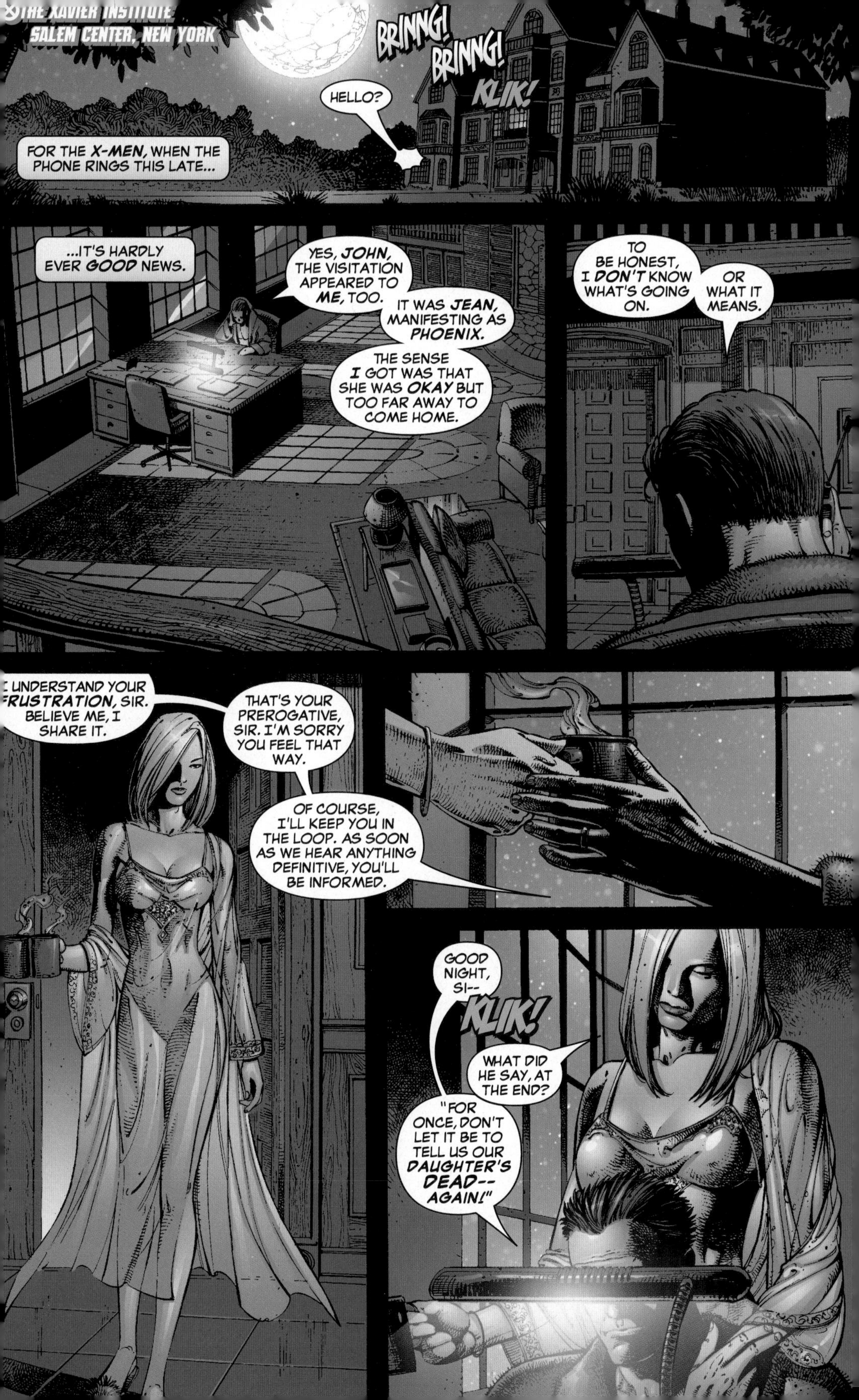
THE XAVIER INSTITUTE
SALEM CENTER, NEW YORK
FOR THE X-MEN, WHEN THE PHONE RINGS THIS LATE...
BRINNG! BRINNG!
KLIK!
HELLO?
...IT'S HARDLY EVER GOOD NEWS.
YES, JOHN, THE VISITATION APPEARED TO ME, TOO.
IT WAS JEAN, MANIFESTING AS PHOENIX.
THE SENSE I GOT WAS THAT SHE WAS OKAY BUT TOO FAR AWAY TO COME HOME.
TO BE HONEST, I DON'T KNOW WHAT'S GOING ON.
OR WHAT IT MEANS.
I UNDERSTAND YOUR FRUSTRATION, SIR. BELIEVE ME, I SHARE IT.
THAT'S YOUR PREROGATIVE, SIR. I'M SORRY YOU FEEL THAT WAY.
OF COURSE, I'LL KEEP YOU IN THE LOOP. AS SOON AS WE HEAR ANYTHING DEFINITIVE, YOU'LL BE INFORMED.
GOOD NIGHT, SI--
KLIK!
WHAT DID HE SAY, AT THE END?
"FOR ONCE, DON'T LET IT BE TO TELL US OUR DAUGHTER'S DEAD-- AGAIN!"

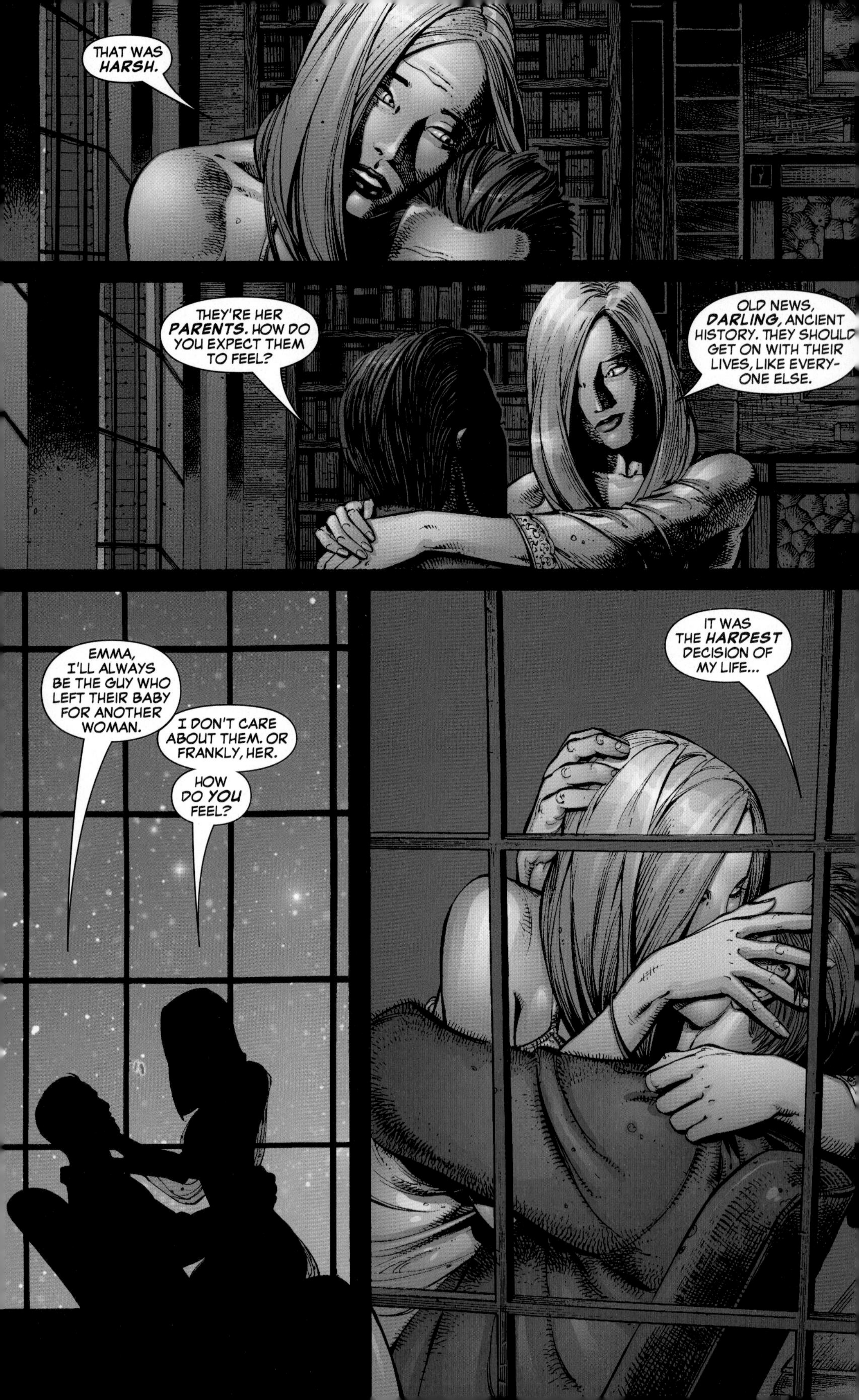
THAT WAS HARSH.
THEY'RE HER PARENTS. HOW DO YOU EXPECT THEM TO FEEL?
OLD NEWS, DARLING, ANCIENT HISTORY. THEY SHOULD GET ON WITH THEIR LIVES, LIKE EVERY-ONE ELSE.
EMMA, I'LL ALWAYS BE THE GUY WHO LEFT THEIR BABY FOR ANOTHER WOMAN.
I DON'T CARE ABOUT THEM. OR FRANKLY, HER.
HOW DO YOU FEEL?
IT WAS THE HARDEST DECISION OF MY LIFE...

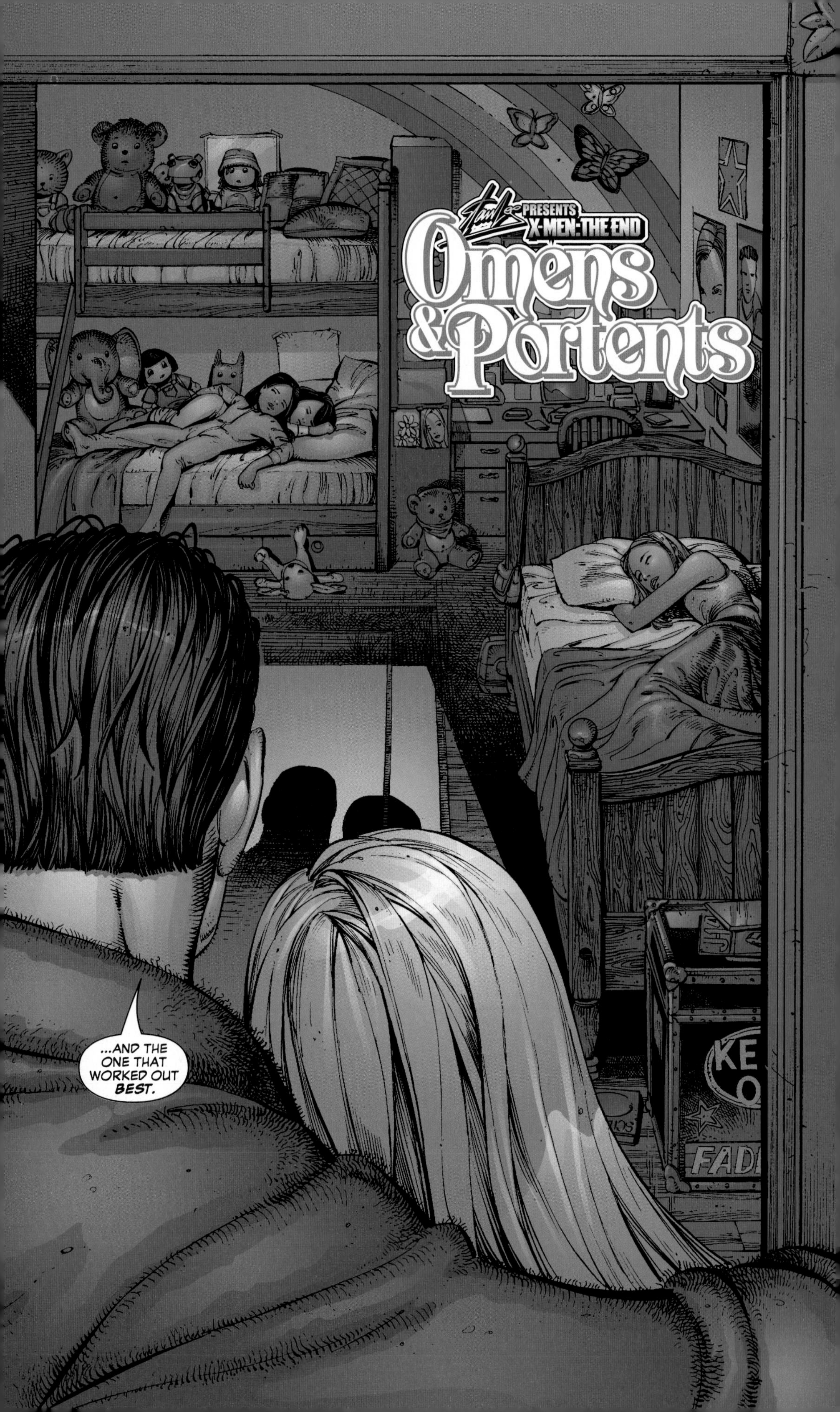
PRESENTS
X-MEN: THE END
Omens & Portents
...AND THE ONE THAT WORKED OUT BEST.

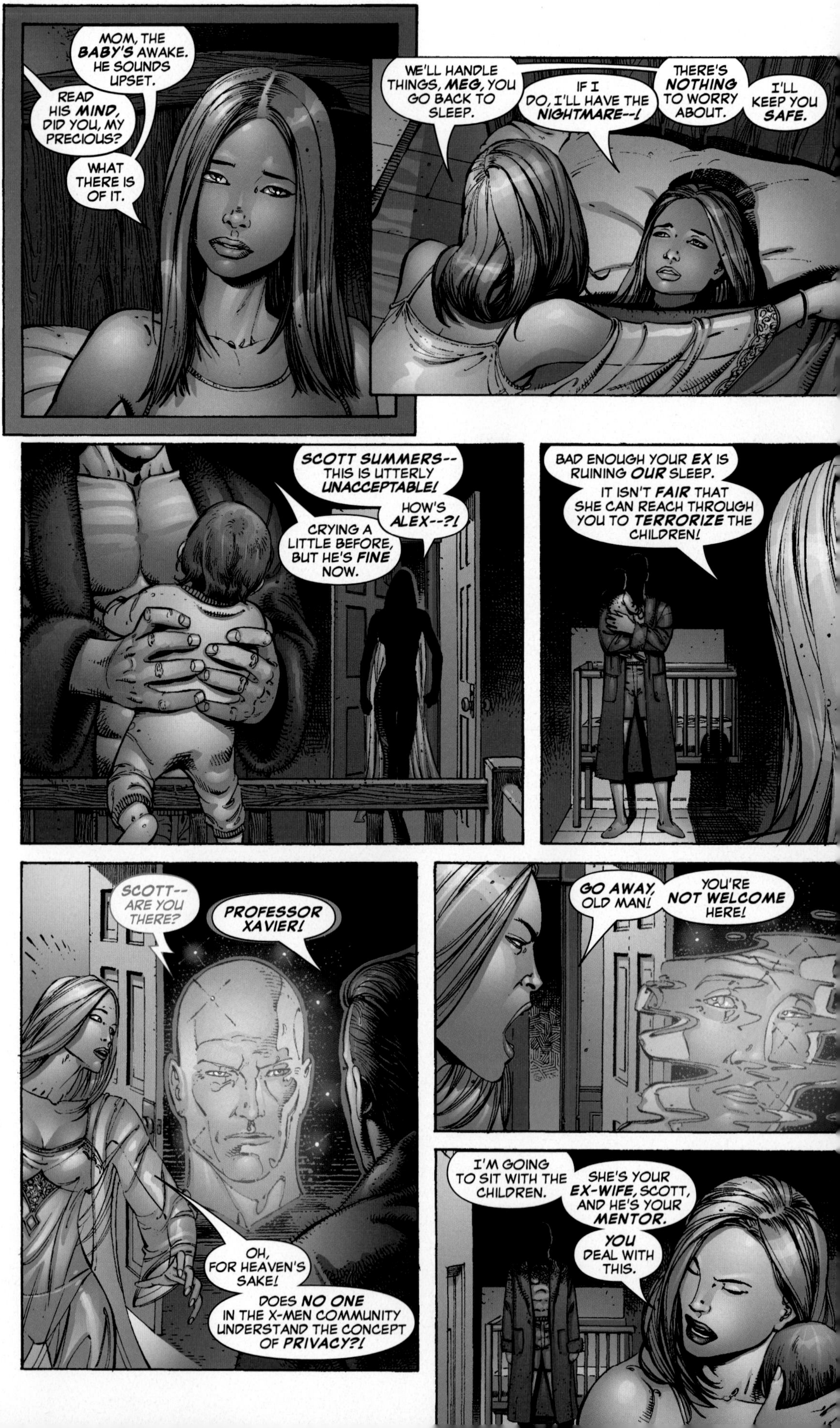
MOM, THE BABY'S AWAKE. HE SOUNDS UPSET.
READ HIS MIND, DID YOU, MY PRECIOUS?
WHAT THERE IS OF IT.
WE'LL HANDLE THINGS, MEG, YOU GO BACK TO SLEEP.
IF I DO, I'LL HAVE THE NIGHTMARE--!
THERE'S NOTHING TO WORRY ABOUT.
I'LL KEEP YOU SAFE.
SCOTT SUMMERS-- THIS IS UTTERLY UNACCEPTABLE!
HOW'S ALEX--?!
CRYING A LITTLE BEFORE, BUT HE'S FINE NOW.
BAD ENOUGH YOUR EX IS RUINING OUR SLEEP.
IT ISN'T FAIR THAT SHE CAN REACH THROUGH YOU TO TERRORIZE THE CHILDREN!
SCOTT-- ARE YOU THERE?
PROFESSOR XAVIER!
OH, FOR HEAVEN'S SAKE!
DOES NO ONE IN THE X-MEN COMMUNITY UNDERSTAND THE CONCEPT OF PRIVACY?!
GO AWAY, OLD MAN!
YOU'RE NOT WELCOME HERE!
I'M GOING TO SIT WITH THE CHILDREN.
SHE'S YOUR EX-WIFE, SCOTT, AND HE'S YOUR MENTOR.
YOU DEAL WITH THIS.

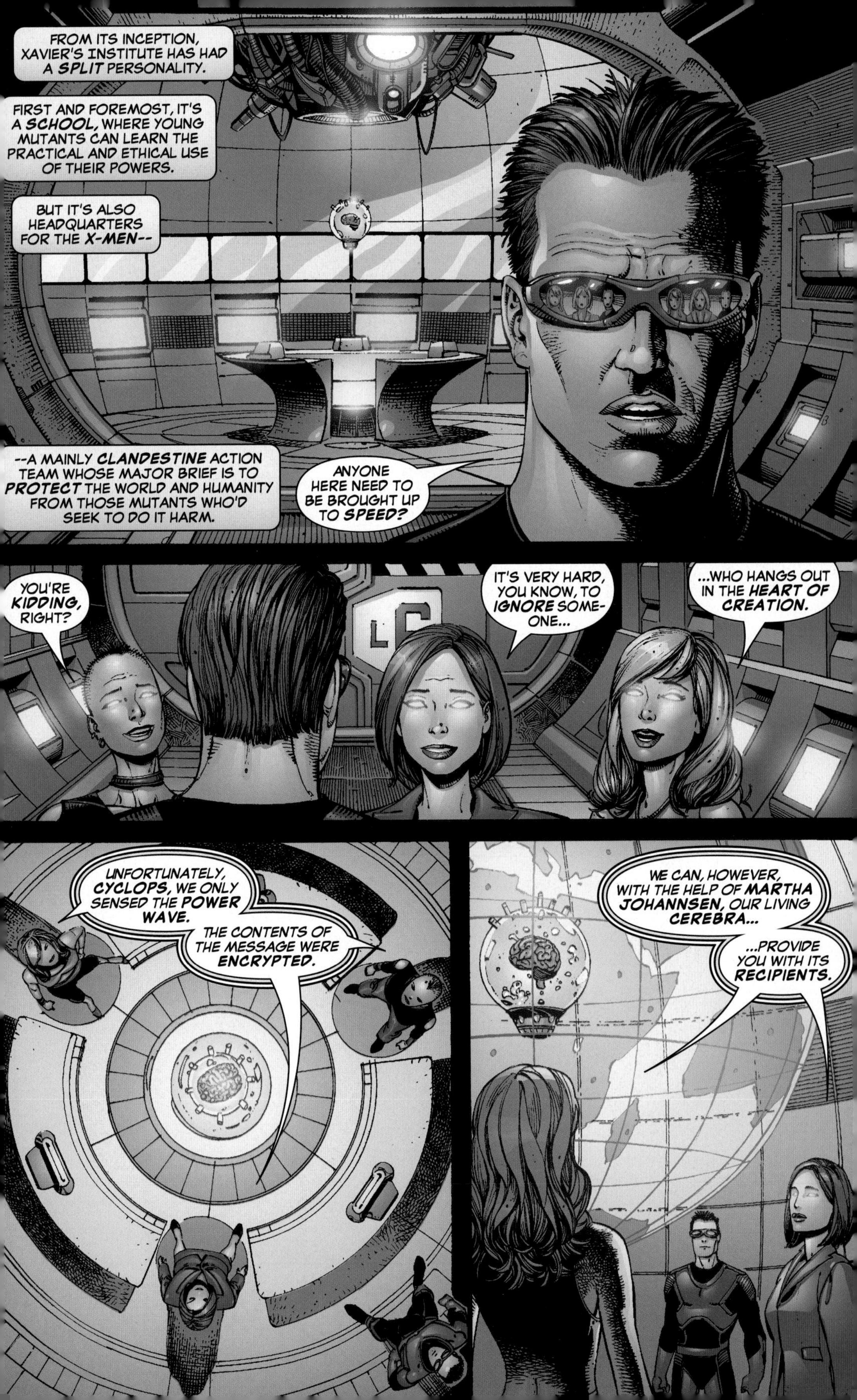
FROM ITS INCEPTION, XAVIER'S INSTITUTE HAS HAD A SPLIT PERSONALITY.
FIRST AND FOREMOST, IT'S A SCHOOL, WHERE YOUNG MUTANTS CAN LEARN THE PRACTICAL AND ETHICAL USE OF THEIR POWERS.
BUT IT'S ALSO HEADQUARTERS FOR THE X-MEN--
--A MAINLY CLANDESTINE ACTION TEAM WHOSE MAJOR BRIEF IS TO PROTECT THE WORLD AND HUMANITY FROM THOSE MUTANTS WHO'D SEEK TO DO IT HARM.
ANYONE HERE NEED TO BE BROUGHT UP TO SPEED?
YOU'RE KIDDING, RIGHT?
IT'S VERY HARD, YOU KNOW, TO IGNORE SOME-ONE...
...WHO HANGS OUT IN THE HEART OF CREATION.
UNFORTUNATELY, CYCLOPS, WE ONLY SENSED THE POWER WAVE.
THE CONTENTS OF THE MESSAGE WERE ENCRYPTED.
WE CAN, HOWEVER, WITH THE HELP OF MARTHA JOHANNSEN, OUR LIVING CEREBRA...
...PROVIDE YOU WITH ITS RECIPIENTS.

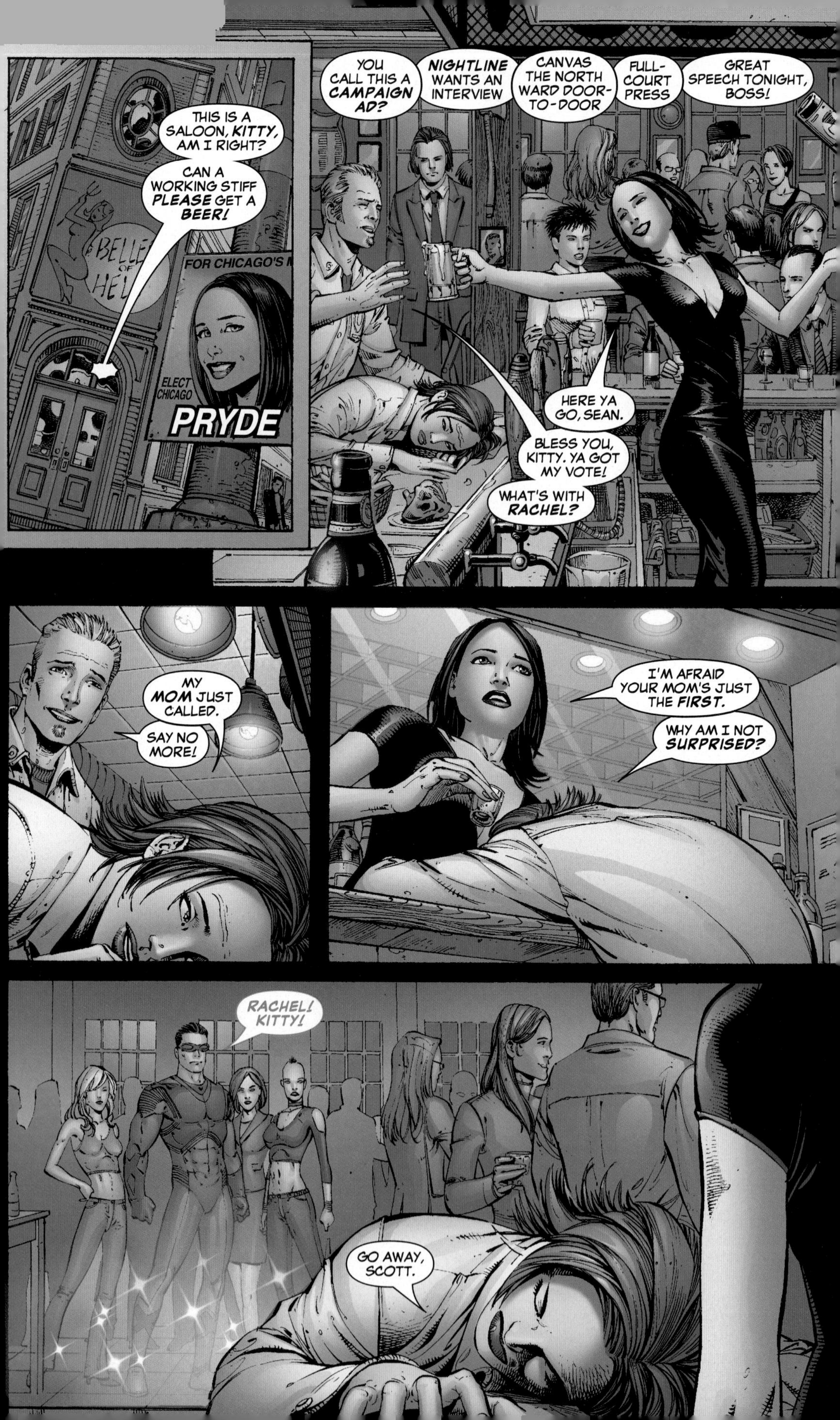

THIS IS A SALOON, *KITTY*, AM I RIGHT?
CAN A WORKING STIFF *PLEASE* GET A *BEER!*
BELLE OF HELL
FOR CHICAGO'S
ELECT CHICAGO
PRYDE
YOU CALL THIS A *CAMPAIGN AD?*
NIGHTLINE WANTS AN INTERVIEW
CANVAS THE NORTH WARD DOOR-TO-DOOR
FULL-COURT PRESS
GREAT SPEECH TONIGHT, BOSS!
HERE YA GO, SEAN.
BLESS YOU, KITTY. YA GOT MY VOTE!
WHAT'S WITH *RACHEL?*
MY *MOM* JUST CALLED.
SAY NO MORE!
I'M AFRAID YOUR MOM'S JUST THE *FIRST.*
WHY AM I NOT *SURPRISED?*
RACHEL! KITTY!
GO AWAY, SCOTT.

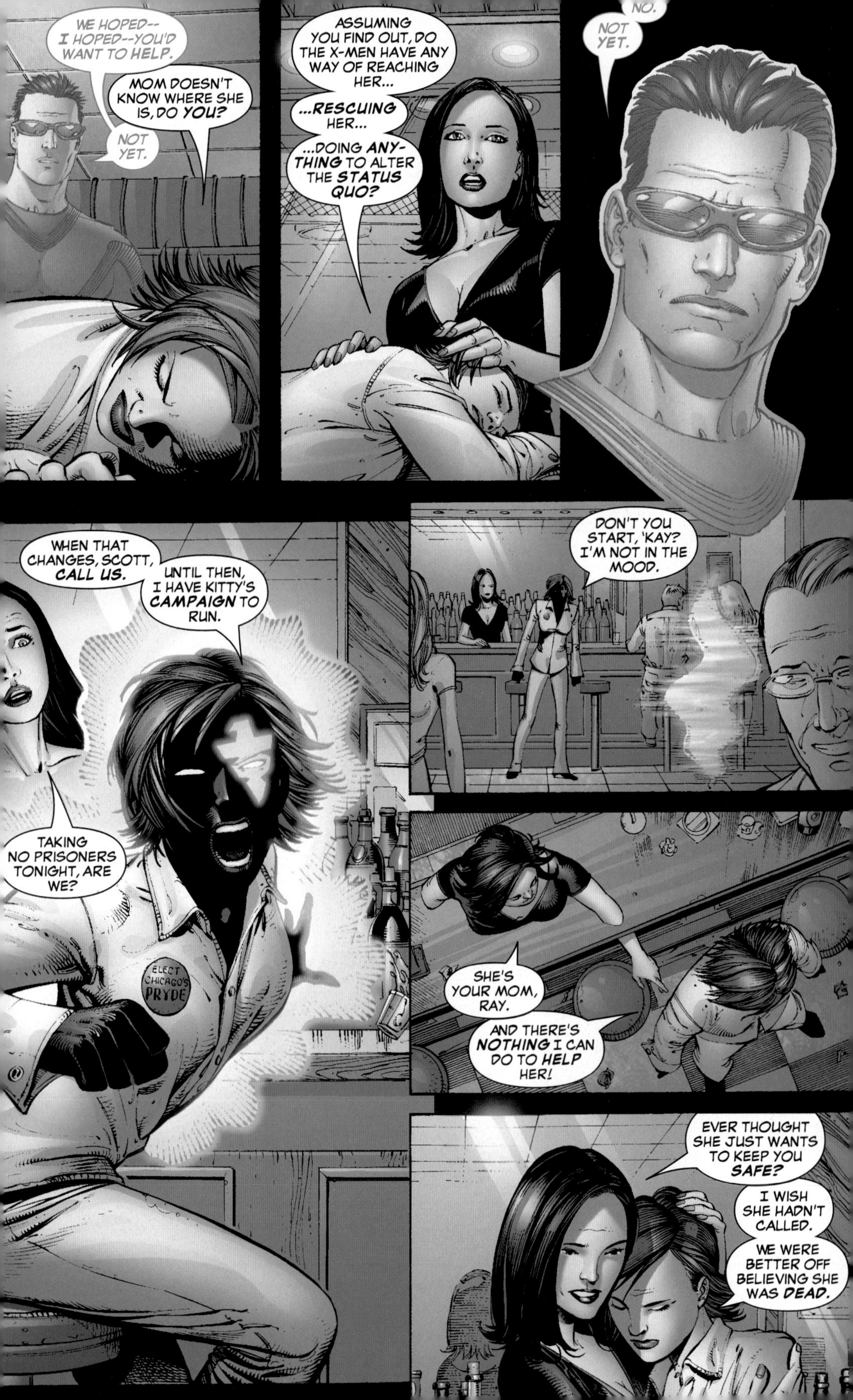
WE HOPED-- I HOPED--YOU'D WANT TO HELP.
MOM DOESN'T KNOW WHERE SHE IS, DO YOU?
NOT YET.
ASSUMING YOU FIND OUT, DO THE X-MEN HAVE ANY WAY OF REACHING HER...
...RESCUING HER...
...DOING ANY-THING TO ALTER THE STATUS QUO?
NO.
NOT YET.
WHEN THAT CHANGES, SCOTT, CALL US.
UNTIL THEN, I HAVE KITTY'S CAMPAIGN TO RUN.
TAKING NO PRISONERS TONIGHT, ARE WE?
ELECT CHICAGO'S PRYDE
DON'T YOU START, 'KAY? I'M NOT IN THE MOOD.
SHE'S YOUR MOM, RAY.
AND THERE'S NOTHING I CAN DO TO HELP HER!
EVER THOUGHT SHE JUST WANTS TO KEEP YOU SAFE?
I WISH SHE HADN'T CALLED.
WE WERE BETTER OFF BELIEVING SHE WAS DEAD.

IS THIS A BAD TIME, CABLE?

NOT AT ALL, *CYCLOPS*. THEY'RE ONLY *TERRORISTS*.

THANKS FOR BRINGING ME UP TO *SPEED*.

I HAVE AN *ULTERIOR MOTIVE*, CABLE.

AND WE'VE HAD THIS CONVERSATION *BEFORE*.

SKKOOM!

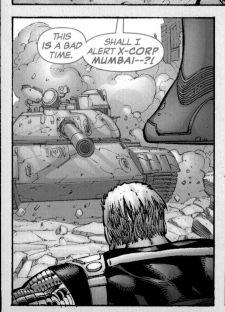

THIS IS A BAD TIME.

SHALL I ALERT X-CORP MUMBAI--?!

WRENCH

NEVER NEEDED THEIR HELP BEFORE.

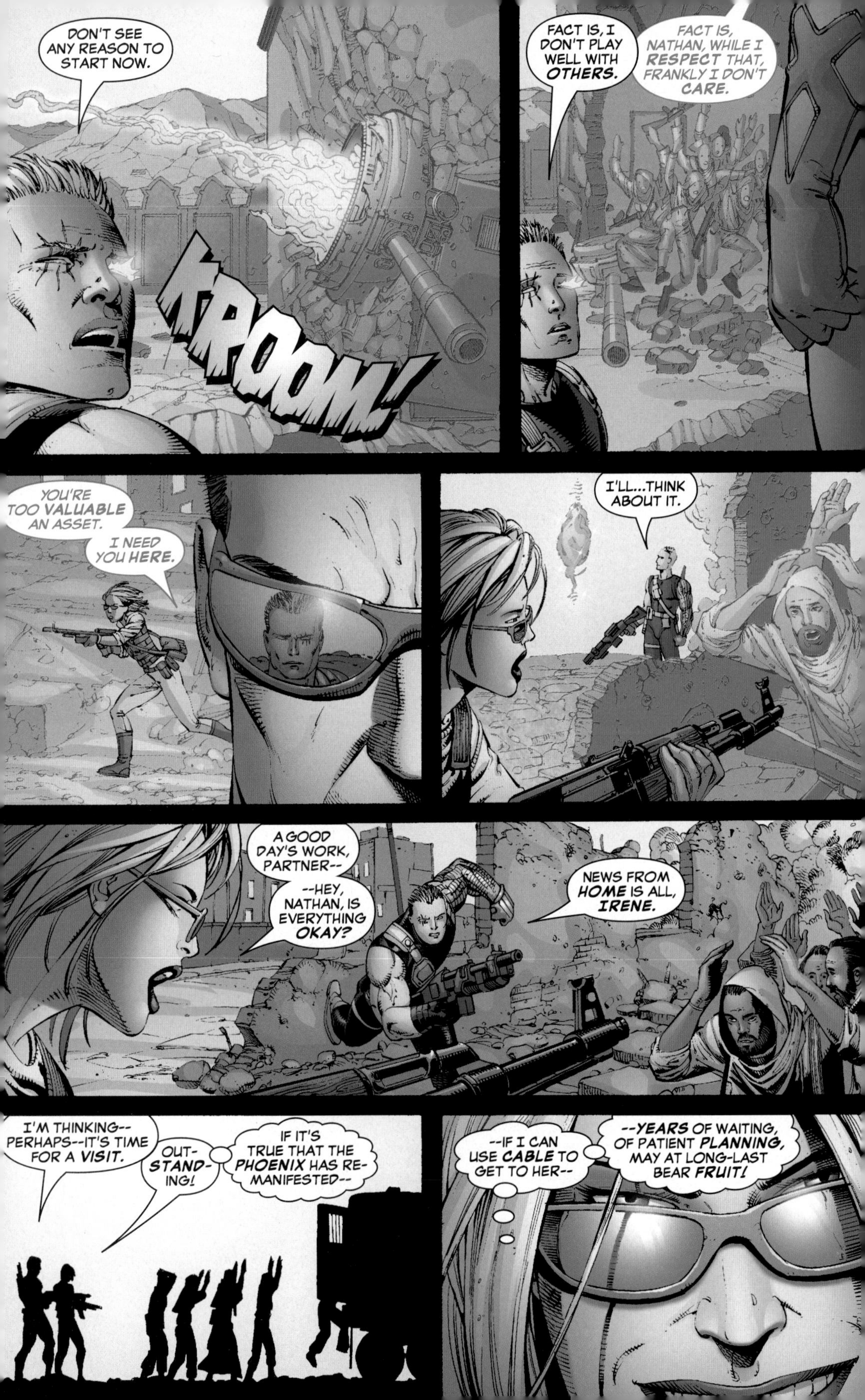
DON'T SEE ANY REASON TO START NOW.
KROOM!
FACT IS, I DON'T PLAY WELL WITH OTHERS.
FACT IS, NATHAN, WHILE I RESPECT THAT, FRANKLY I DON'T CARE.
YOU'RE TOO VALUABLE AN ASSET.
I NEED YOU HERE.
I'LL...THINK ABOUT IT.
A GOOD DAY'S WORK, PARTNER--
--HEY, NATHAN, IS EVERYTHING OKAY?
NEWS FROM HOME IS ALL, IRENE.
I'M THINKING-- PERHAPS--IT'S TIME FOR A VISIT.
OUT-STAND-ING!
IF IT'S TRUE THAT THE PHOENIX HAS RE-MANIFESTED--
--IF I CAN USE CABLE TO GET TO HER--
--YEARS OF WAITING, OF PATIENT PLANNING, MAY AT LONG-LAST BEAR FRUIT!

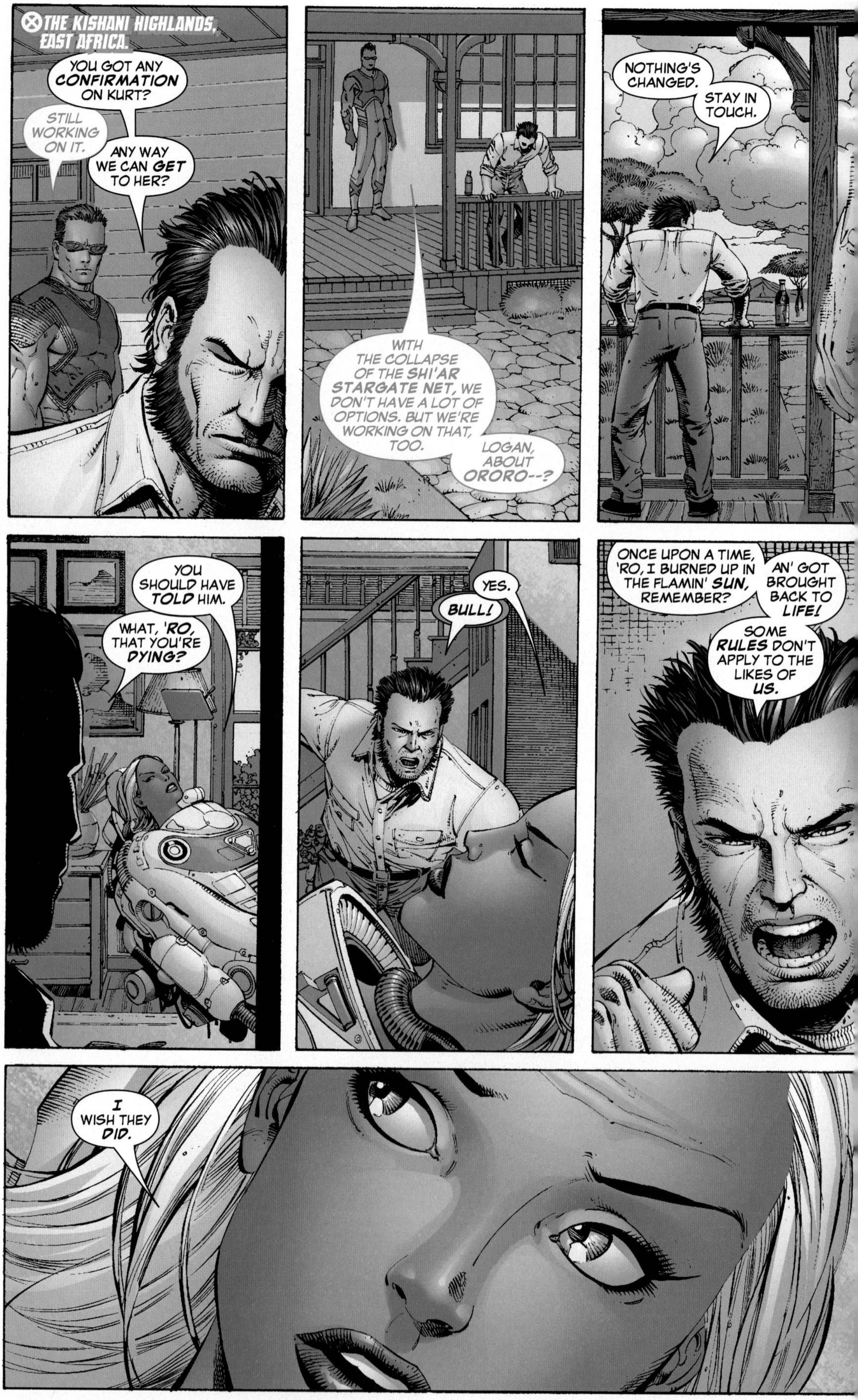
THE KISHANI HIGHLANDS, EAST AFRICA.
YOU GOT ANY CONFIRMATION ON KURT?
STILL WORKING ON IT.
ANY WAY WE CAN GET TO HER?
WITH THE COLLAPSE OF THE SHI'AR STARGATE NET, WE DON'T HAVE A LOT OF OPTIONS. BUT WE'RE WORKING ON THAT, TOO.
LOGAN, ABOUT ORORO--?
NOTHING'S CHANGED.
STAY IN TOUCH.
YOU SHOULD HAVE TOLD HIM.
WHAT, 'RO, THAT YOU'RE DYING?
YES.
BULL!
ONCE UPON A TIME, 'RO, I BURNED UP IN THE FLAMIN' SUN, REMEMBER?
AN' GOT BROUGHT BACK TO LIFE!
SOME RULES DON'T APPLY TO THE LIKES OF US.
I WISH THEY DID.

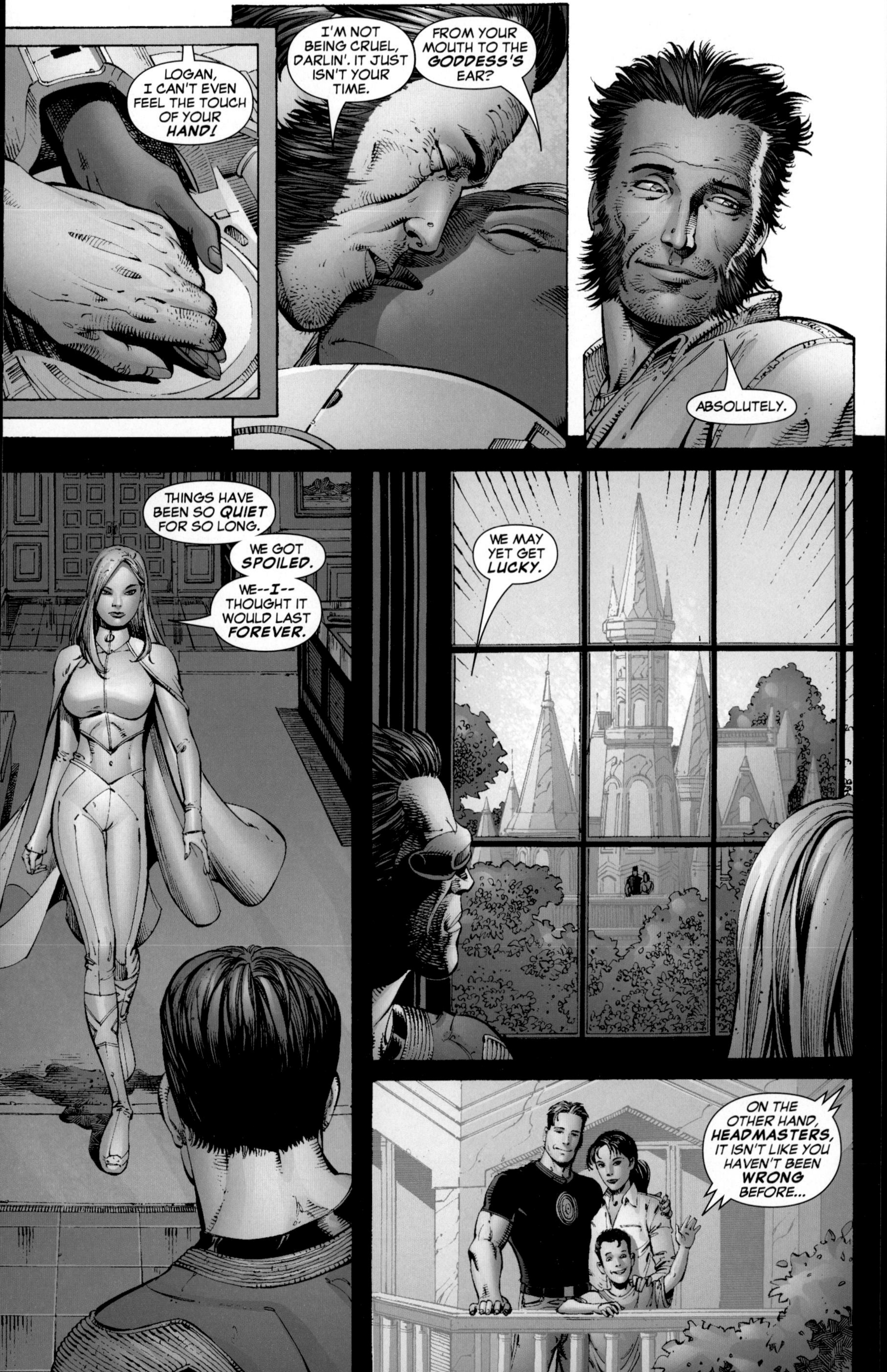
LOGAN, I CAN'T EVEN FEEL THE TOUCH OF YOUR HAND!
I'M NOT BEING CRUEL, DARLIN'. IT JUST ISN'T YOUR TIME.
FROM YOUR MOUTH TO THE GODDESS'S EAR?
ABSOLUTELY.
THINGS HAVE BEEN SO QUIET FOR SO LONG.
WE GOT SPOILED.
WE--I--THOUGHT IT WOULD LAST FOREVER.
WE MAY YET GET LUCKY.
ON THE OTHER HAND, HEADMASTERS, IT ISN'T LIKE YOU HAVEN'T BEEN WRONG BEFORE...

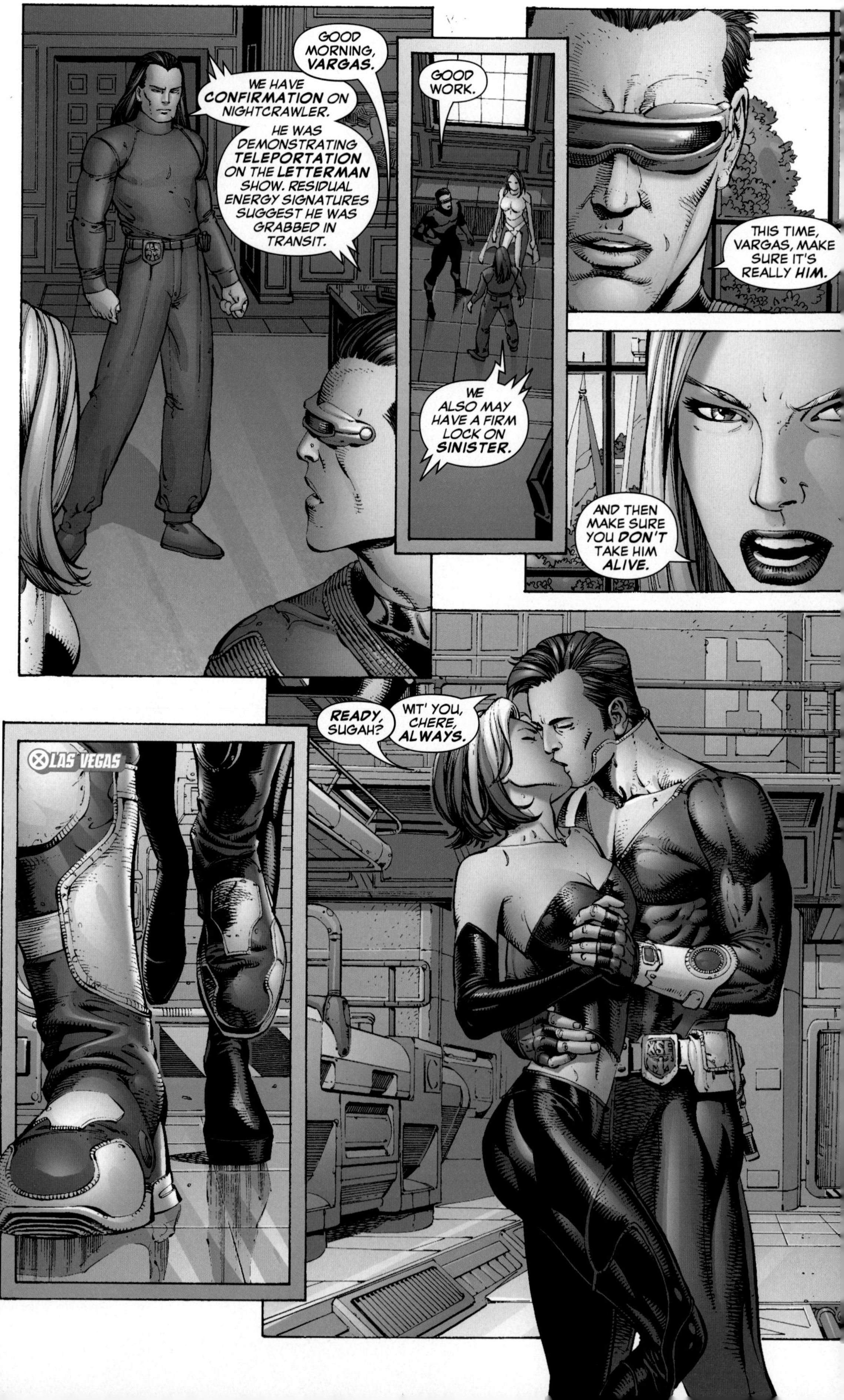
GOOD MORNING, VARGAS.
WE HAVE CONFIRMATION ON NIGHTCRAWLER.
HE WAS DEMONSTRATING TELEPORTATION ON THE LETTERMAN SHOW. RESIDUAL ENERGY SIGNATURES SUGGEST HE WAS GRABBED IN TRANSIT.
GOOD WORK.
WE ALSO MAY HAVE A FIRM LOCK ON SINISTER.
THIS TIME, VARGAS, MAKE SURE IT'S REALLY HIM.
AND THEN MAKE SURE YOU DON'T TAKE HIM ALIVE.
LAS VEGAS
READY, SUGAH?
WIT' YOU, CHERE, ALWAYS.

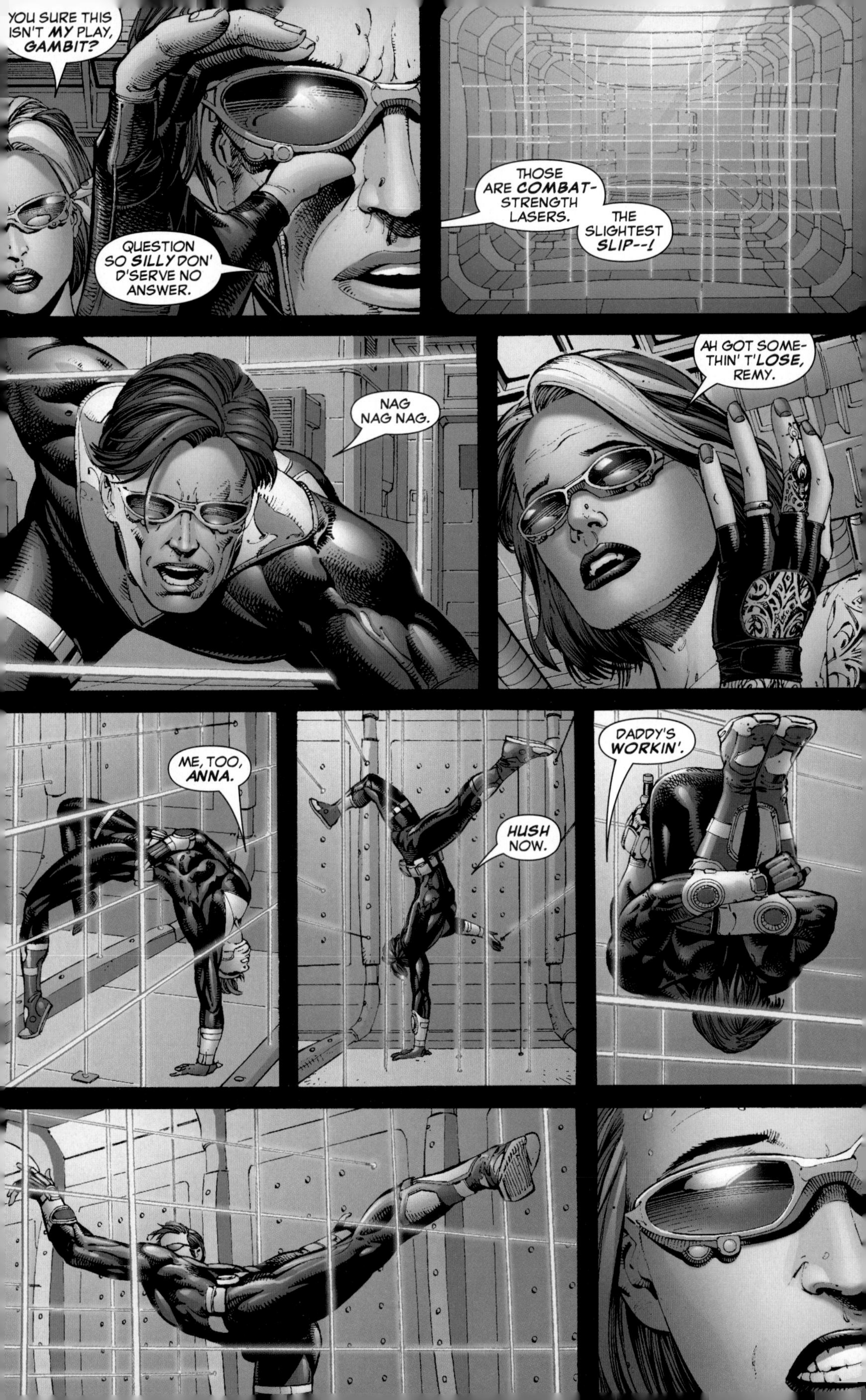
YOU SURE THIS ISN'T MY PLAY, GAMBIT?
QUESTION SO SILLY DON' D'SERVE NO ANSWER.
THOSE ARE COMBAT-STRENGTH LASERS.
THE SLIGHTEST SLIP--!
NAG NAG NAG.
AH GOT SOME-THIN' T'LOSE, REMY.
ME, TOO, ANNA.
HUSH NOW.
DADDY'S WORKIN'.

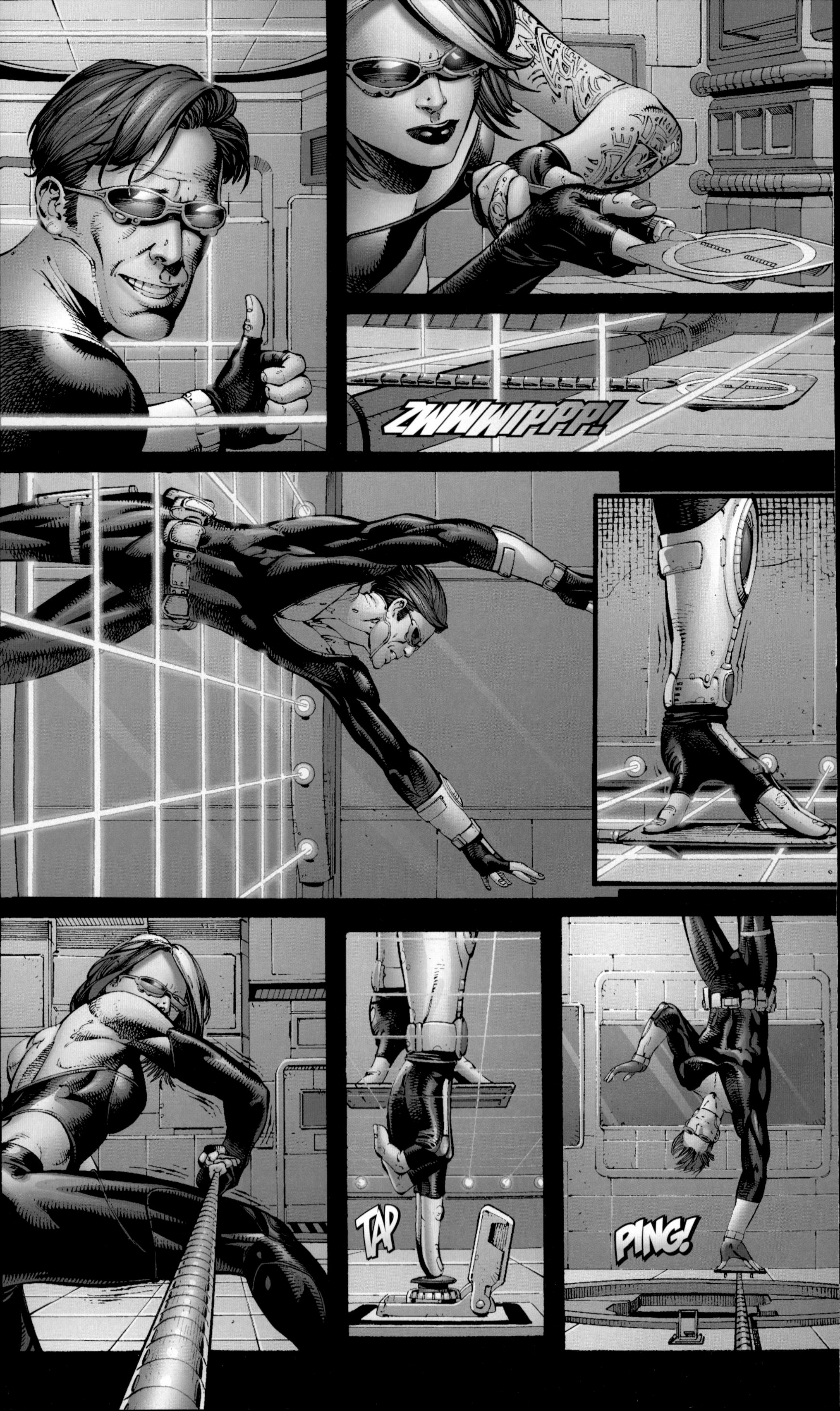
ZWWWIPPP!
TAP
PING!

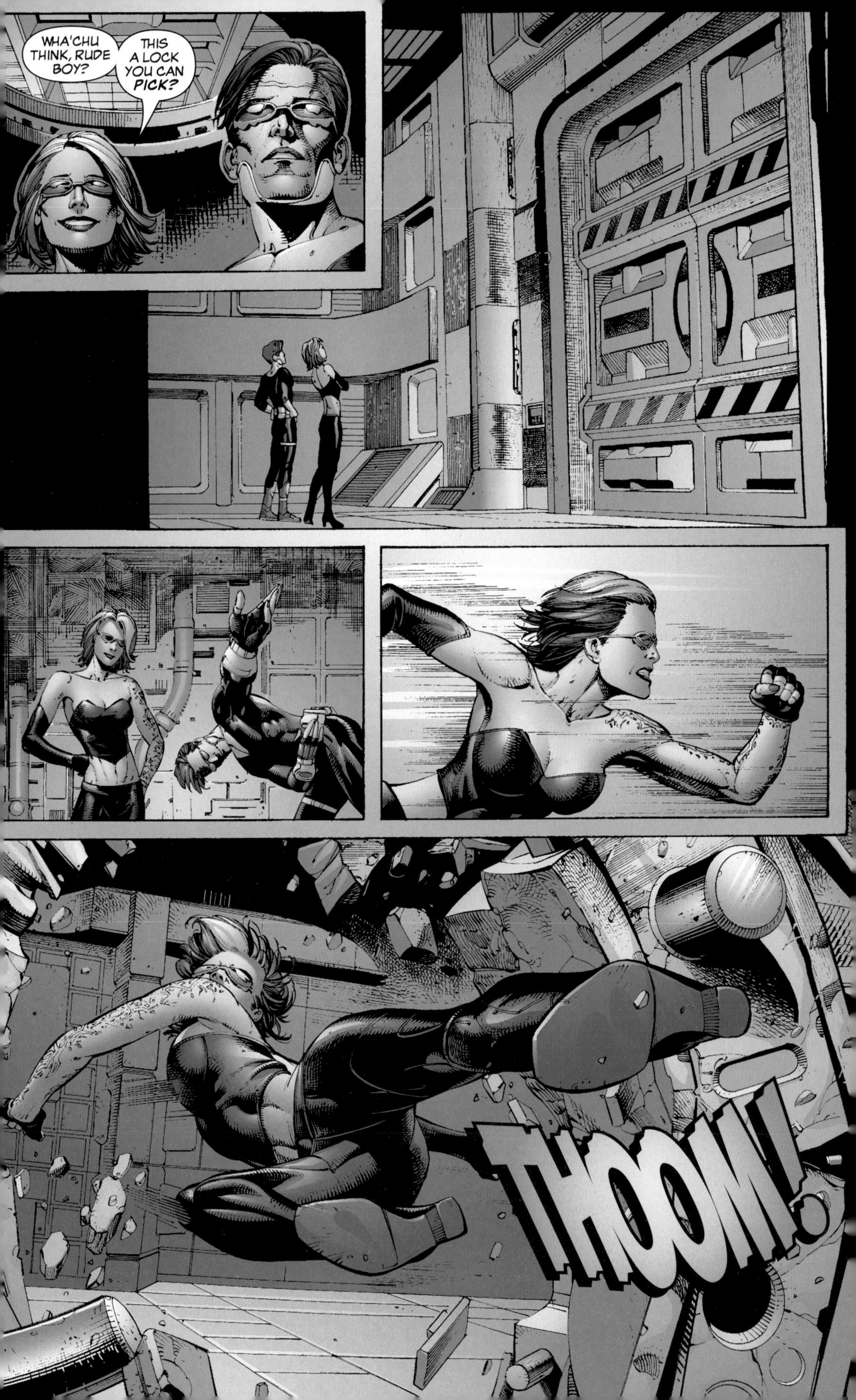
WHA'CHU THINK, RUDE BOY?
THIS A LOCK YOU CAN PICK?
THOOM!

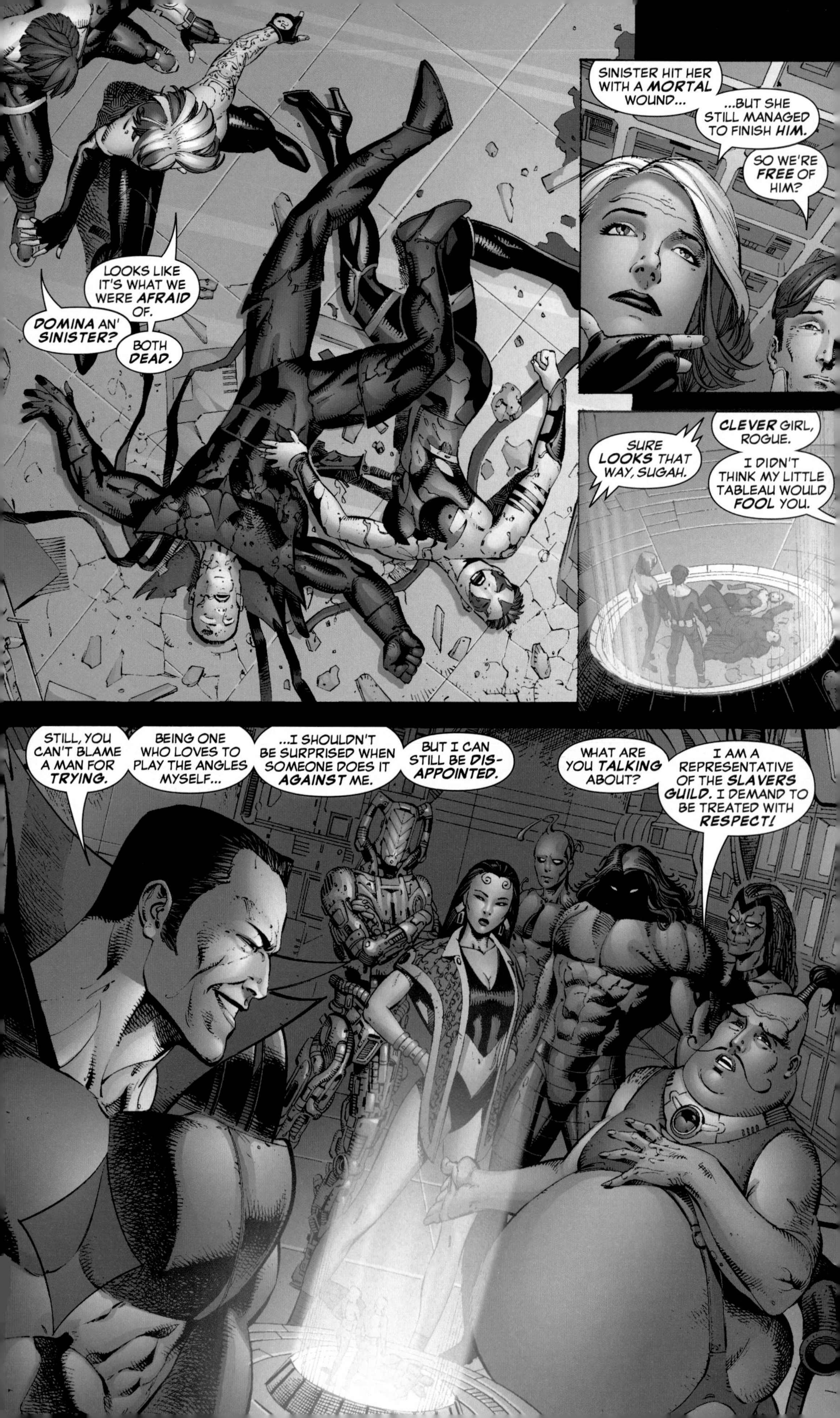
LOOKS LIKE IT'S WHAT WE WERE AFRAID OF.
DOMINA AN' SINISTER?
BOTH DEAD.
SINISTER HIT HER WITH A MORTAL WOUND...
...BUT SHE STILL MANAGED TO FINISH HIM.
SO WE'RE FREE OF HIM?
SURE LOOKS THAT WAY, SUGAH.
CLEVER GIRL, ROGUE.
I DIDN'T THINK MY LITTLE TABLEAU WOULD FOOL YOU.
STILL, YOU CAN'T BLAME A MAN FOR TRYING.
BEING ONE WHO LOVES TO PLAY THE ANGLES MYSELF...
...I SHOULDN'T BE SURPRISED WHEN SOMEONE DOES IT AGAINST ME.
BUT I CAN STILL BE DIS-APPOINTED.
WHAT ARE YOU TALKING ABOUT?
I AM A REPRESENTATIVE OF THE SLAVERS GUILD. I DEMAND TO BE TREATED WITH RESPECT!

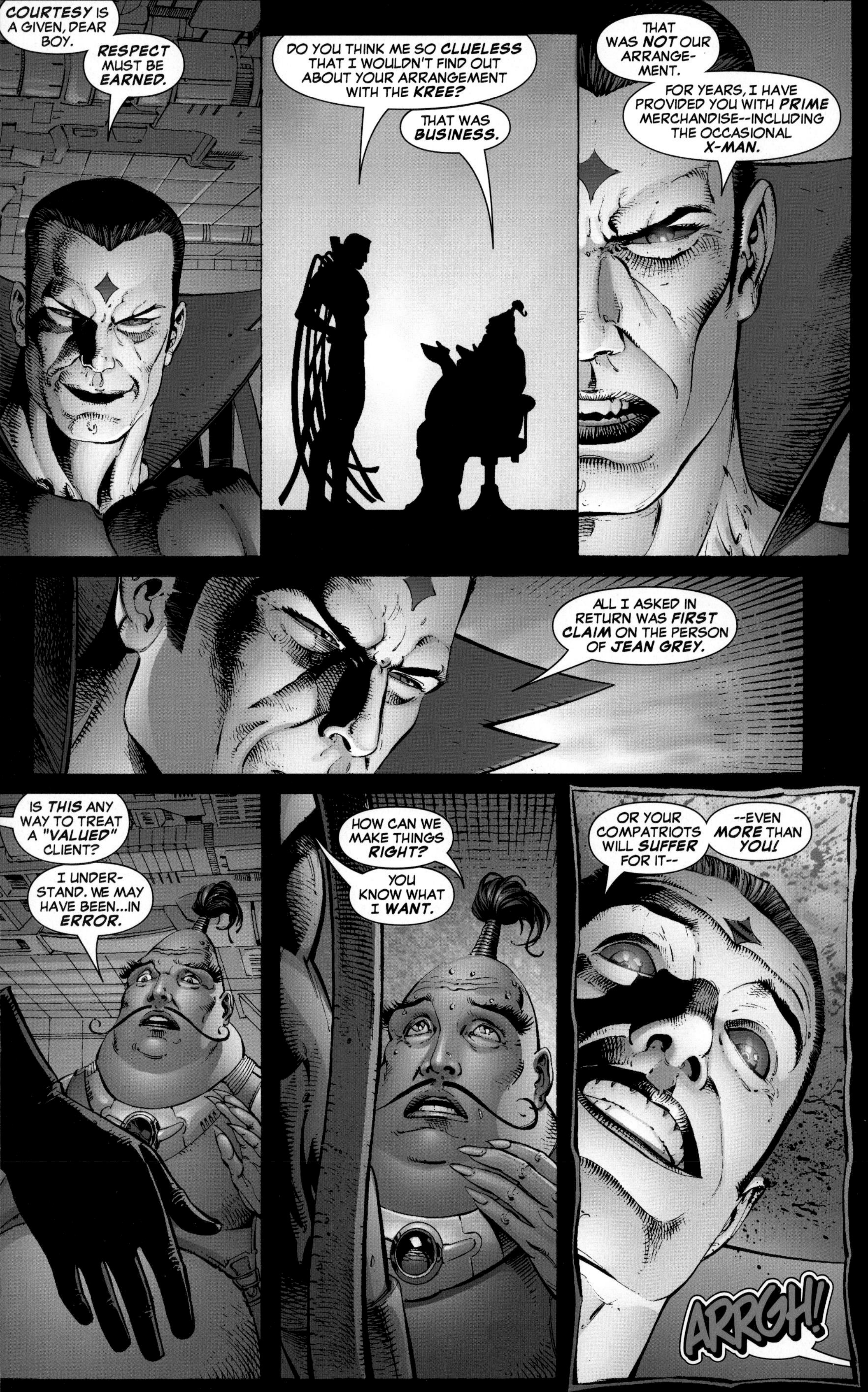

COURTESY IS A GIVEN, DEAR BOY.
RESPECT MUST BE EARNED.
DO YOU THINK ME SO CLUELESS THAT I WOULDN'T FIND OUT ABOUT YOUR ARRANGEMENT WITH THE KREE?
THAT WAS BUSINESS.
THAT WAS NOT OUR ARRANGE-MENT.
FOR YEARS, I HAVE PROVIDED YOU WITH PRIME MERCHANDISE--INCLUDING THE OCCASIONAL X-MAN.
ALL I ASKED IN RETURN WAS FIRST CLAIM ON THE PERSON OF JEAN GREY.
IS THIS ANY WAY TO TREAT A "VALUED" CLIENT?
I UNDER-STAND. WE MAY HAVE BEEN...IN ERROR.
HOW CAN WE MAKE THINGS RIGHT?
YOU KNOW WHAT I WANT.
OR YOUR COMPATRIOTS WILL SUFFER FOR IT--
--EVEN MORE THAN YOU!
ARRGH!!

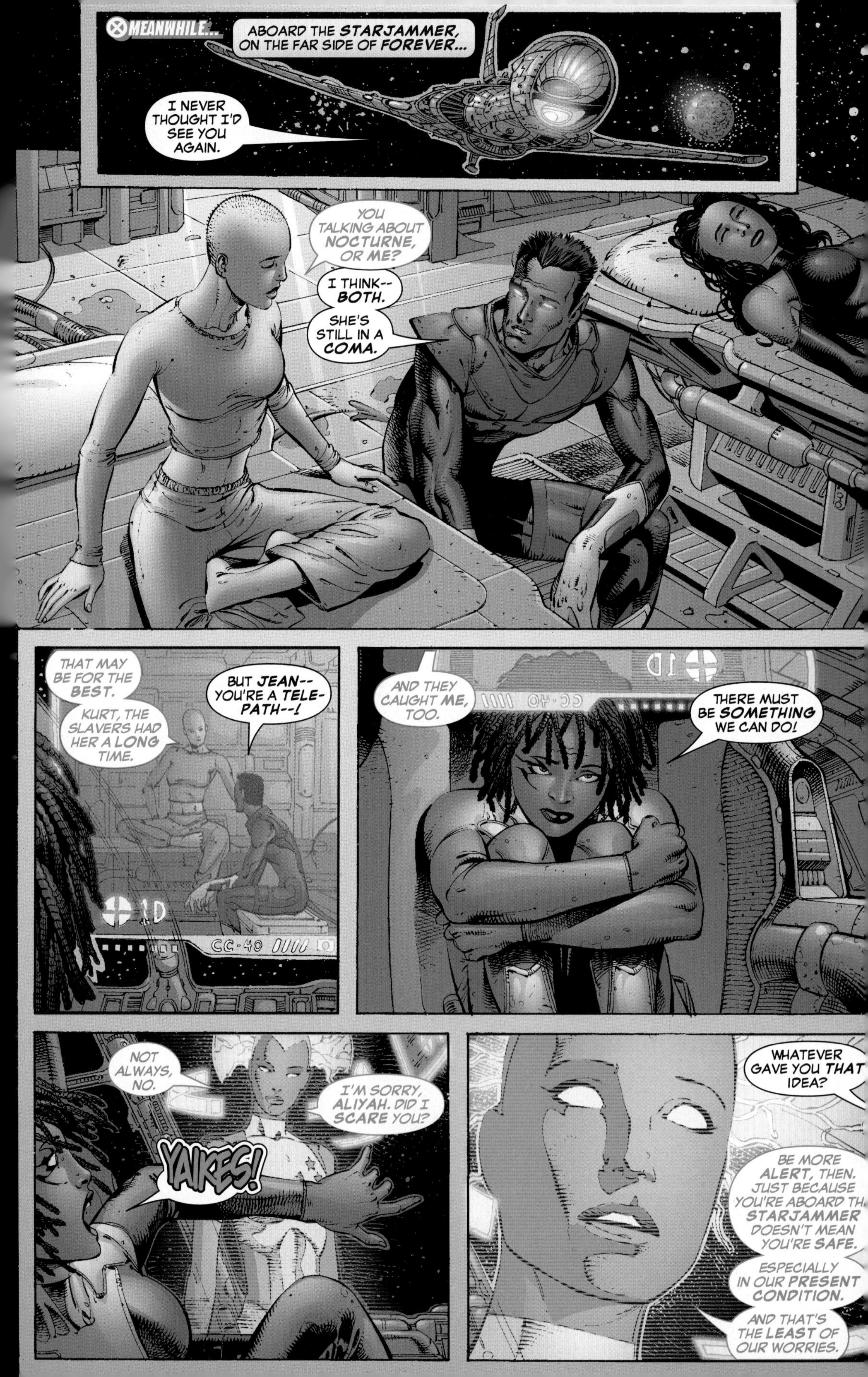
MEANWHILE...
ABOARD THE STARJAMMER, ON THE FAR SIDE OF FOREVER...
I NEVER THOUGHT I'D SEE YOU AGAIN.
YOU TALKING ABOUT NOCTURNE, OR ME?
I THINK-- BOTH.
SHE'S STILL IN A COMA.
THAT MAY BE FOR THE BEST.
KURT, THE SLAVERS HAD HER A LONG TIME.
BUT JEAN-- YOU'RE A TELE-PATH--!
AND THEY CAUGHT ME, TOO.
THERE MUST BE SOMETHING WE CAN DO!
NOT ALWAYS, NO.
YAIKES!
I'M SORRY, ALIYAH. DID I SCARE YOU?
WHATEVER GAVE YOU THAT IDEA?
BE MORE ALERT, THEN. JUST BECAUSE YOU'RE ABOARD TH STARJAMMER DOESN'T MEAN YOU'RE SAFE.
ESPECIALLY IN OUR PRESENT CONDITION.
AND THAT'S THE LEAST OF OUR WORRIES.

THOSE ARE THE CRITTERS WE FOUGHT.

THEY'RE AN EVOLUTION OF THE *BROOD*.

CAROL, THEY'RE SUPPOSED TO BE *DEAD!*

EXTINCT, ACTUALLY, THANKS TO *STORM* AND ME.

IT WAS MY *LAST* MISSION AS *WARBIRD*-- BEFORE ...

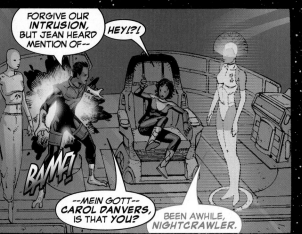

FORGIVE OUR *INTRUSION*, BUT JEAN HEARD MENTION OF--

HEY!?!

BAMF!

--MEIN GOTT-- *CAROL DANVERS*, IS THAT *YOU*?

BEEN AWHILE, *NIGHTCRAWLER*.

I DON'T KNOW WHAT TO SAY. I DON'T KNOW WHY I'M EVEN *HERE*.

MY FAULT, I'M AFRAID, KURT.

I REACHED OUT BLIND FOR SOMEONE I COULD *TRUST*.

CAN YOU SEND ME *HOME*?

REAL QUESTION IS *SHOULD* WE?

I'M NOT AN *X-MAN* ANYMORE, CAROL. I'M AN *ACTOR*.

AND THIS ISN'T JUST ABOUT *YOU*.

THE SHI'AR EMPIRE'S BEEN IN *CHAOS* FOR YEARS, EVER SINCE A MONSTER MASQUERADING AS CHARLES XAVIER DROVE EMPRESS LILANDRA INSANE.

CASSANDRA NOVA, I REMEMBER.

UNDER THE NEW *CHANCELLOR*, CENTRAL AUTHORITY'S BEEN GRADUALLY *RESTORED*. ALONG WITH THE EMPIRE'S AGGRESSIVE, EXPANSIONIST *FOREIGN POLICY*.

TO FULFILL THOSE AMBITIONS, THE EMPIRE NEEDS A NEW *STARGATE* NETWORK.

THE *SLAVERS* ARE THE PERFECT SOLUTION. THEIR TRANSIT NET STRETCHES ACROSS ENTIRE *DIMENSIONS*.

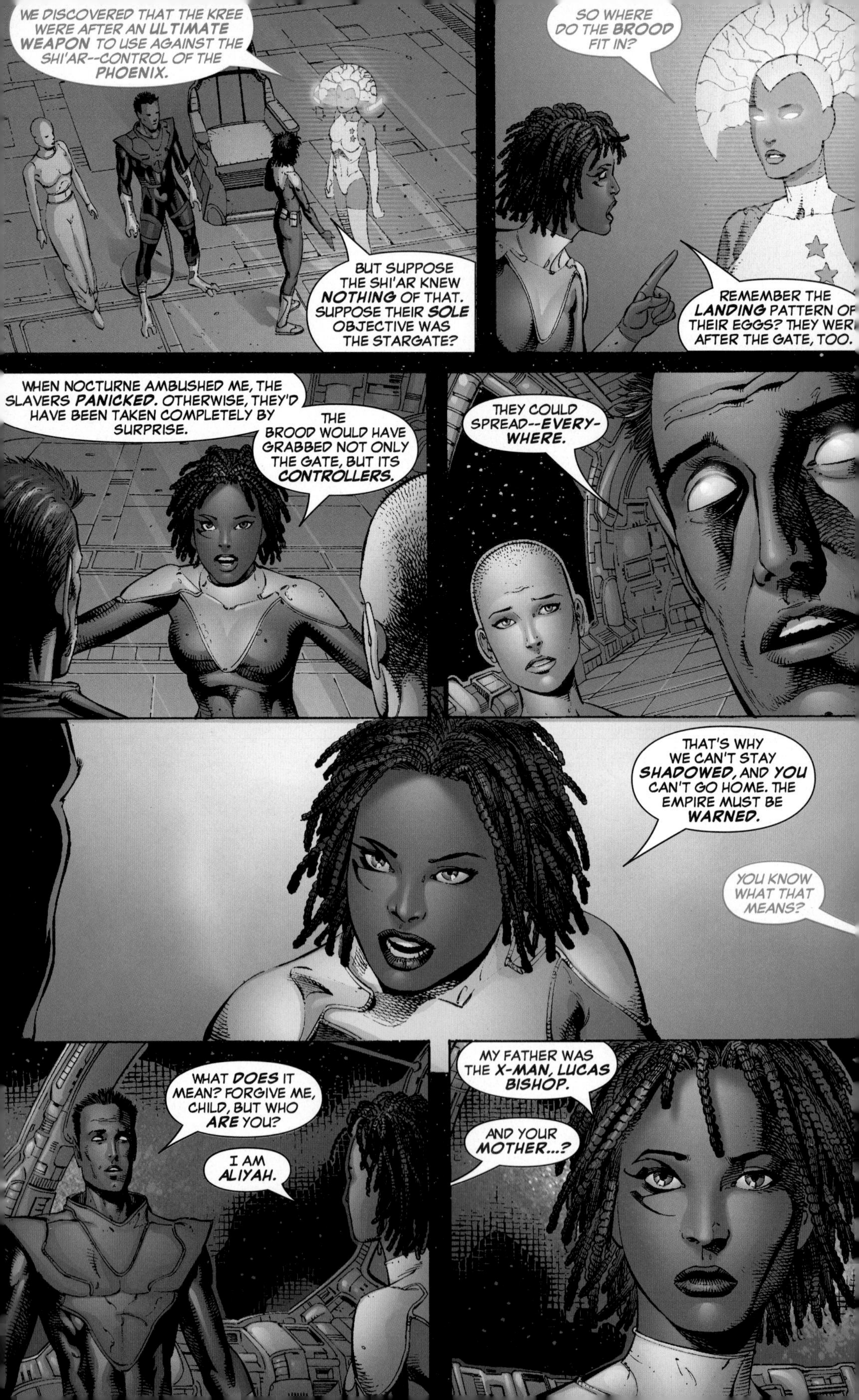
WE DISCOVERED THAT THE KREE WERE AFTER AN ULTIMATE WEAPON TO USE AGAINST THE SHI'AR--CONTROL OF THE PHOENIX.
BUT SUPPOSE THE SHI'AR KNEW NOTHING OF THAT. SUPPOSE THEIR SOLE OBJECTIVE WAS THE STARGATE?
SO WHERE DO THE BROOD FIT IN?
REMEMBER THE LANDING PATTERN OF THEIR EGGS? THEY WER AFTER THE GATE, TOO.
WHEN NOCTURNE AMBUSHED ME, THE SLAVERS PANICKED. OTHERWISE, THEY'D HAVE BEEN TAKEN COMPLETELY BY SURPRISE.
THE BROOD WOULD HAVE GRABBED NOT ONLY THE GATE, BUT ITS CONTROLLERS.
THEY COULD SPREAD--EVERY-WHERE.
THAT'S WHY WE CAN'T STAY SHADOWED, AND YOU CAN'T GO HOME. THE EMPIRE MUST BE WARNED.
YOU KNOW WHAT THAT MEANS?
WHAT DOES IT MEAN? FORGIVE ME, CHILD, BUT WHO ARE YOU?
I AM ALIYAH.
MY FATHER WAS THE X-MAN, LUCAS BISHOP.
AND YOUR MOTHER...?

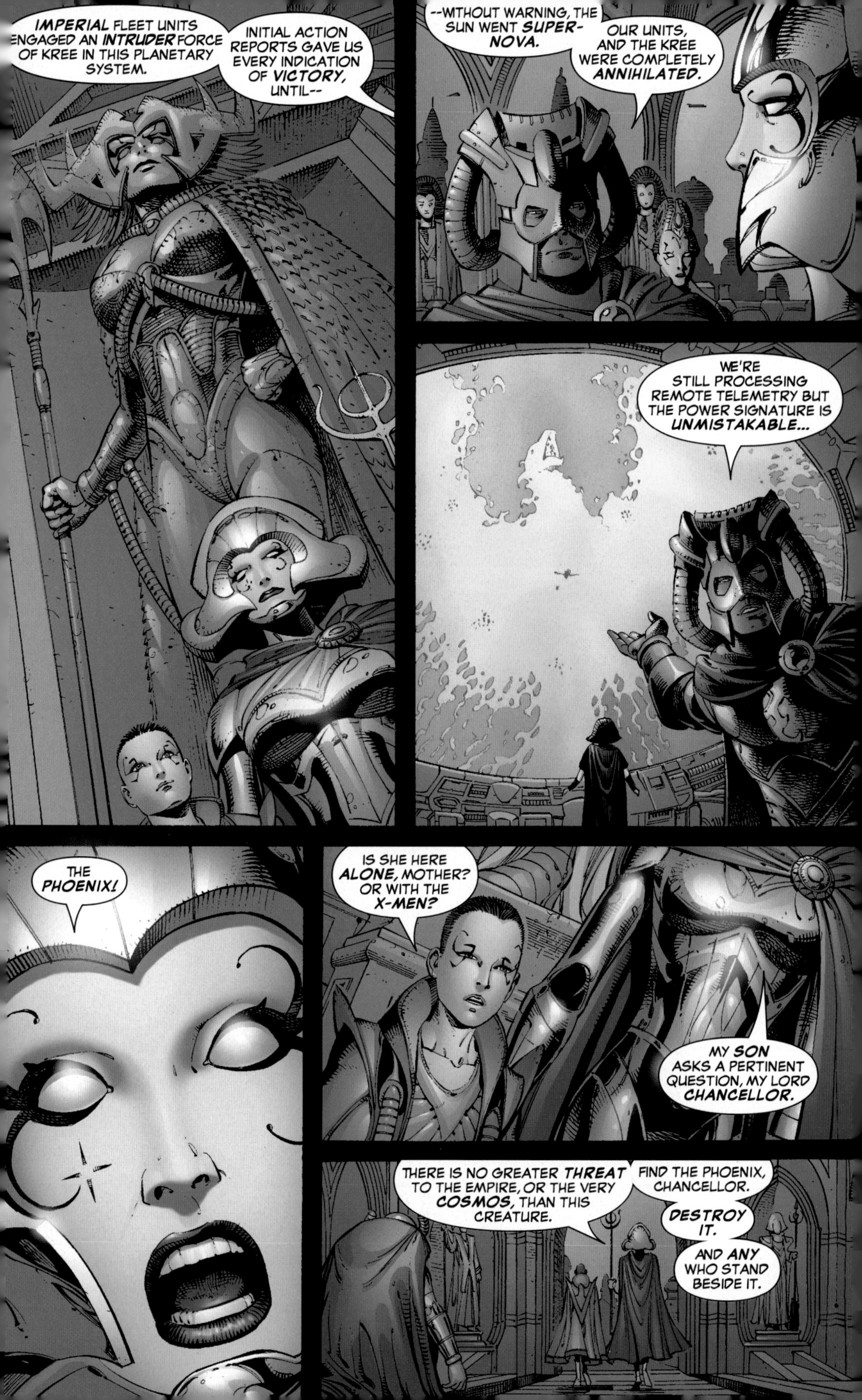
IMPERIAL FLEET UNITS ENGAGED AN INTRUDER FORCE OF KREE IN THIS PLANETARY SYSTEM.
INITIAL ACTION REPORTS GAVE US EVERY INDICATION OF VICTORY, UNTIL--
--WITHOUT WARNING, THE SUN WENT SUPER-NOVA.
OUR UNITS, AND THE KREE WERE COMPLETELY ANNIHILATED.
WE'RE STILL PROCESSING REMOTE TELEMETRY BUT THE POWER SIGNATURE IS UNMISTAKABLE...
THE PHOENIX!
IS SHE HERE ALONE, MOTHER? OR WITH THE X-MEN?
MY SON ASKS A PERTINENT QUESTION, MY LORD CHANCELLOR.
THERE IS NO GREATER THREAT TO THE EMPIRE, OR THE VERY COSMOS, THAN THIS CREATURE.
FIND THE PHOENIX, CHANCELLOR.
DESTROY IT.
AND ANY WHO STAND BESIDE IT.

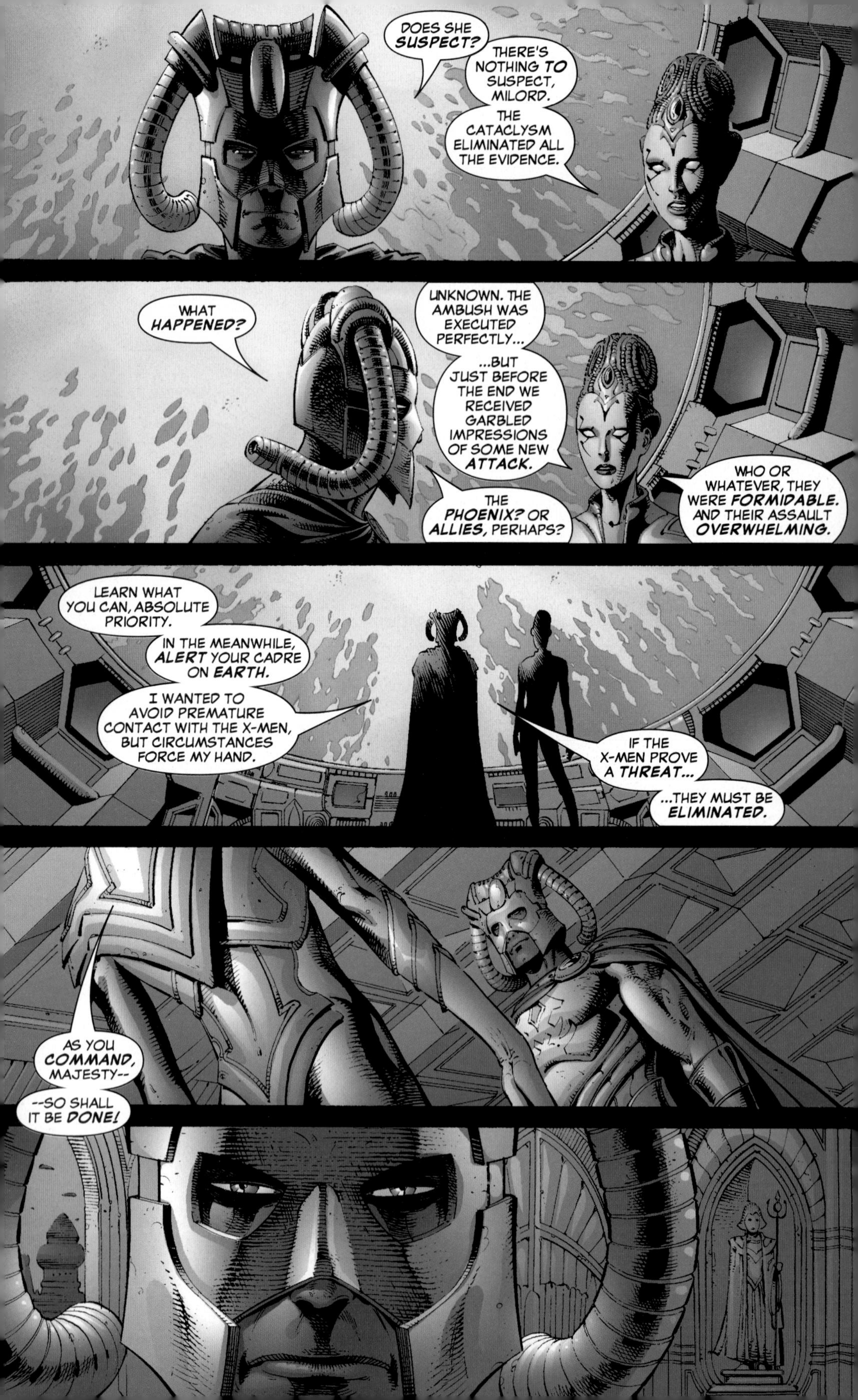
DOES SHE SUSPECT?
THERE'S NOTHING TO SUSPECT, MILORD.
THE CATACLYSM ELIMINATED ALL THE EVIDENCE.
WHAT HAPPENED?
UNKNOWN. THE AMBUSH WAS EXECUTED PERFECTLY...
...BUT JUST BEFORE THE END WE RECEIVED GARBLED IMPRESSIONS OF SOME NEW ATTACK.
THE PHOENIX? OR ALLIES, PERHAPS?
WHO OR WHATEVER, THEY WERE FORMIDABLE. AND THEIR ASSAULT OVERWHELMING.
LEARN WHAT YOU CAN, ABSOLUTE PRIORITY.
IN THE MEANWHILE, ALERT YOUR CADRE ON EARTH.
I WANTED TO AVOID PREMATURE CONTACT WITH THE X-MEN, BUT CIRCUMSTANCES FORCE MY HAND.
IF THE X-MEN PROVE A THREAT...
...THEY MUST BE ELIMINATED.
AS YOU COMMAND, MAJESTY--
--SO SHALL IT BE DONE!

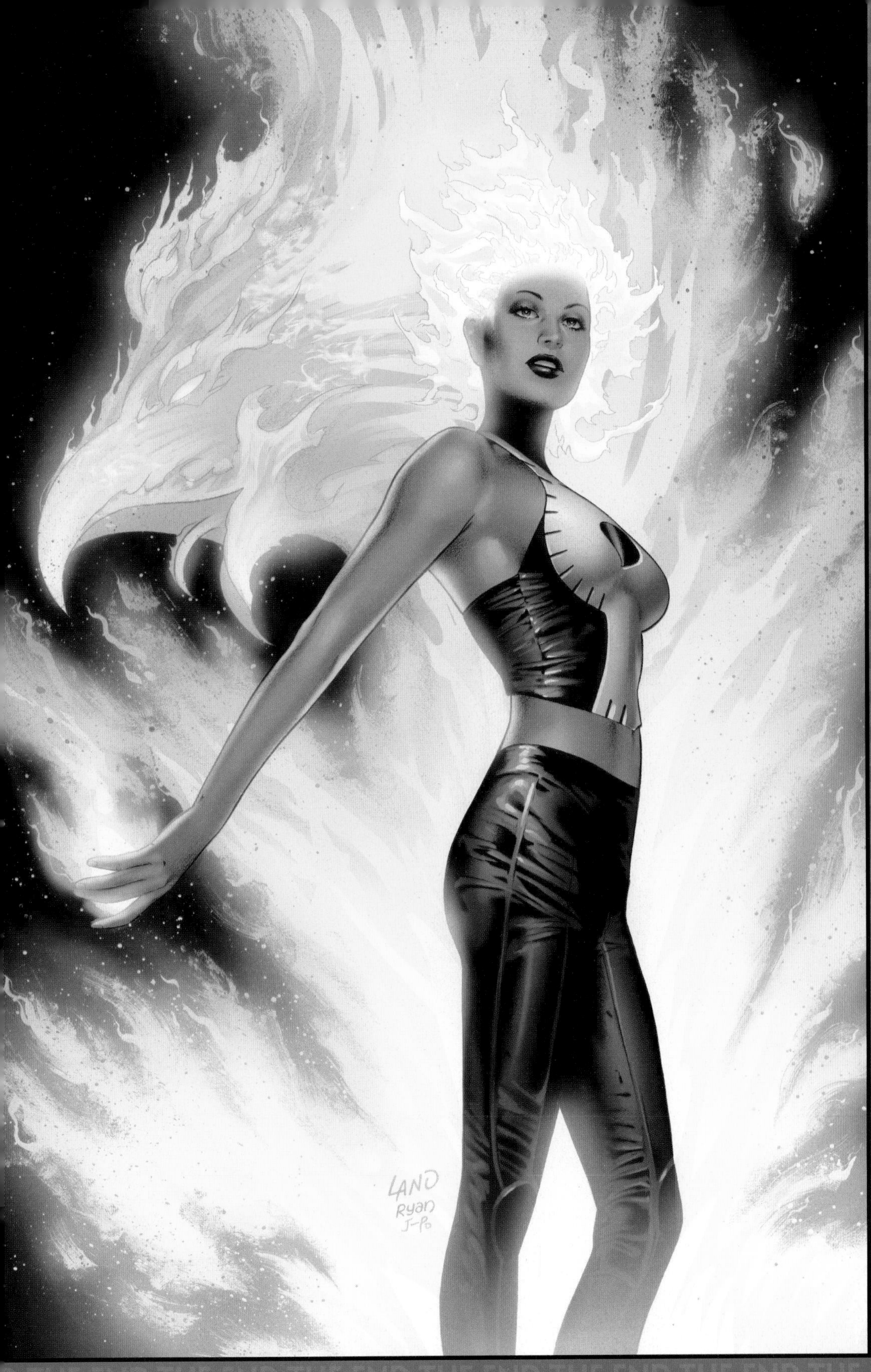
LAND
Ryan
J-Po

THE END THE END THE END THE END THE END THE END

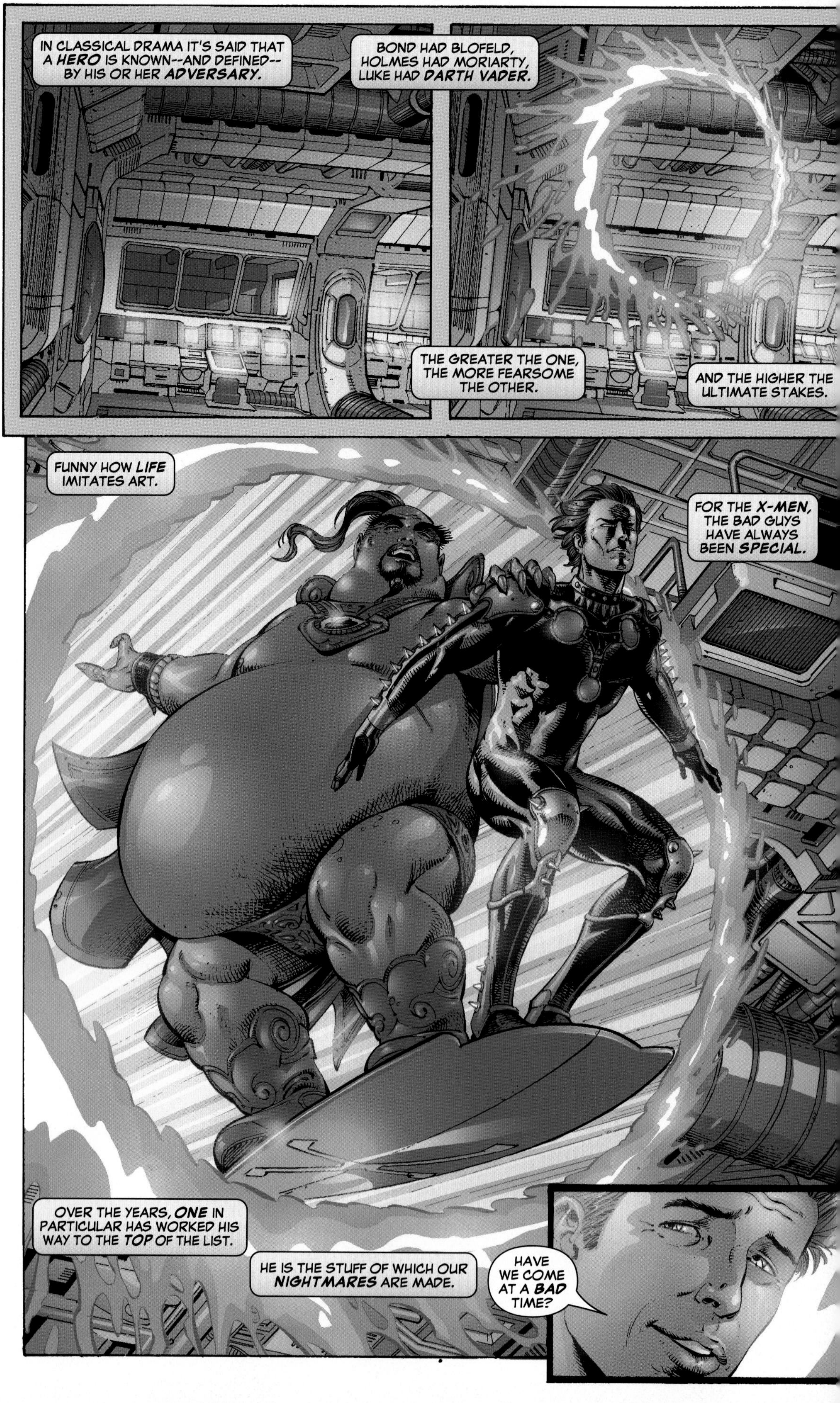

IN CLASSICAL DRAMA IT'S SAID THAT A HERO IS KNOWN--AND DEFINED-- BY HIS OR HER ADVERSARY.
BOND HAD BLOFELD, HOLMES HAD MORIARTY, LUKE HAD DARTH VADER.
THE GREATER THE ONE, THE MORE FEARSOME THE OTHER.
AND THE HIGHER THE ULTIMATE STAKES.
FUNNY HOW LIFE IMITATES ART.
FOR THE X-MEN, THE BAD GUYS HAVE ALWAYS BEEN SPECIAL.
OVER THE YEARS, ONE IN PARTICULAR HAS WORKED HIS WAY TO THE TOP OF THE LIST.
HE IS THE STUFF OF WHICH OUR NIGHTMARES ARE MADE.
HAVE WE COME AT A BAD TIME?

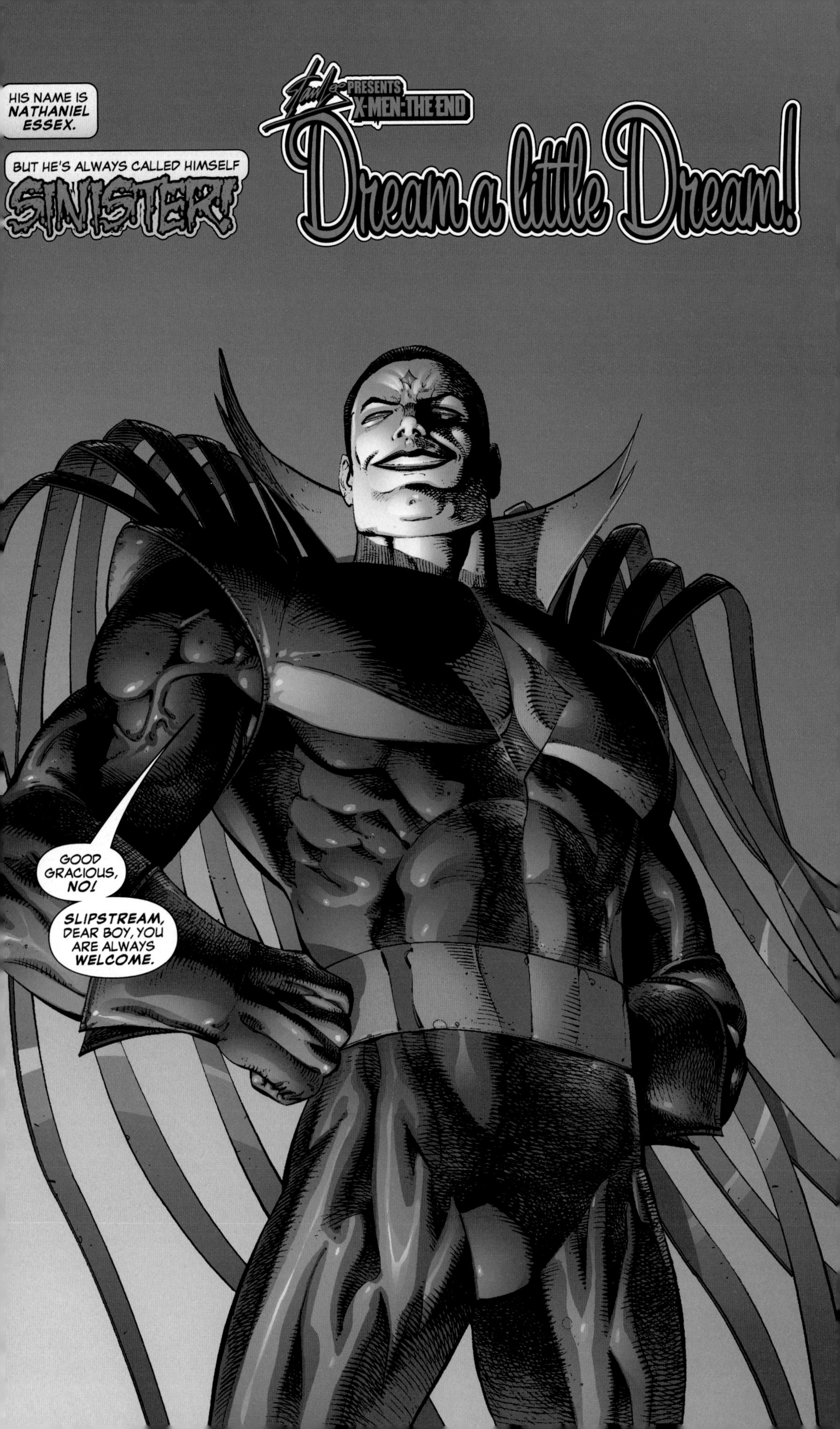
HIS NAME IS NATHANIEL ESSEX.
BUT HE'S ALWAYS CALLED HIMSELF
SINISTER!
PRESENTS X-MEN: THE END
Dream a little Dream!
GOOD GRACIOUS, NO!
SLIPSTREAM, DEAR BOY, YOU ARE ALWAYS WELCOME.

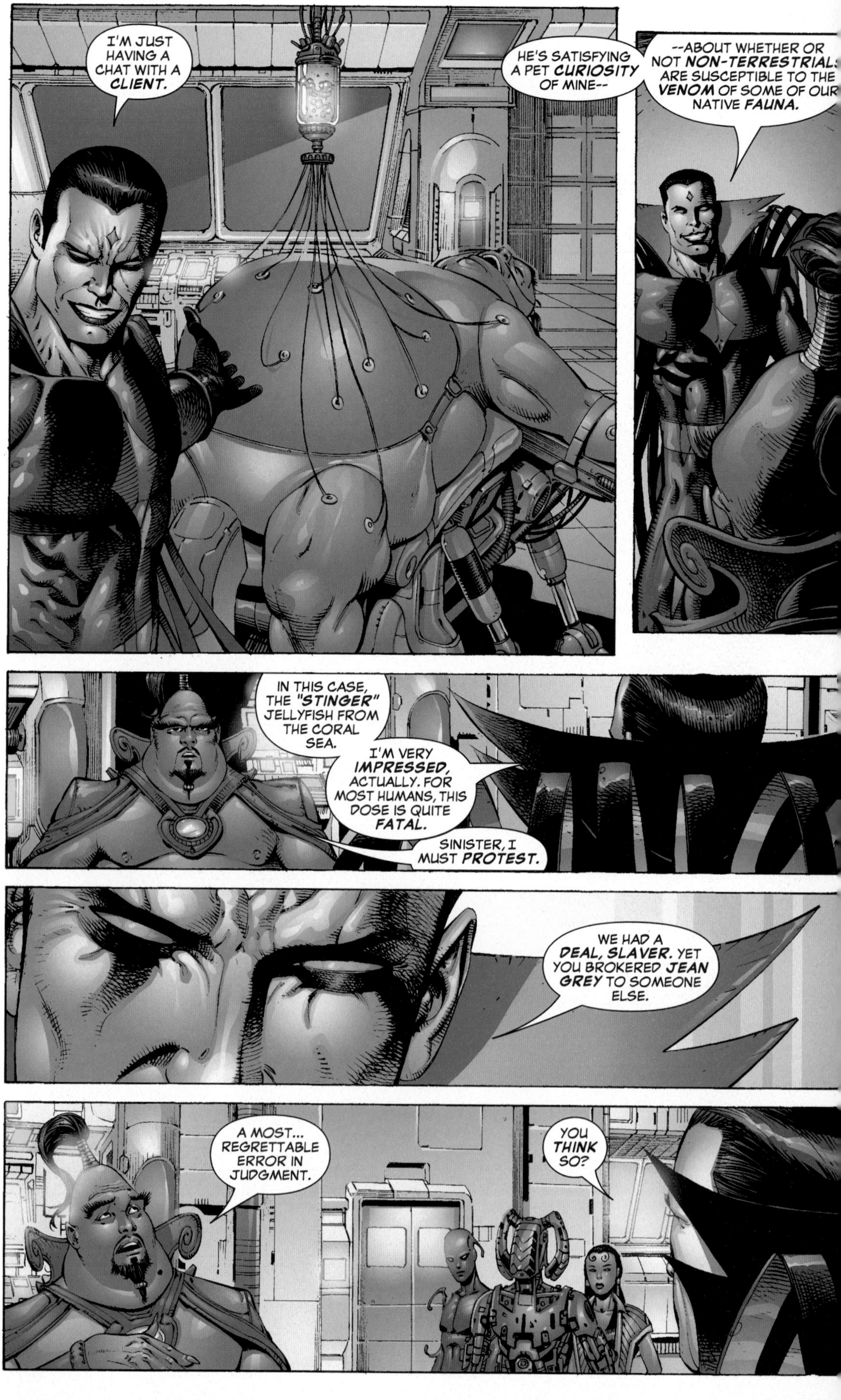
I'M JUST HAVING A CHAT WITH A CLIENT.
HE'S SATISFYING A PET CURIOSITY OF MINE--
--ABOUT WHETHER OR NOT NON-TERRESTRIALS ARE SUSCEPTIBLE TO THE VENOM OF SOME OF OUR NATIVE FAUNA.
IN THIS CASE, THE "STINGER" JELLYFISH FROM THE CORAL SEA.
I'M VERY IMPRESSED, ACTUALLY. FOR MOST HUMANS, THIS DOSE IS QUITE FATAL.
SINISTER, I MUST PROTEST.
WE HAD A DEAL, SLAVER. YET YOU BROKERED JEAN GREY TO SOMEONE ELSE.
A MOST... REGRETTABLE ERROR IN JUDGMENT.
YOU THINK SO?

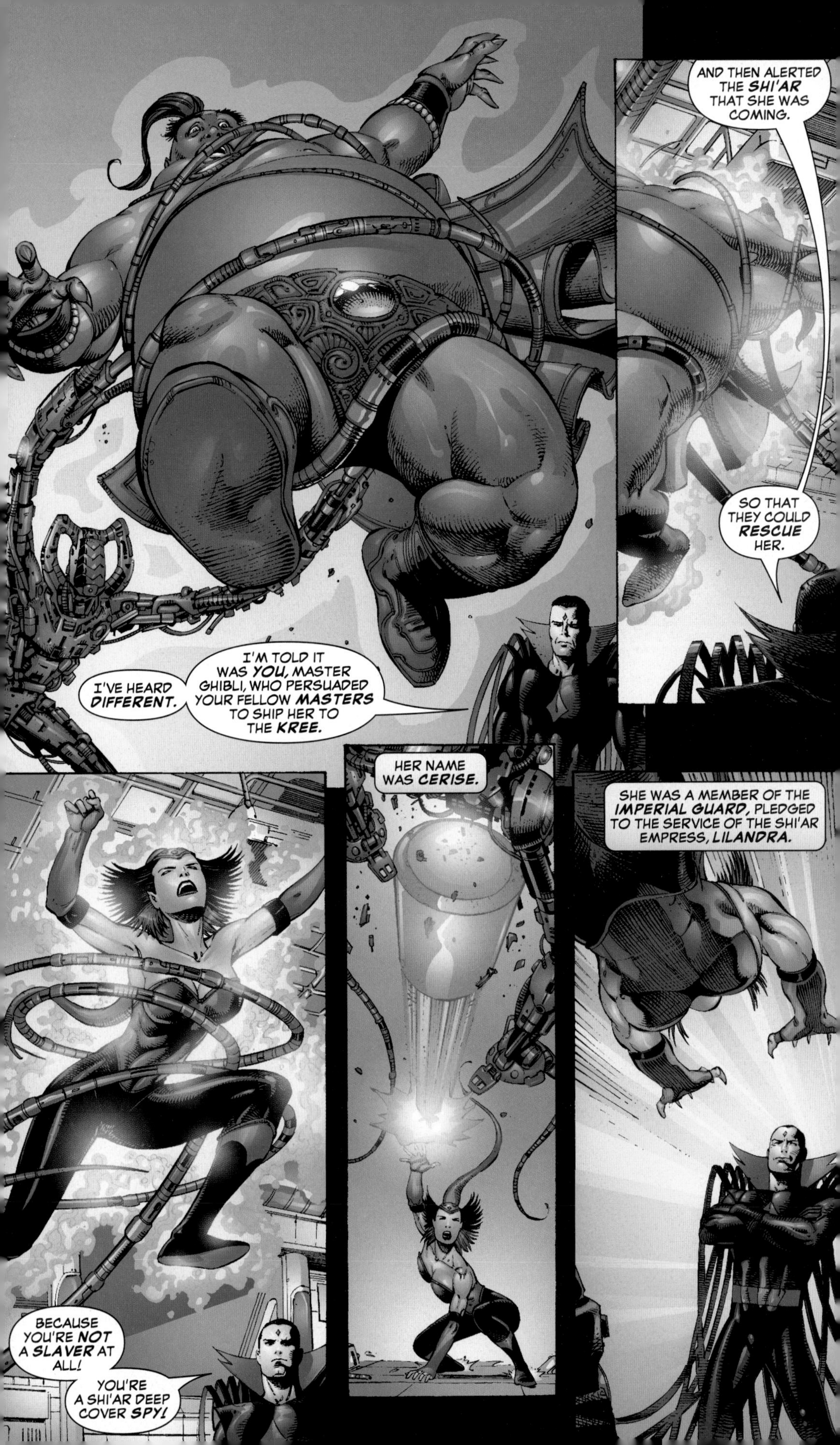
I'M TOLD IT WAS YOU, MASTER GHIBLI, WHO PERSUADED YOUR FELLOW MASTERS TO SHIP HER TO THE KREE.
I'VE HEARD DIFFERENT.
AND THEN ALERTED THE SHI'AR THAT SHE WAS COMING.
SO THAT THEY COULD RESCUE HER.
HER NAME WAS CERISE.
SHE WAS A MEMBER OF THE IMPERIAL GUARD, PLEDGED TO THE SERVICE OF THE SHI'AR EMPRESS, LILANDRA.
BECAUSE YOU'RE NOT A SLAVER AT ALL!
YOU'RE A SHI'AR DEEP COVER SPY!

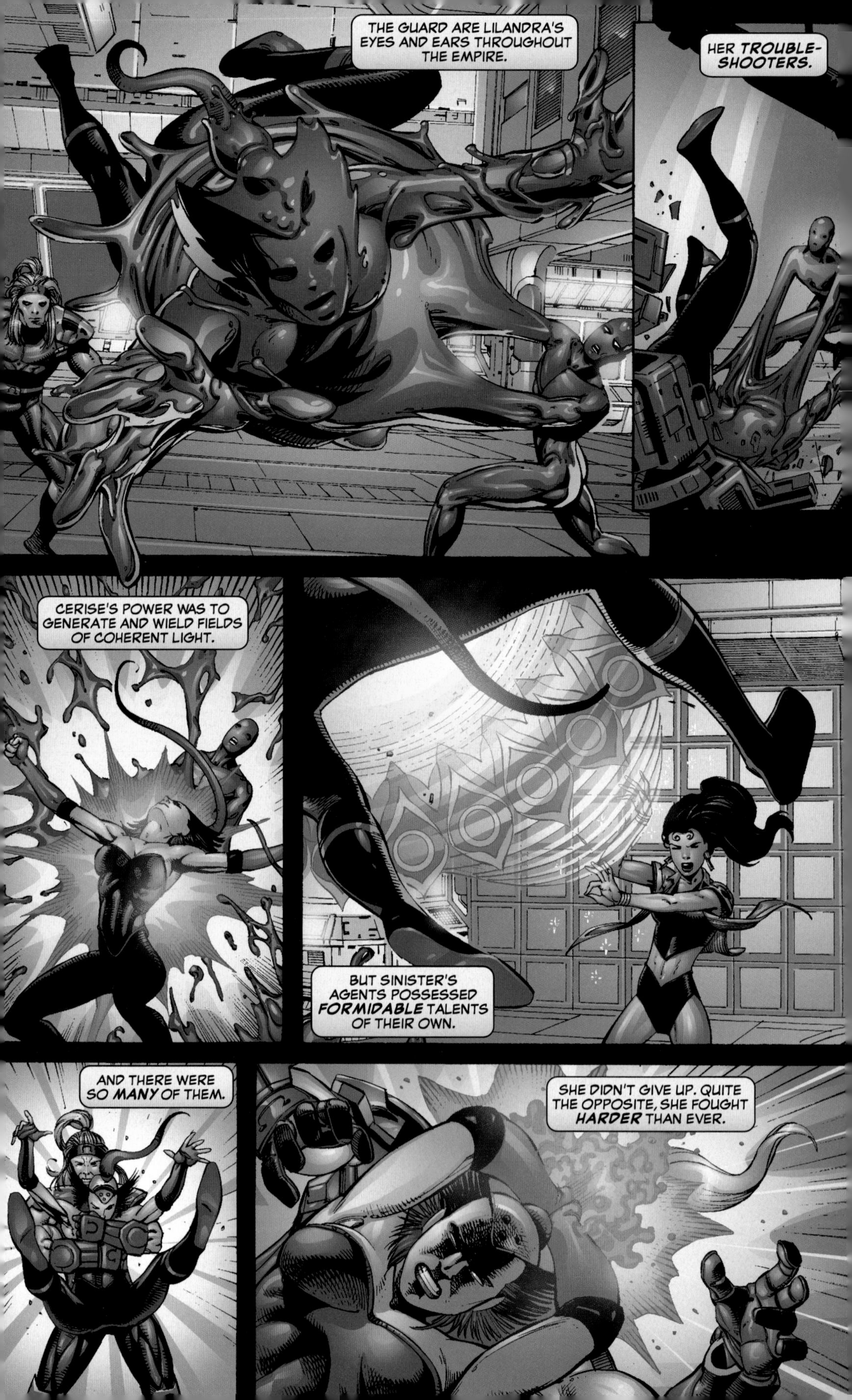
THE GUARD ARE LILANDRA'S EYES AND EARS THROUGHOUT THE EMPIRE.
HER TROUBLE-SHOOTERS.
CERISE'S POWER WAS TO GENERATE AND WIELD FIELDS OF COHERENT LIGHT.
BUT SINISTER'S AGENTS POSSESSED FORMIDABLE TALENTS OF THEIR OWN.
AND THERE WERE SO MANY OF THEM.
SHE DIDN'T GIVE UP. QUITE THE OPPOSITE, SHE FOUGHT HARDER THAN EVER.

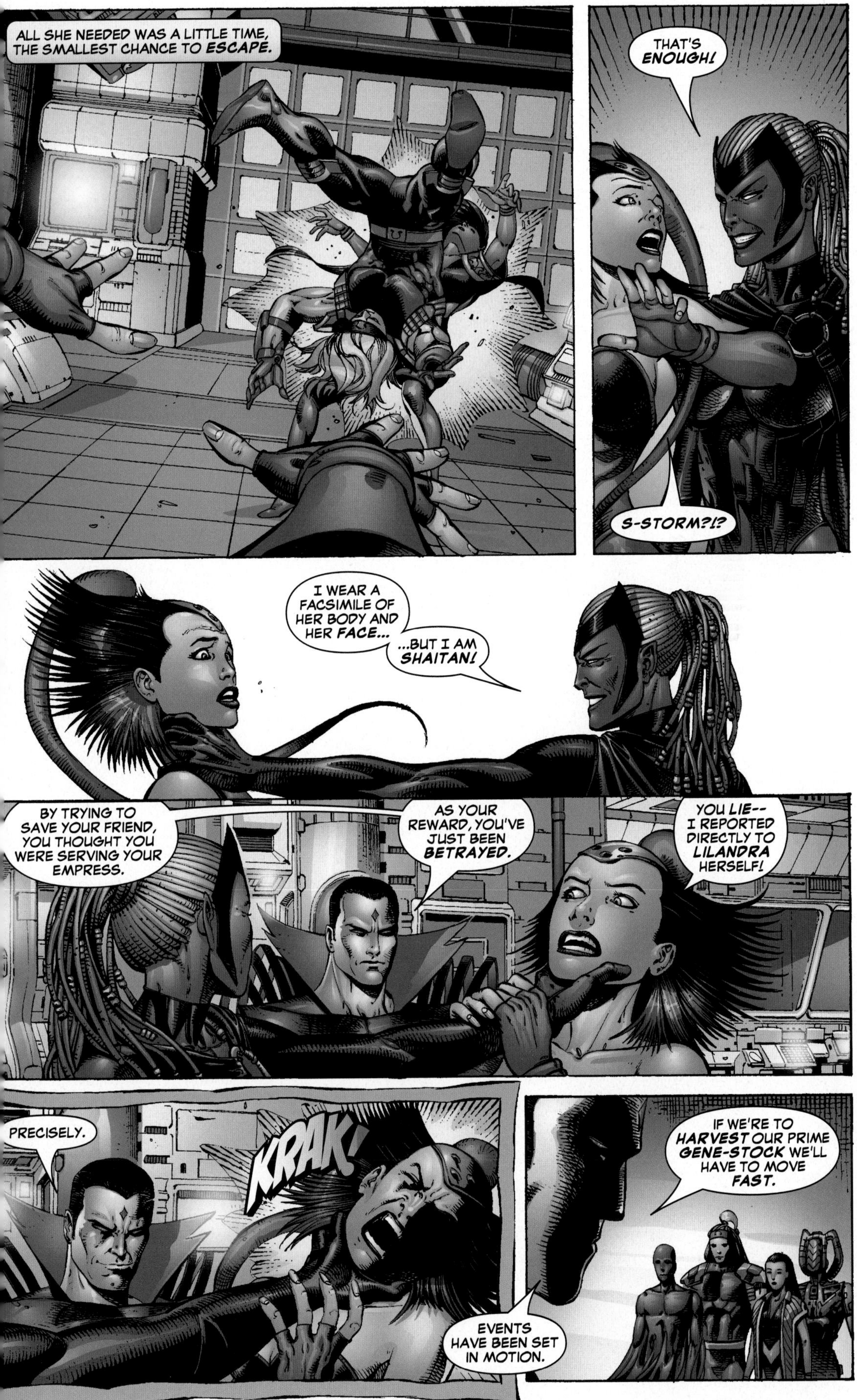
ALL SHE NEEDED WAS A LITTLE TIME, THE SMALLEST CHANCE TO ESCAPE.
THAT'S ENOUGH!
S-STORM?!?
I WEAR A FACSIMILE OF HER BODY AND HER FACE...
...BUT I AM SHAITAN!
BY TRYING TO SAVE YOUR FRIEND, YOU THOUGHT YOU WERE SERVING YOUR EMPRESS.
AS YOUR REWARD, YOU'VE JUST BEEN BETRAYED.
YOU LIE-- I REPORTED DIRECTLY TO LILANDRA HERSELF!
PRECISELY.
KRAK!
EVENTS HAVE BEEN SET IN MOTION.
IF WE'RE TO HARVEST OUR PRIME GENE-STOCK WE'LL HAVE TO MOVE FAST.

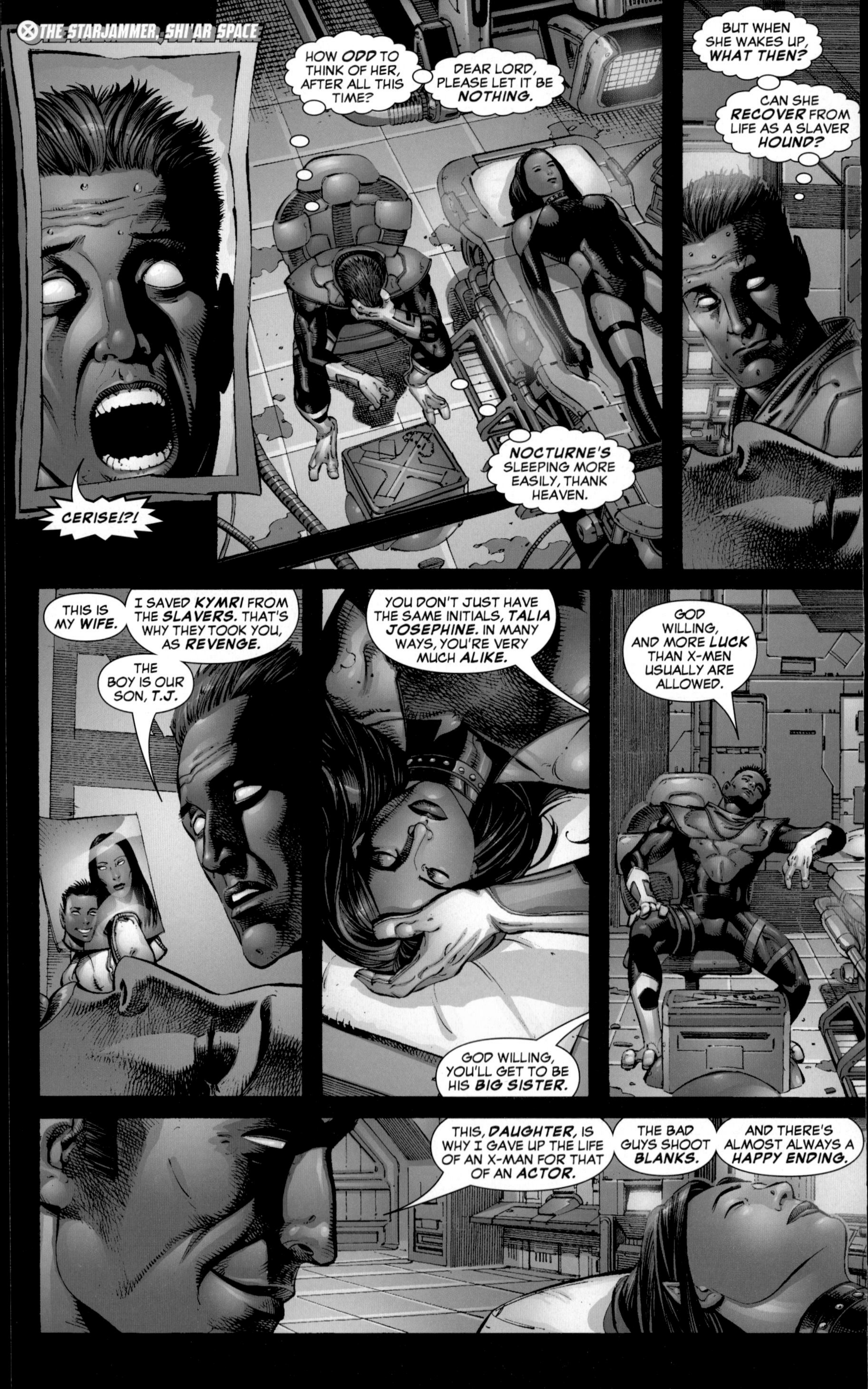
THE STARJAMMER, SHI'AR SPACE
CERISE!?!
HOW ODD TO THINK OF HER, AFTER ALL THIS TIME?
DEAR LORD, PLEASE LET IT BE NOTHING.
NOCTURNE'S SLEEPING MORE EASILY, THANK HEAVEN.
BUT WHEN SHE WAKES UP, WHAT THEN?
CAN SHE RECOVER FROM LIFE AS A SLAVER HOUND?
THIS IS MY WIFE.
I SAVED KYMRI FROM THE SLAVERS. THAT'S WHY THEY TOOK YOU, AS REVENGE.
THE BOY IS OUR SON, T.J.
YOU DON'T JUST HAVE THE SAME INITIALS, TALIA JOSEPHINE. IN MANY WAYS, YOU'RE VERY MUCH ALIKE.
GOD WILLING, YOU'LL GET TO BE HIS BIG SISTER.
GOD WILLING, AND MORE LUCK THAN X-MEN USUALLY ARE ALLOWED.
THIS, DAUGHTER, IS WHY I GAVE UP THE LIFE OF AN X-MAN FOR THAT OF AN ACTOR.
THE BAD GUYS SHOOT BLANKS.
AND THERE'S ALMOST ALWAYS A HAPPY ENDING.

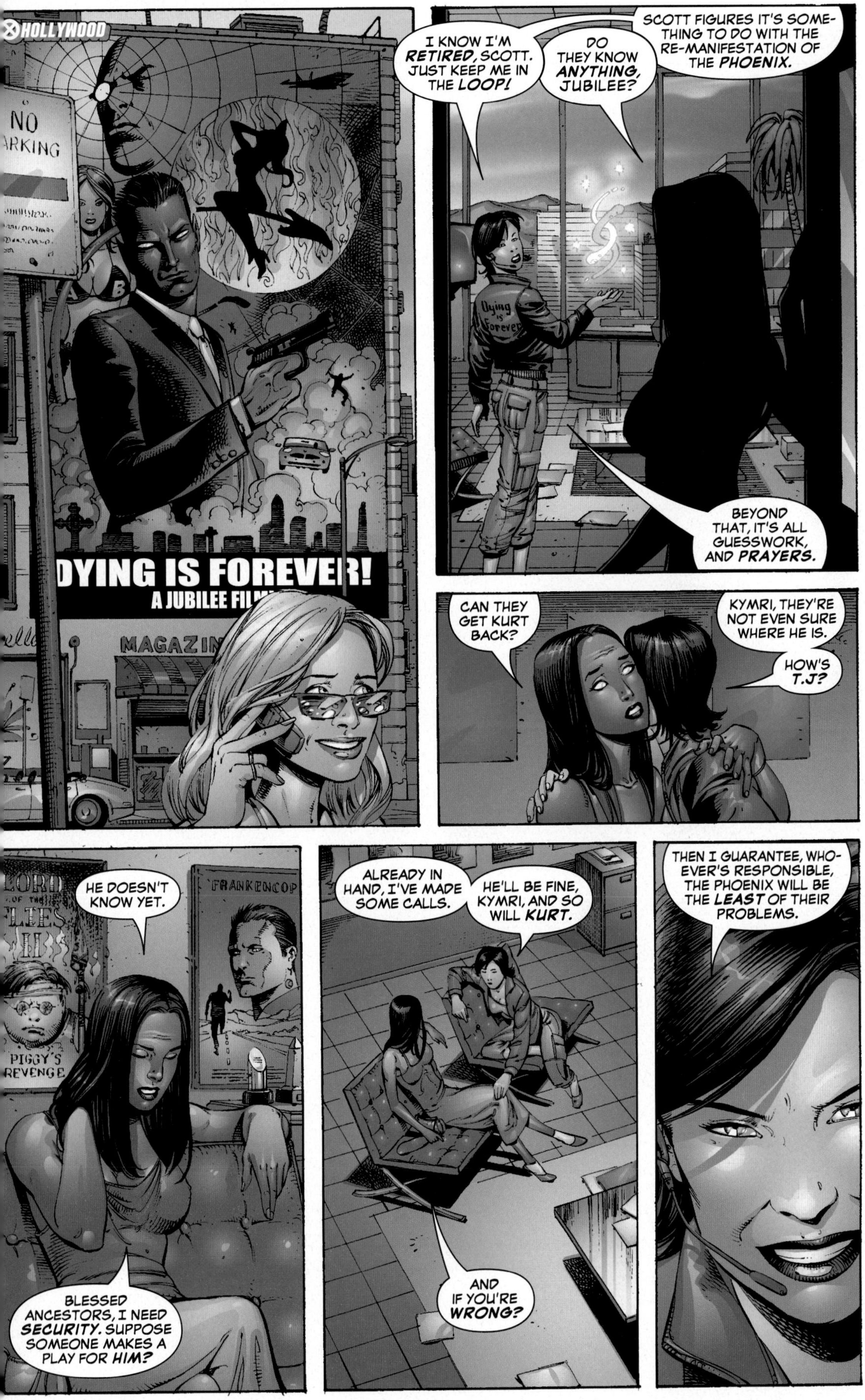

HOLLYWOOD
NO PARKING
DYING IS FOREVER!
A JUBILEE FILM
MAGAZIN
I KNOW I'M RETIRED, SCOTT. JUST KEEP ME IN THE LOOP!
DO THEY KNOW ANYTHING, JUBILEE?
SCOTT FIGURES IT'S SOMETHING TO DO WITH THE RE-MANIFESTATION OF THE PHOENIX.
Dying is Forever
BEYOND THAT, IT'S ALL GUESSWORK, AND PRAYERS.
CAN THEY GET KURT BACK?
KYMRI, THEY'RE NOT EVEN SURE WHERE HE IS.
HOW'S T.J?
LORD OF THE FLIES II
PIGGY'S REVENGE
FRANKENCOP
HE DOESN'T KNOW YET.
BLESSED ANCESTORS, I NEED SECURITY. SUPPOSE SOMEONE MAKES A PLAY FOR HIM?
ALREADY IN HAND, I'VE MADE SOME CALLS.
HE'LL BE FINE, KYMRI, AND SO WILL KURT.
AND IF YOU'RE WRONG?
THEN I GUARANTEE, WHOEVER'S RESPONSIBLE, THE PHOENIX WILL BE THE LEAST OF THEIR PROBLEMS.

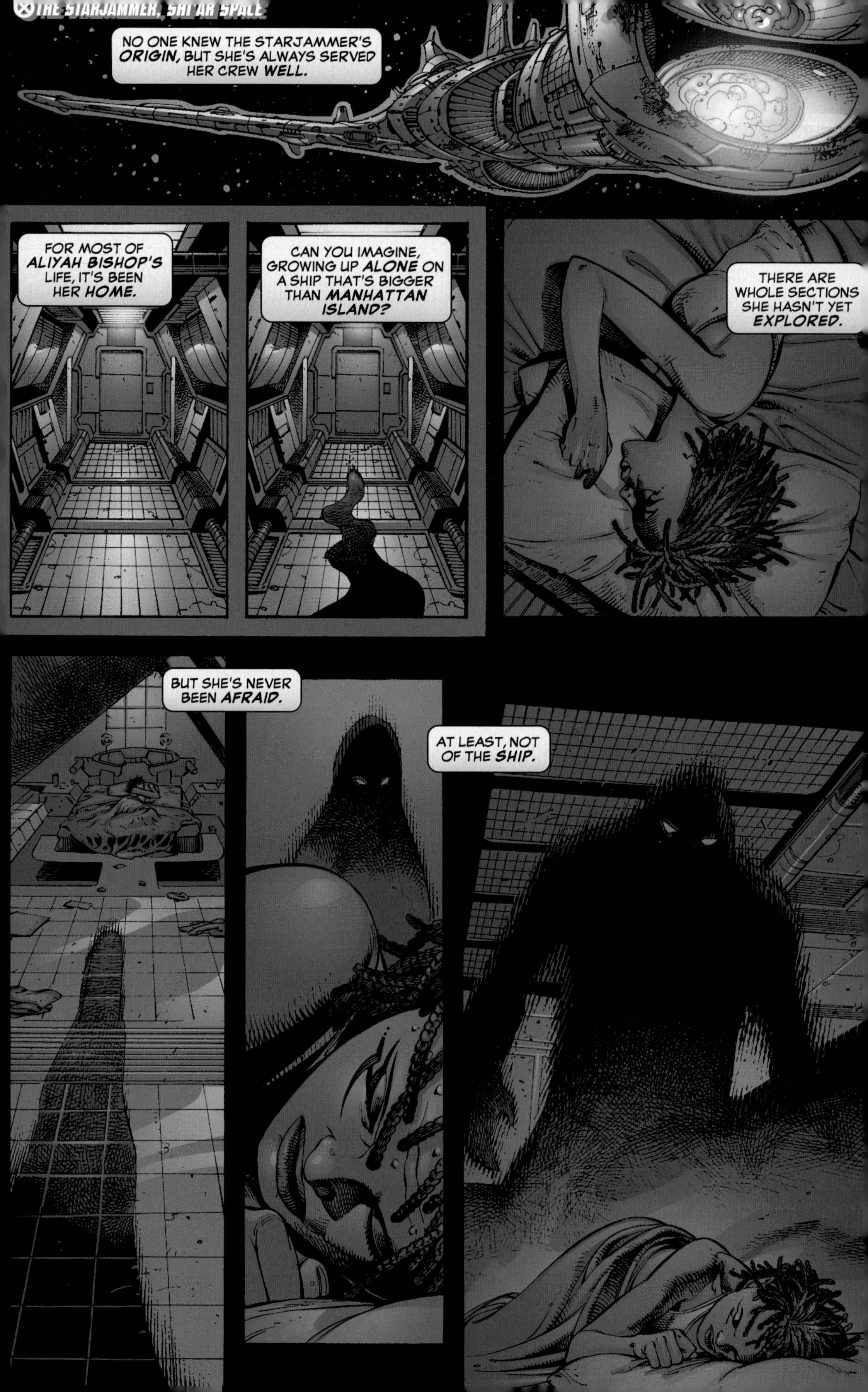
THE STARJAMMER, SHI'AR SPACE
NO ONE KNEW THE STARJAMMER'S ORIGIN, BUT SHE'S ALWAYS SERVED HER CREW WELL.
FOR MOST OF ALIYAH BISHOP'S LIFE, IT'S BEEN HER HOME.
CAN YOU IMAGINE, GROWING UP ALONE ON A SHIP THAT'S BIGGER THAN MANHATTAN ISLAND?
THERE ARE WHOLE SECTIONS SHE HASN'T YET EXPLORED.
BUT SHE'S NEVER BEEN AFRAID.
AT LEAST, NOT OF THE SHIP.

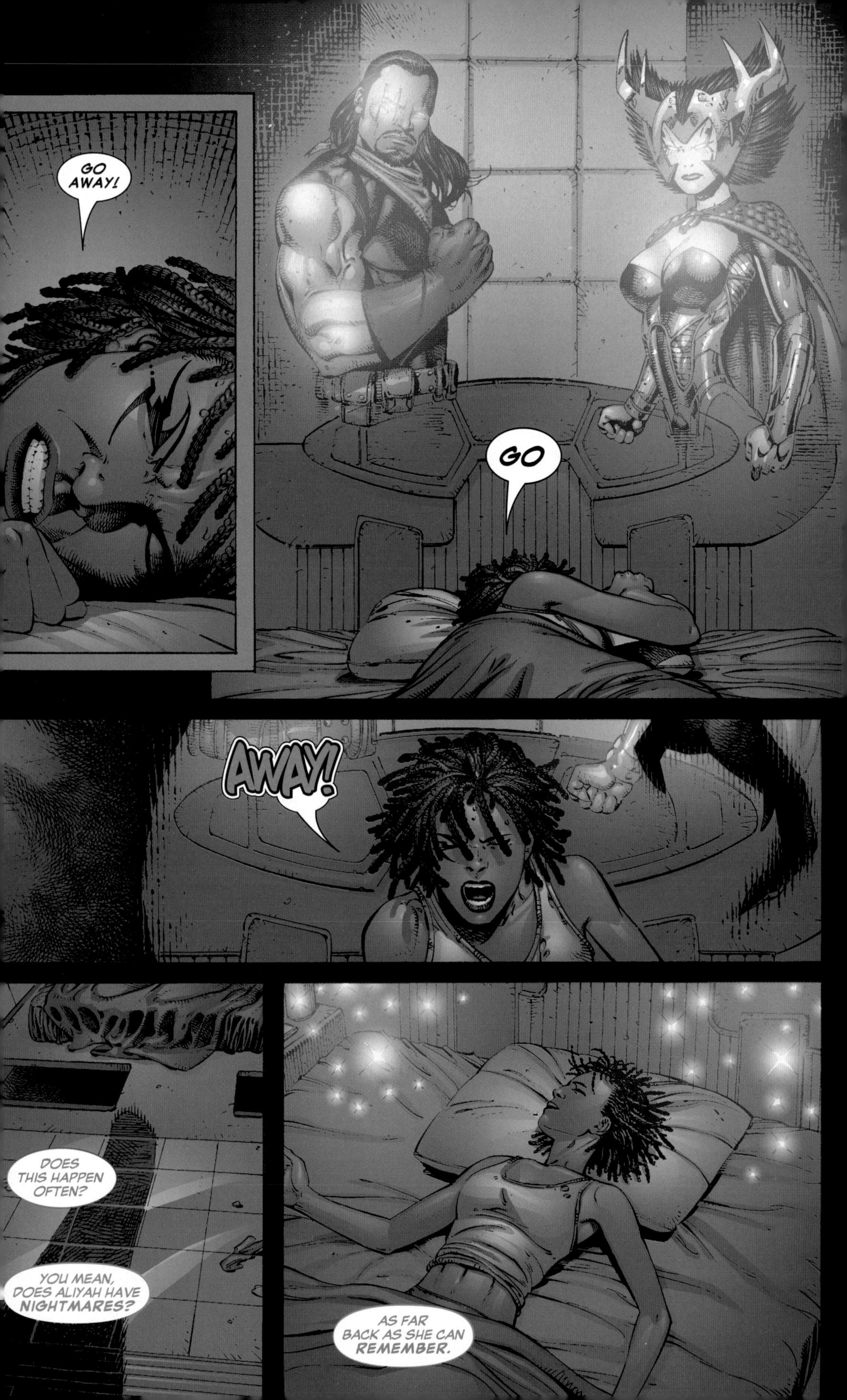
GO AWAY!
GO
AWAY!
DOES THIS HAPPEN OFTEN?
YOU MEAN, DOES ALIYAH HAVE NIGHTMARES?
AS FAR BACK AS SHE CAN REMEMBER.

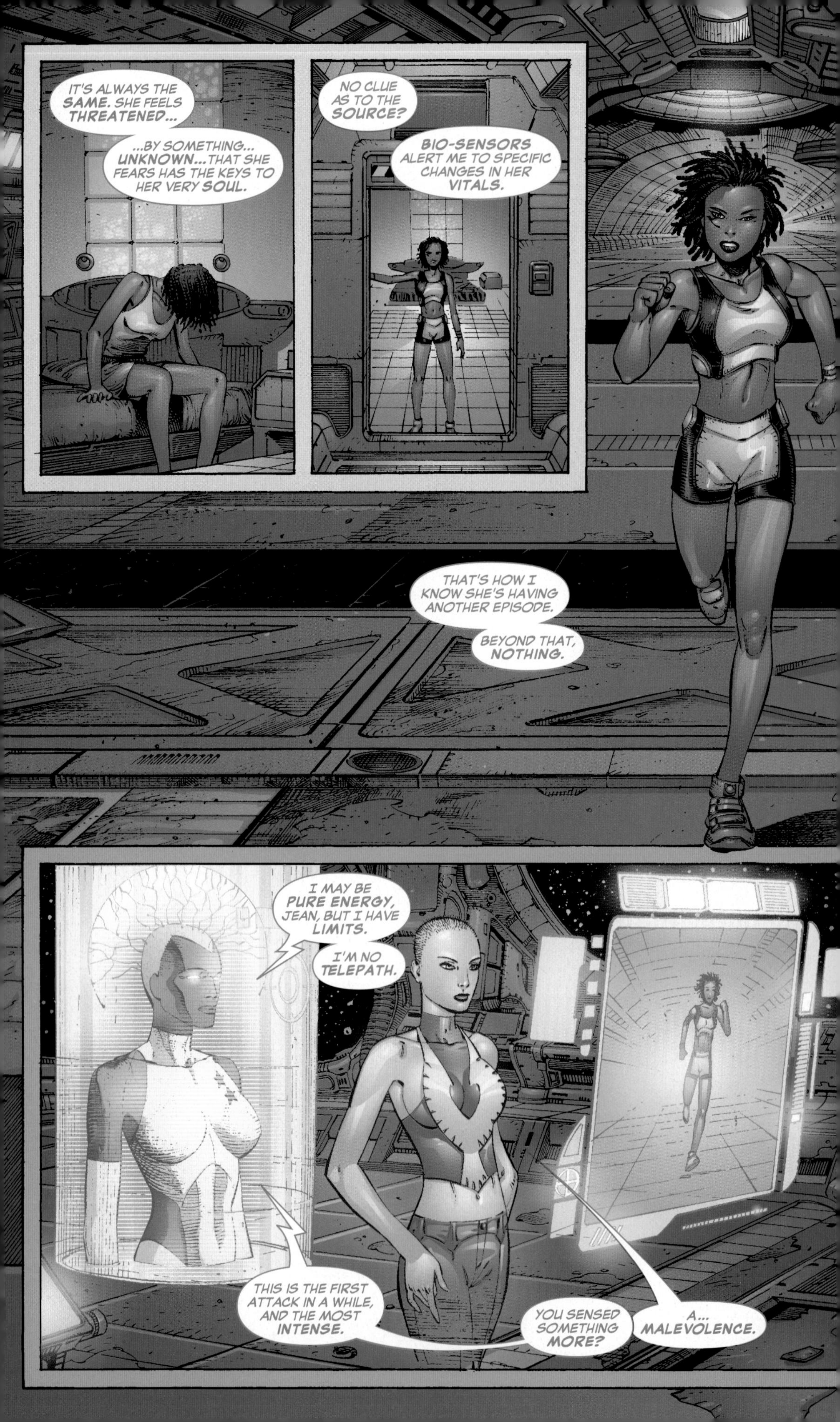
IT'S ALWAYS THE SAME. SHE FEELS THREATENED...
...BY SOMETHING... UNKNOWN...THAT SHE FEARS HAS THE KEYS TO HER VERY SOUL.
NO CLUE AS TO THE SOURCE?
BIO-SENSORS ALERT ME TO SPECIFIC CHANGES IN HER VITALS.
THAT'S HOW I KNOW SHE'S HAVING ANOTHER EPISODE.
BEYOND THAT, NOTHING.
I MAY BE PURE ENERGY, JEAN, BUT I HAVE LIMITS.
I'M NO TELEPATH.
THIS IS THE FIRST ATTACK IN A WHILE, AND THE MOST INTENSE.
YOU SENSED SOMETHING MORE?
A... MALEVOLENCE.

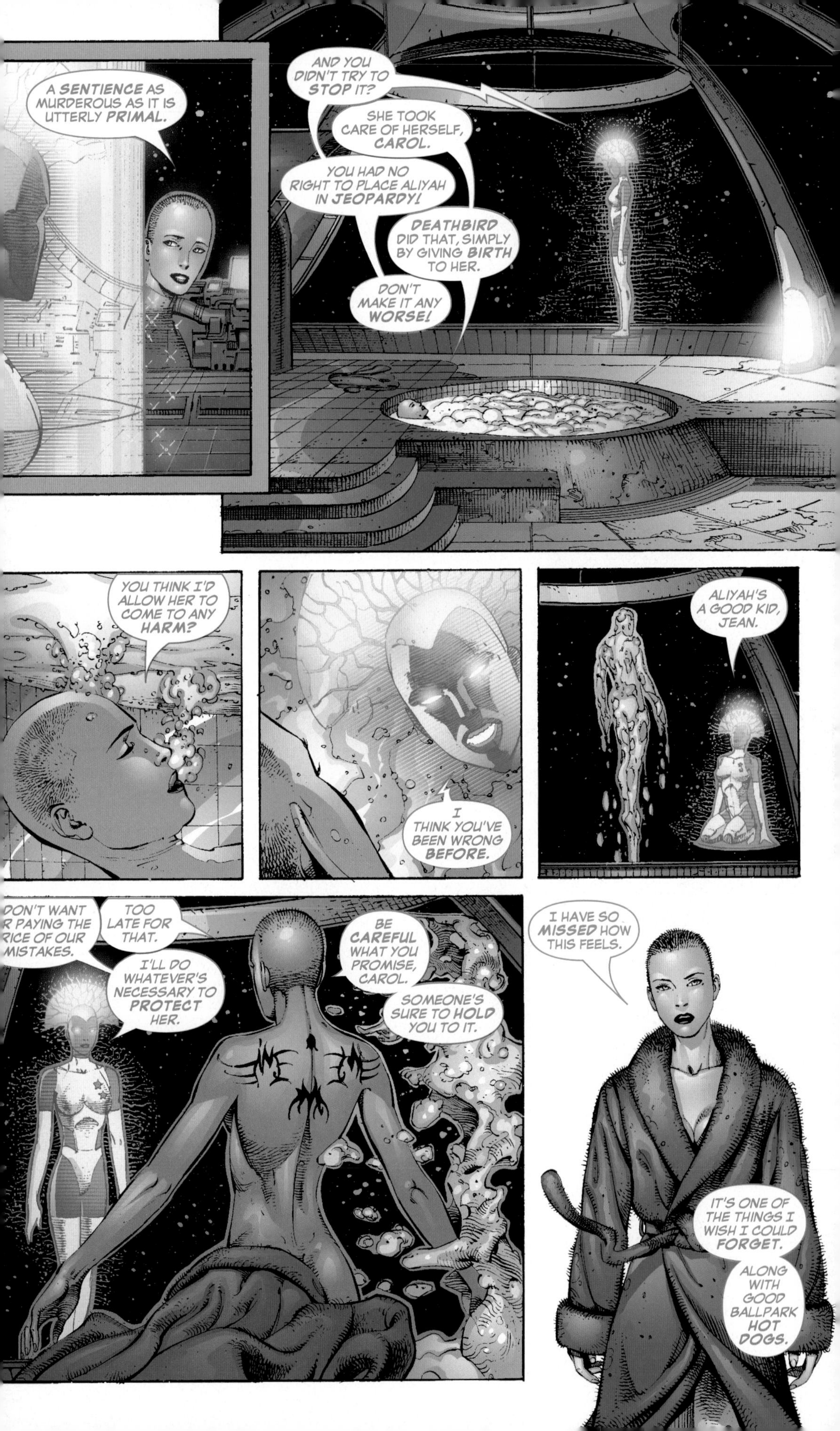
A SENTIENCE AS MURDEROUS AS IT IS UTTERLY PRIMAL.
AND YOU DIDN'T TRY TO STOP IT?
SHE TOOK CARE OF HERSELF, CAROL.
YOU HAD NO RIGHT TO PLACE ALIYAH IN JEOPARDY!
DEATHBIRD DID THAT, SIMPLY BY GIVING BIRTH TO HER.
DON'T MAKE IT ANY WORSE!
YOU THINK I'D ALLOW HER TO COME TO ANY HARM?
I THINK YOU'VE BEEN WRONG BEFORE.
ALIYAH'S A GOOD KID, JEAN.
DON'T WANT R PAYING THE RICE OF OUR MISTAKES.
TOO LATE FOR THAT.
I'LL DO WHATEVER'S NECESSARY TO PROTECT HER.
BE CAREFUL WHAT YOU PROMISE, CAROL.
SOMEONE'S SURE TO HOLD YOU TO IT.
I HAVE SO MISSED HOW THIS FEELS.
IT'S ONE OF THE THINGS I WISH I COULD FORGET.
ALONG WITH GOOD BALLPARK HOT DOGS.

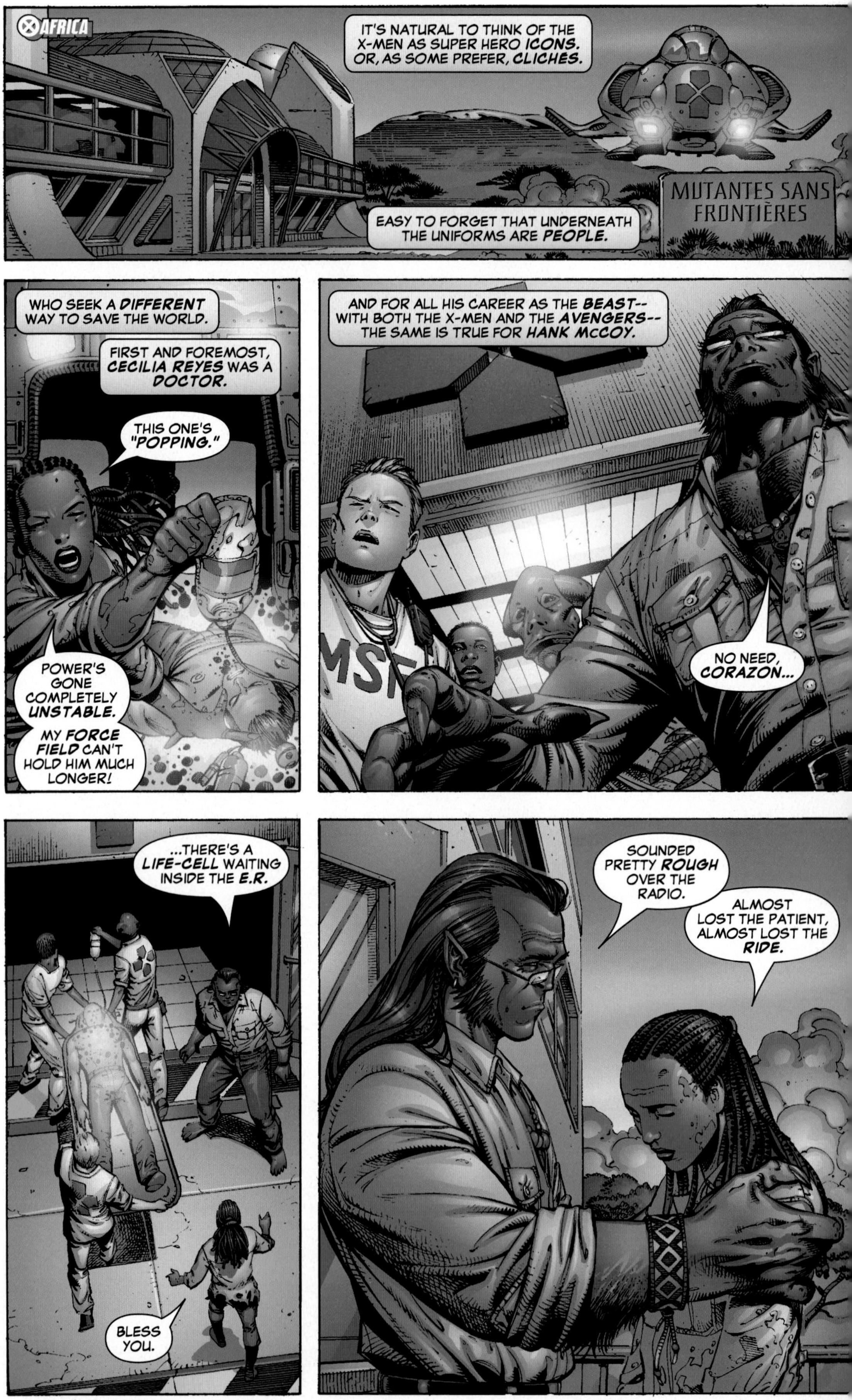
AFRICA
IT'S NATURAL TO THINK OF THE X-MEN AS SUPER HERO ICONS. OR, AS SOME PREFER, CLICHÉS.
MUTANTES SANS FRONTIÈRES
EASY TO FORGET THAT UNDERNEATH THE UNIFORMS ARE PEOPLE.
WHO SEEK A DIFFERENT WAY TO SAVE THE WORLD.
FIRST AND FOREMOST, CECILIA REYES WAS A DOCTOR.
THIS ONE'S "POPPING."
POWER'S GONE COMPLETELY UNSTABLE.
MY FORCE FIELD CAN'T HOLD HIM MUCH LONGER!
AND FOR ALL HIS CAREER AS THE BEAST-- WITH BOTH THE X-MEN AND THE AVENGERS-- THE SAME IS TRUE FOR HANK McCOY.
MSF
NO NEED, CORAZON...
...THERE'S A LIFE-CELL WAITING INSIDE THE E.R.
BLESS YOU.
SOUNDED PRETTY ROUGH OVER THE RADIO.
ALMOST LOST THE PATIENT, ALMOST LOST THE RIDE.

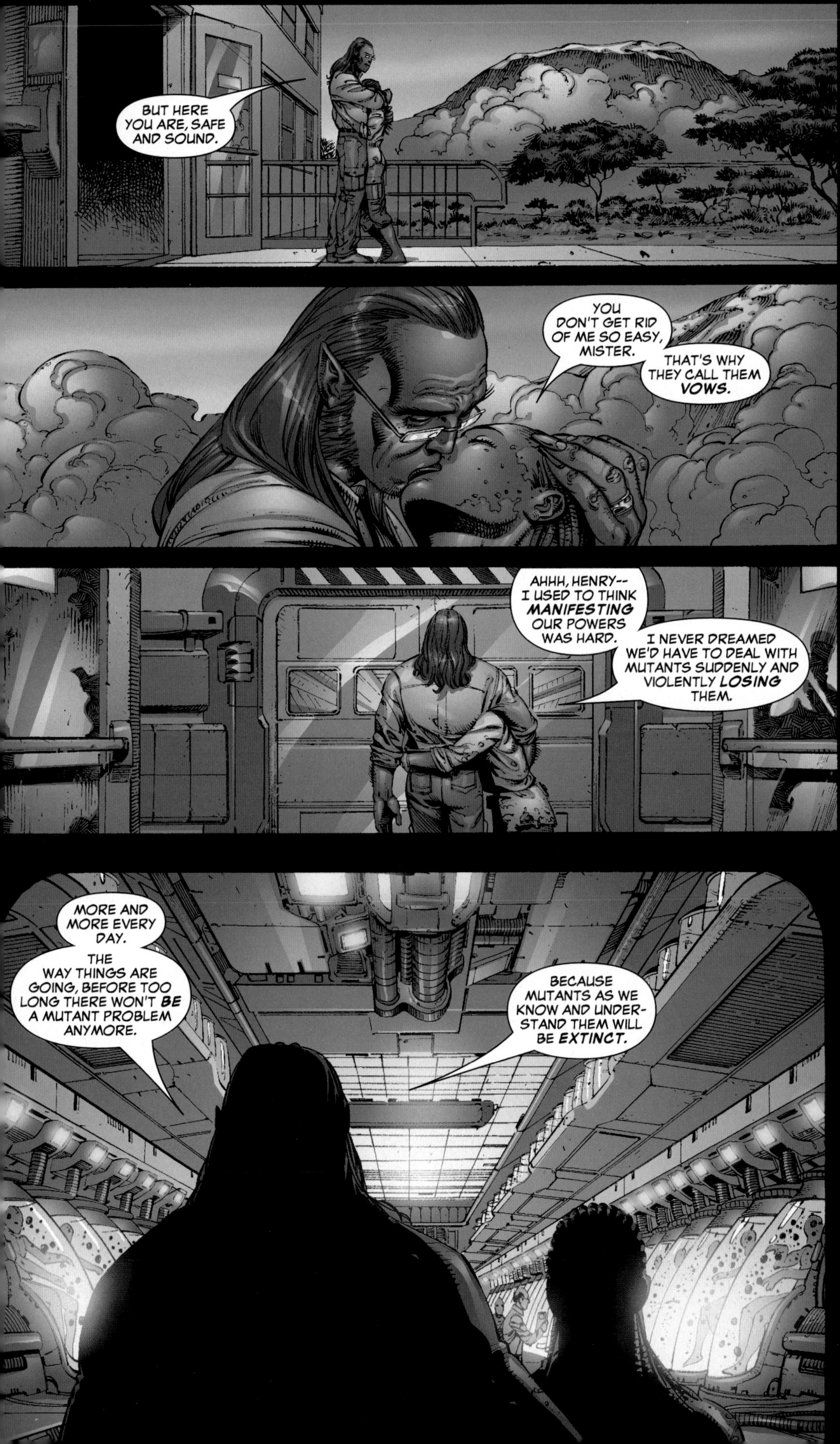
BUT HERE YOU ARE, SAFE AND SOUND.
YOU DON'T GET RID OF ME SO EASY, MISTER.
THAT'S WHY THEY CALL THEM **VOWS.**
AHHH, HENRY-- I USED TO THINK **MANIFESTING** OUR POWERS WAS HARD.
I NEVER DREAMED WE'D HAVE TO DEAL WITH MUTANTS SUDDENLY AND VIOLENTLY **LOSING** THEM.
MORE AND MORE EVERY DAY.
THE WAY THINGS ARE GOING, BEFORE TOO LONG THERE WON'T **BE** A MUTANT PROBLEM ANYMORE.
BECAUSE MUTANTS AS WE KNOW AND UNDER- STAND THEM WILL BE **EXTINCT.**

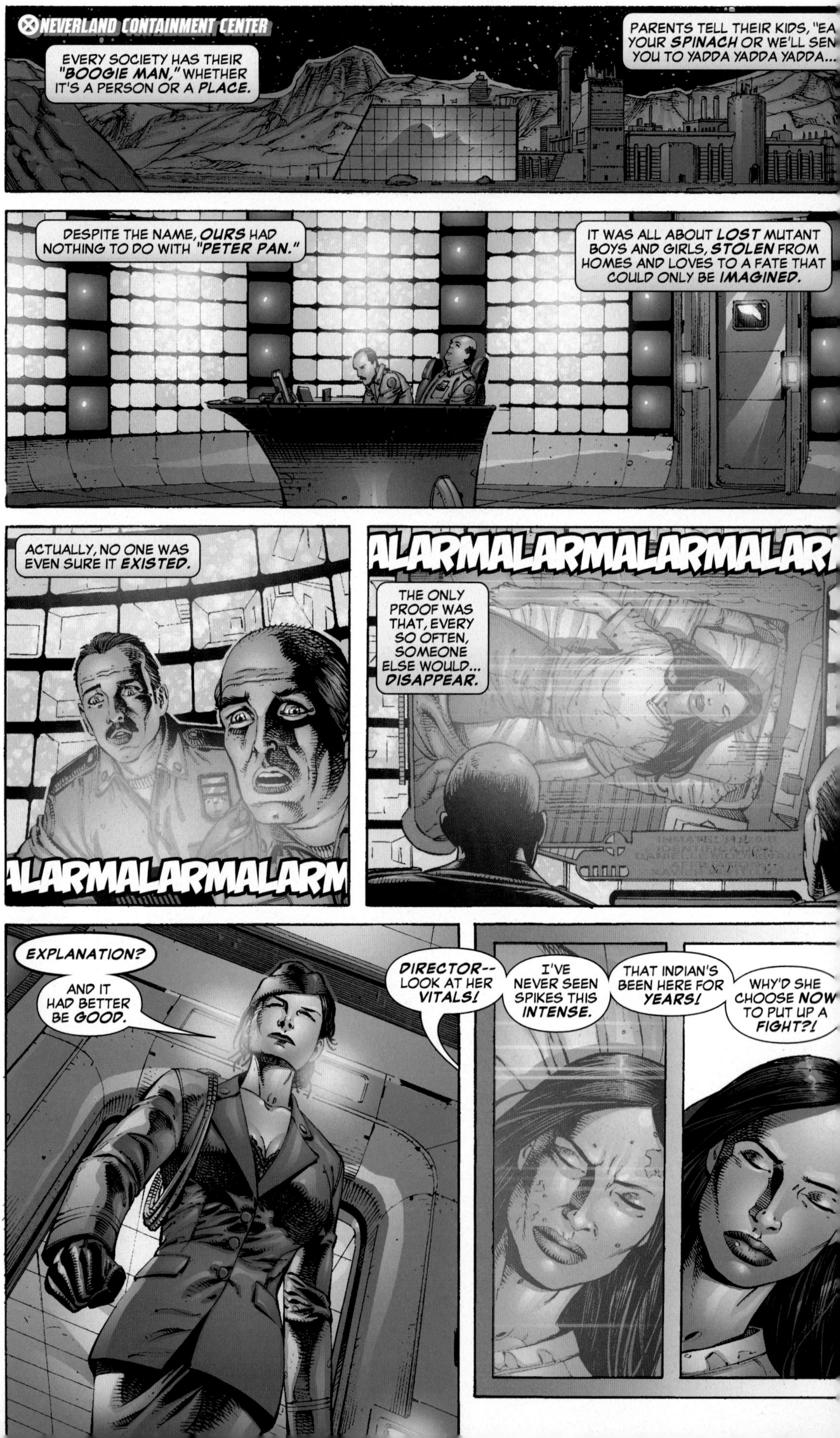
NEVERLAND CONTAINMENT CENTER
EVERY SOCIETY HAS THEIR "BOOGIE MAN," WHETHER IT'S A PERSON OR A PLACE.
PARENTS TELL THEIR KIDS, "EA YOUR SPINACH OR WE'LL SEN YOU TO YADDA YADDA YADDA...
DESPITE THE NAME, OURS HAD NOTHING TO DO WITH "PETER PAN."
IT WAS ALL ABOUT LOST MUTANT BOYS AND GIRLS, STOLEN FROM HOMES AND LOVES TO A FATE THAT COULD ONLY BE IMAGINED.
ACTUALLY, NO ONE WAS EVEN SURE IT EXISTED.
ALARMALARMALARM
ALARMALARMALARMALAR
THE ONLY PROOF WAS THAT, EVERY SO OFTEN, SOMEONE ELSE WOULD... DISAPPEAR.
EXPLANATION?
AND IT HAD BETTER BE GOOD.
DIRECTOR-- LOOK AT HER VITALS!
I'VE NEVER SEEN SPIKES THIS INTENSE.
THAT INDIAN'S BEEN HERE FOR YEARS!
WHY'D SHE CHOOSE NOW TO PUT UP A FIGHT?!

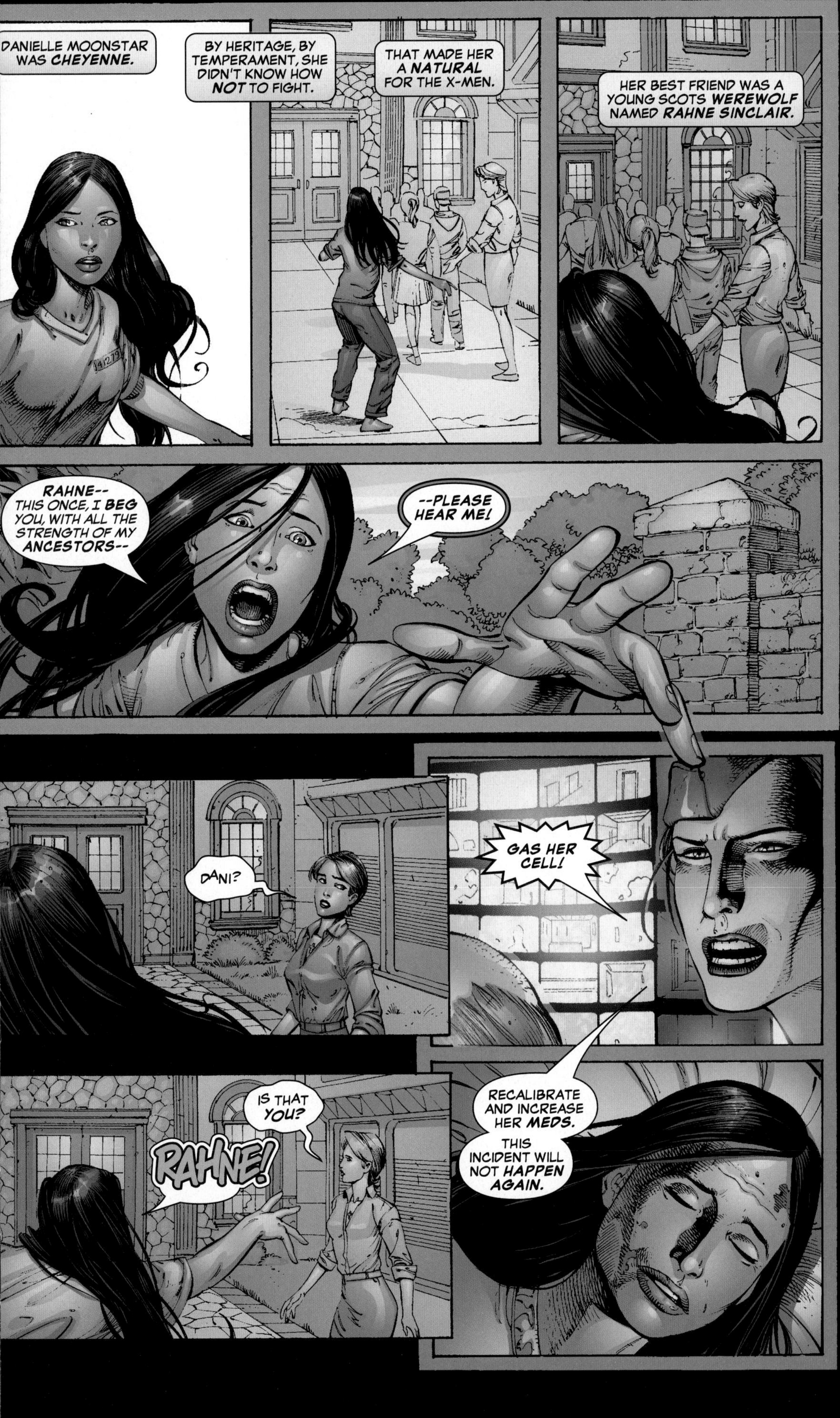
DANIELLE MOONSTAR WAS CHEYENNE.
BY HERITAGE, BY TEMPERAMENT, SHE DIDN'T KNOW HOW NOT TO FIGHT.
THAT MADE HER A NATURAL FOR THE X-MEN.
HER BEST FRIEND WAS A YOUNG SCOTS WEREWOLF NAMED RAHNE SINCLAIR.
RAHNE-- THIS ONCE, I BEG YOU, WITH ALL THE STRENGTH OF MY ANCESTORS--
--PLEASE HEAR ME!
DANI?
GAS HER CELL!
IS THAT YOU?
RAHNE!
RECALIBRATE AND INCREASE HER MEDS.
THIS INCIDENT WILL NOT HAPPEN AGAIN.

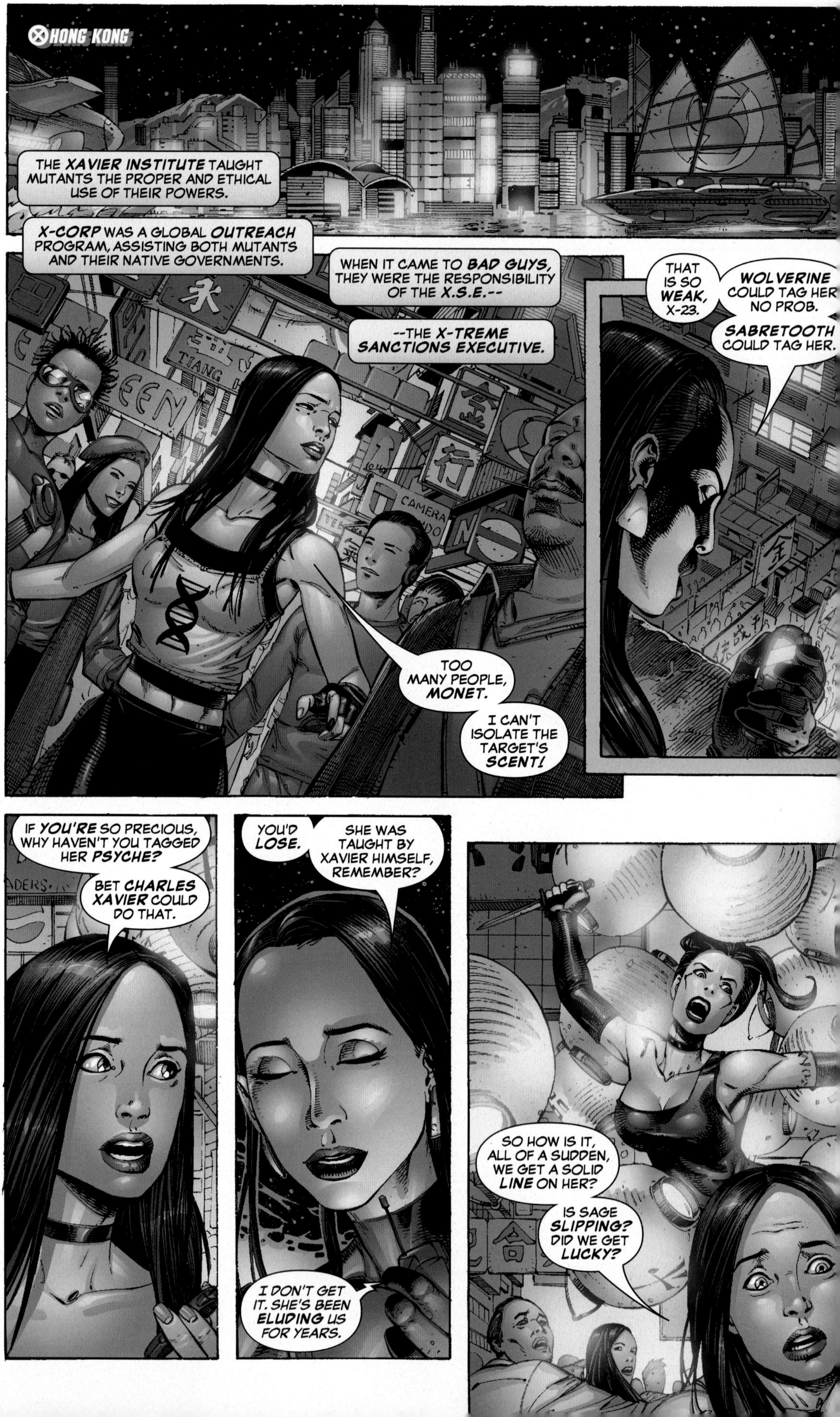
HONG KONG
THE XAVIER INSTITUTE TAUGHT MUTANTS THE PROPER AND ETHICAL USE OF THEIR POWERS.
X-CORP WAS A GLOBAL OUTREACH PROGRAM, ASSISTING BOTH MUTANTS AND THEIR NATIVE GOVERNMENTS.
WHEN IT CAME TO BAD GUYS, THEY WERE THE RESPONSIBILITY OF THE X.S.E.--
--THE X-TREME SANCTIONS EXECUTIVE.
TOO MANY PEOPLE, MONET.
I CAN'T ISOLATE THE TARGET'S SCENT!
THAT IS SO WEAK, X-23.
WOLVERINE COULD TAG HER NO PROB.
SABRETOOTH COULD TAG HER.
IF YOU'RE SO PRECIOUS, WHY HAVEN'T YOU TAGGED HER PSYCHE?
BET CHARLES XAVIER COULD DO THAT.
YOU'D LOSE.
SHE WAS TAUGHT BY XAVIER HIMSELF, REMEMBER?
I DON'T GET IT. SHE'S BEEN ELUDING US FOR YEARS.
SO HOW IS IT, ALL OF A SUDDEN, WE GET A SOLID LINE ON HER?
IS SAGE SLIPPING? DID WE GET LUCKY?

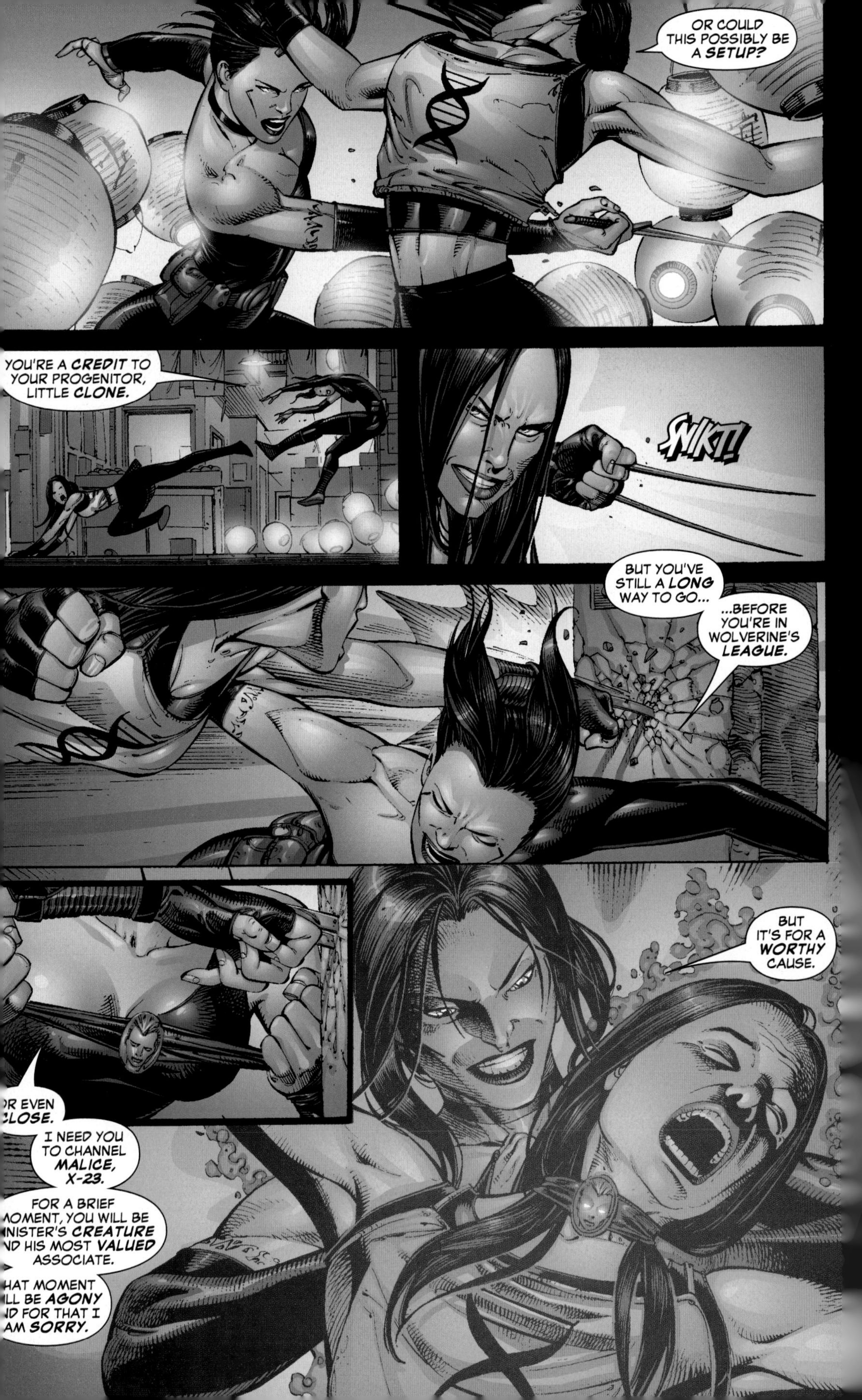
OR COULD THIS POSSIBLY BE A SETUP?
YOU'RE A CREDIT TO YOUR PROGENITOR, LITTLE CLONE.
SNIKT!
BUT YOU'VE STILL A LONG WAY TO GO...
...BEFORE YOU'RE IN WOLVERINE'S LEAGUE.
BUT IT'S FOR A WORTHY CAUSE.
R EVEN CLOSE.
I NEED YOU TO CHANNEL MALICE, X-23.
FOR A BRIEF MOMENT, YOU WILL BE INISTER'S CREATURE ND HIS MOST VALUED ASSOCIATE.
HAT MOMENT ILL BE AGONY ND FOR THAT I AM SORRY.

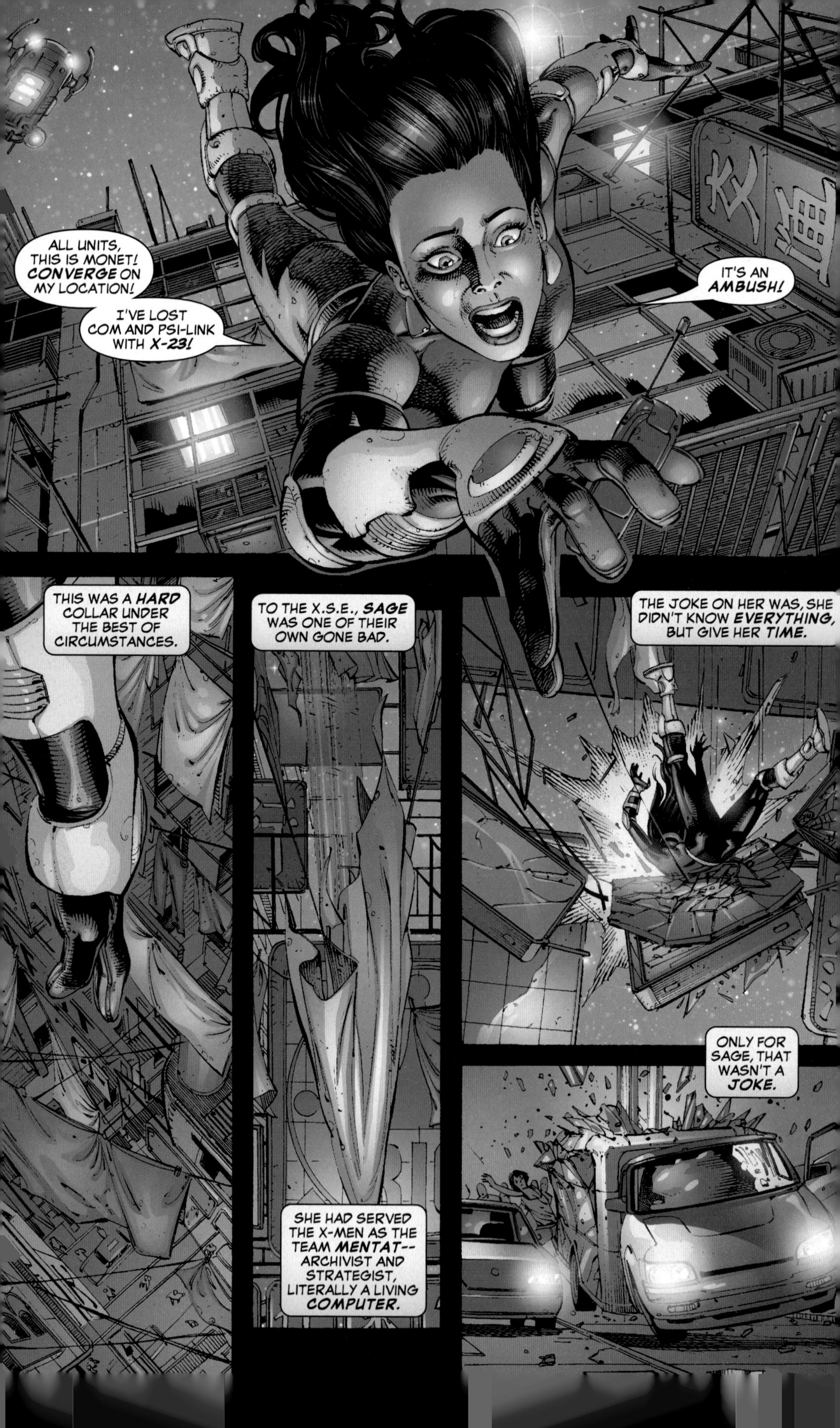

ALL UNITS, THIS IS MONET! CONVERGE ON MY LOCATION!
I'VE LOST COM AND PSI-LINK WITH X-23!
IT'S AN AMBUSH!
THIS WAS A HARD COLLAR UNDER THE BEST OF CIRCUMSTANCES.
TO THE X.S.E., SAGE WAS ONE OF THEIR OWN GONE BAD.
SHE HAD SERVED THE X-MEN AS THE TEAM MENTAT-- ARCHIVIST AND STRATEGIST, LITERALLY A LIVING COMPUTER.
THE JOKE ON HER WAS, SHE DIDN'T KNOW EVERYTHING, BUT GIVE HER TIME.
ONLY FOR SAGE, THAT WASN'T A JOKE.

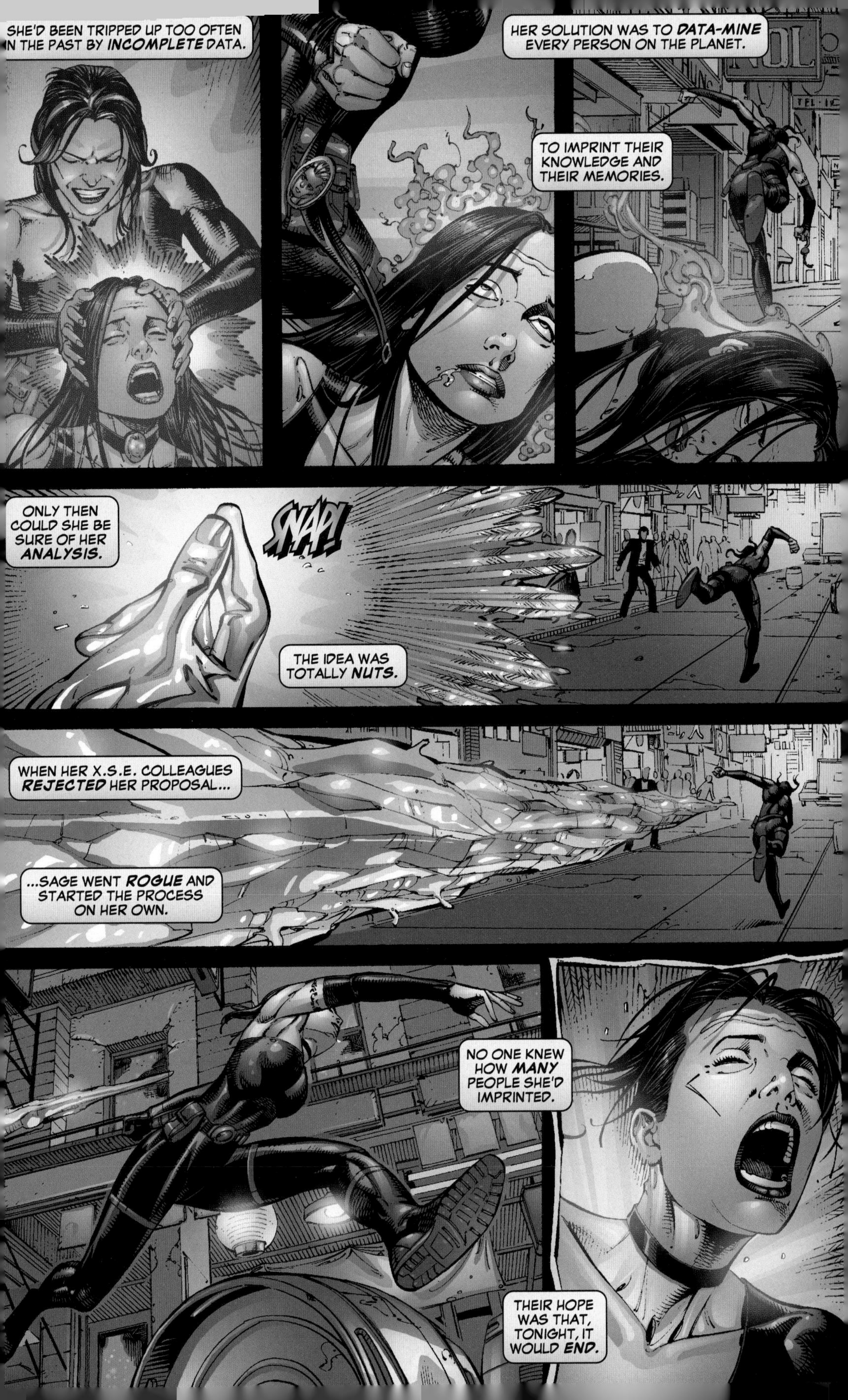
SHE'D BEEN TRIPPED UP TOO OFTEN IN THE PAST BY INCOMPLETE DATA.
HER SOLUTION WAS TO DATA-MINE EVERY PERSON ON THE PLANET.
TO IMPRINT THEIR KNOWLEDGE AND THEIR MEMORIES.
ONLY THEN COULD SHE BE SURE OF HER ANALYSIS.
SNAP!
THE IDEA WAS TOTALLY NUTS.
WHEN HER X.S.E. COLLEAGUES REJECTED HER PROPOSAL...
...SAGE WENT ROGUE AND STARTED THE PROCESS ON HER OWN.
NO ONE KNEW HOW MANY PEOPLE SHE'D IMPRINTED.
THEIR HOPE WAS THAT, TONIGHT, IT WOULD END.

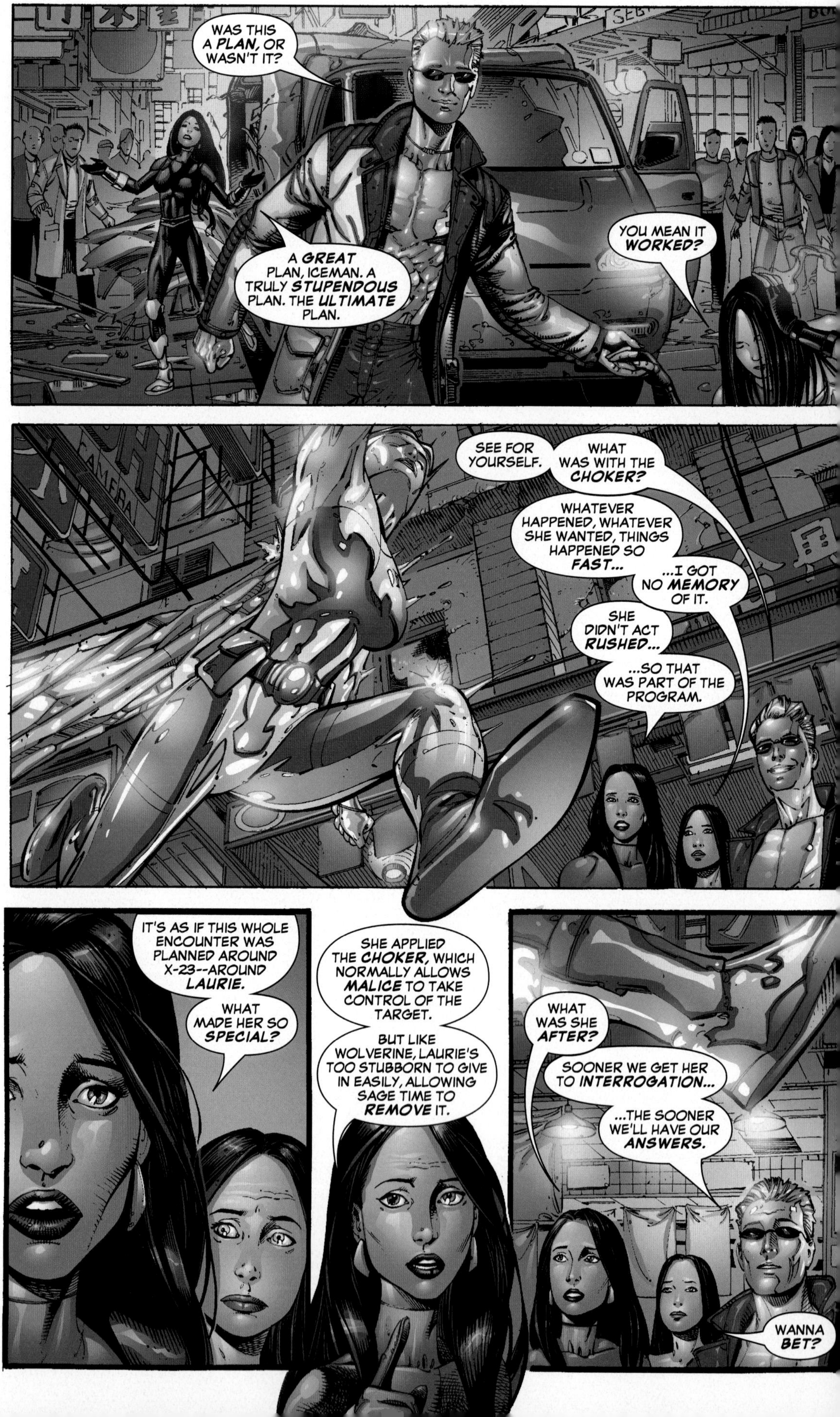
WAS THIS A PLAN, OR WASN'T IT?
A GREAT PLAN, ICEMAN. A TRULY STUPENDOUS PLAN. THE ULTIMATE PLAN.
YOU MEAN IT WORKED?
SEE FOR YOURSELF.
WHAT WAS WITH THE CHOKER?
WHATEVER HAPPENED, WHATEVER SHE WANTED, THINGS HAPPENED SO FAST...
...I GOT NO MEMORY OF IT.
SHE DIDN'T ACT RUSHED...
...SO THAT WAS PART OF THE PROGRAM.
IT'S AS IF THIS WHOLE ENCOUNTER WAS PLANNED AROUND X-23--AROUND LAURIE.
WHAT MADE HER SO SPECIAL?
SHE APPLIED THE CHOKER, WHICH NORMALLY ALLOWS MALICE TO TAKE CONTROL OF THE TARGET.
BUT LIKE WOLVERINE, LAURIE'S TOO STUBBORN TO GIVE IN EASILY, ALLOWING SAGE TIME TO REMOVE IT.
WHAT WAS SHE AFTER?
SOONER WE GET HER TO INTERROGATION...
...THE SOONER WE'LL HAVE OUR ANSWERS.
WANNA BET?

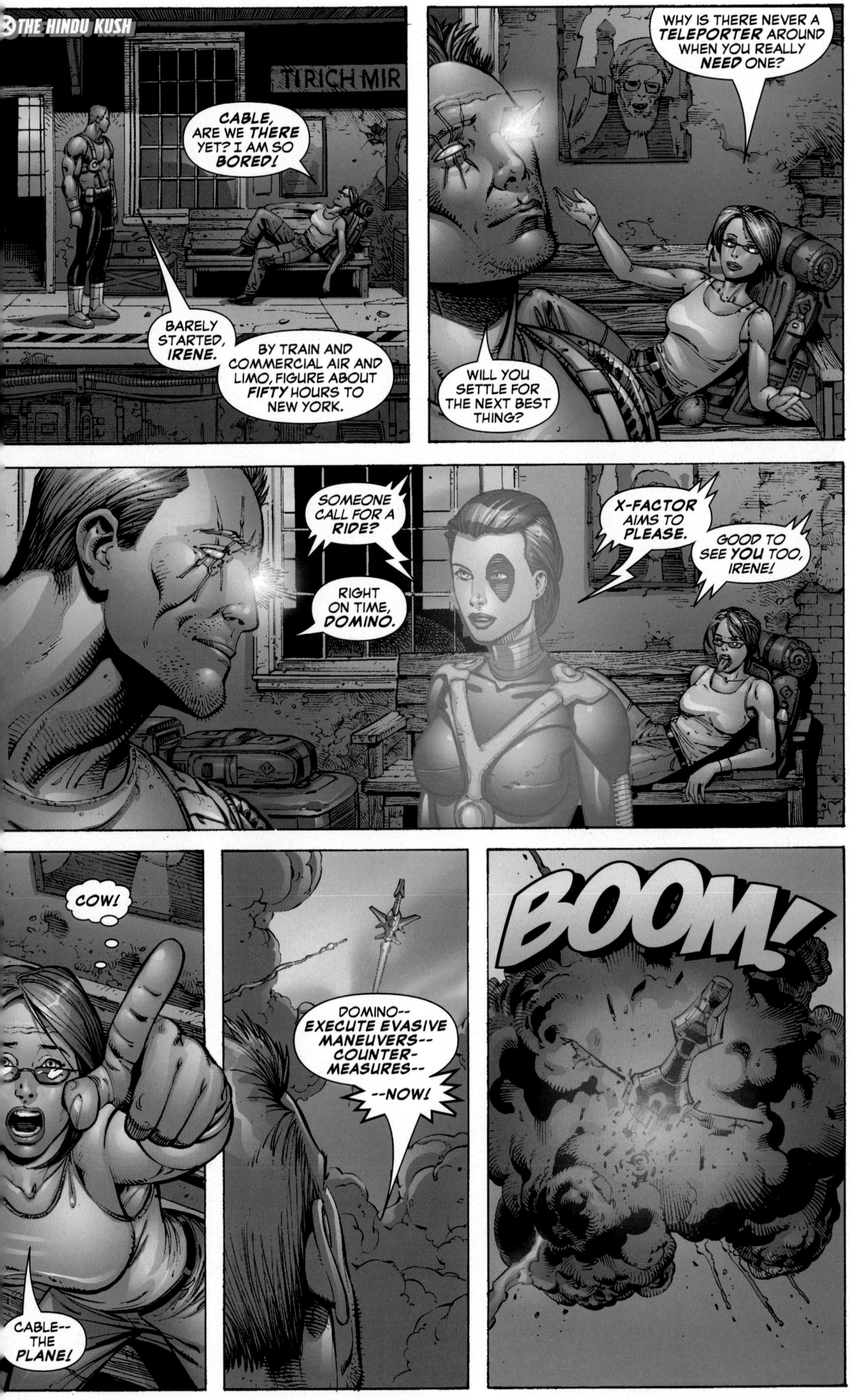
THE HINDU KUSH
TIRICH MIR
CABLE, ARE WE THERE YET? I AM SO BORED!
BARELY STARTED, IRENE.
BY TRAIN AND COMMERCIAL AIR AND LIMO, FIGURE ABOUT FIFTY HOURS TO NEW YORK.
WHY IS THERE NEVER A TELEPORTER AROUND WHEN YOU REALLY NEED ONE?
WILL YOU SETTLE FOR THE NEXT BEST THING?
SOMEONE CALL FOR A RIDE?
RIGHT ON TIME, DOMINO.
X-FACTOR AIMS TO PLEASE.
GOOD TO SEE YOU TOO, IRENE!
COW!
CABLE-- THE PLANE!
DOMINO-- EXECUTE EVASIVE MANEUVERS-- COUNTER-MEASURES--
--NOW!
BOOM!

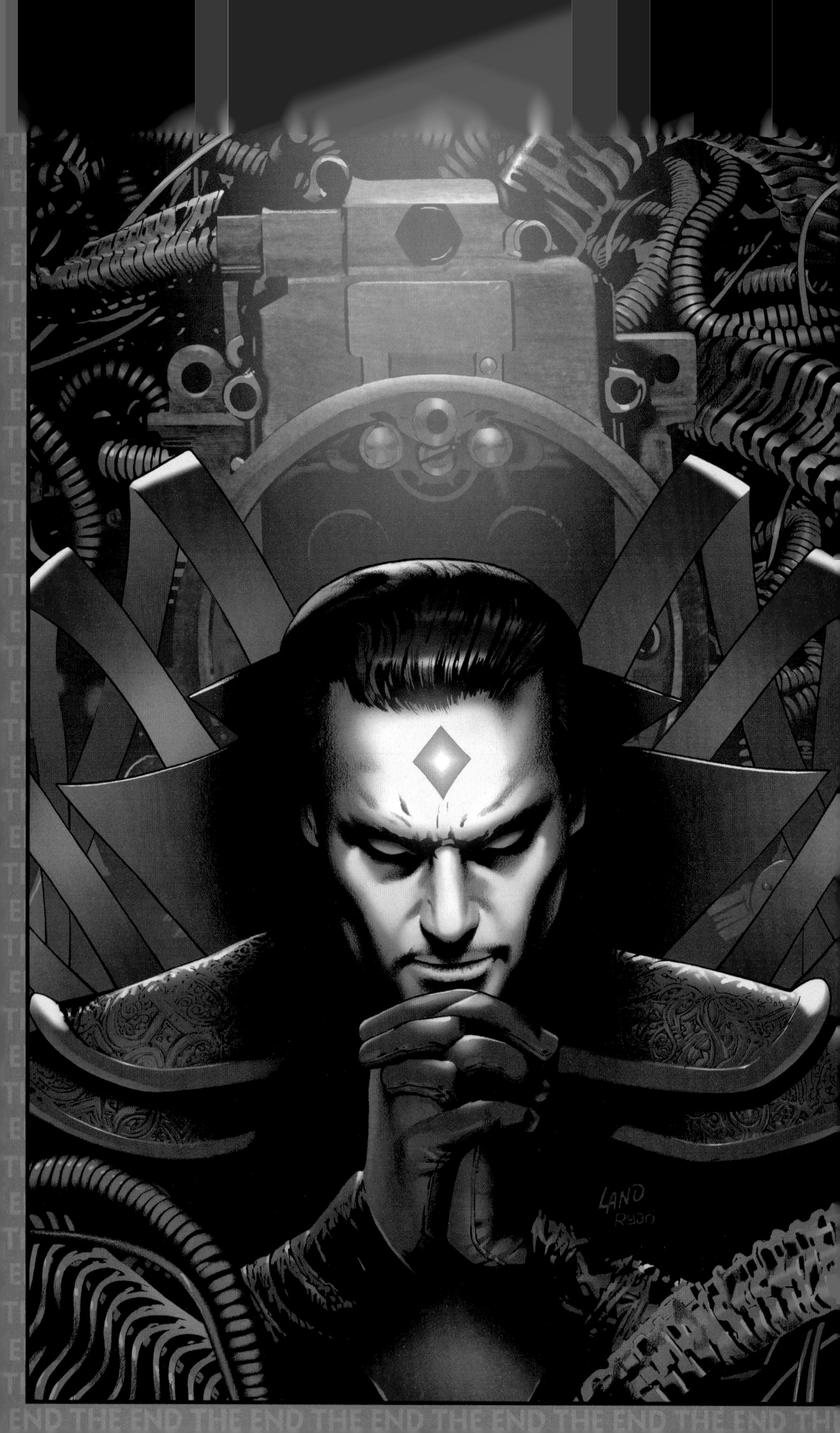
LAND
Ryan

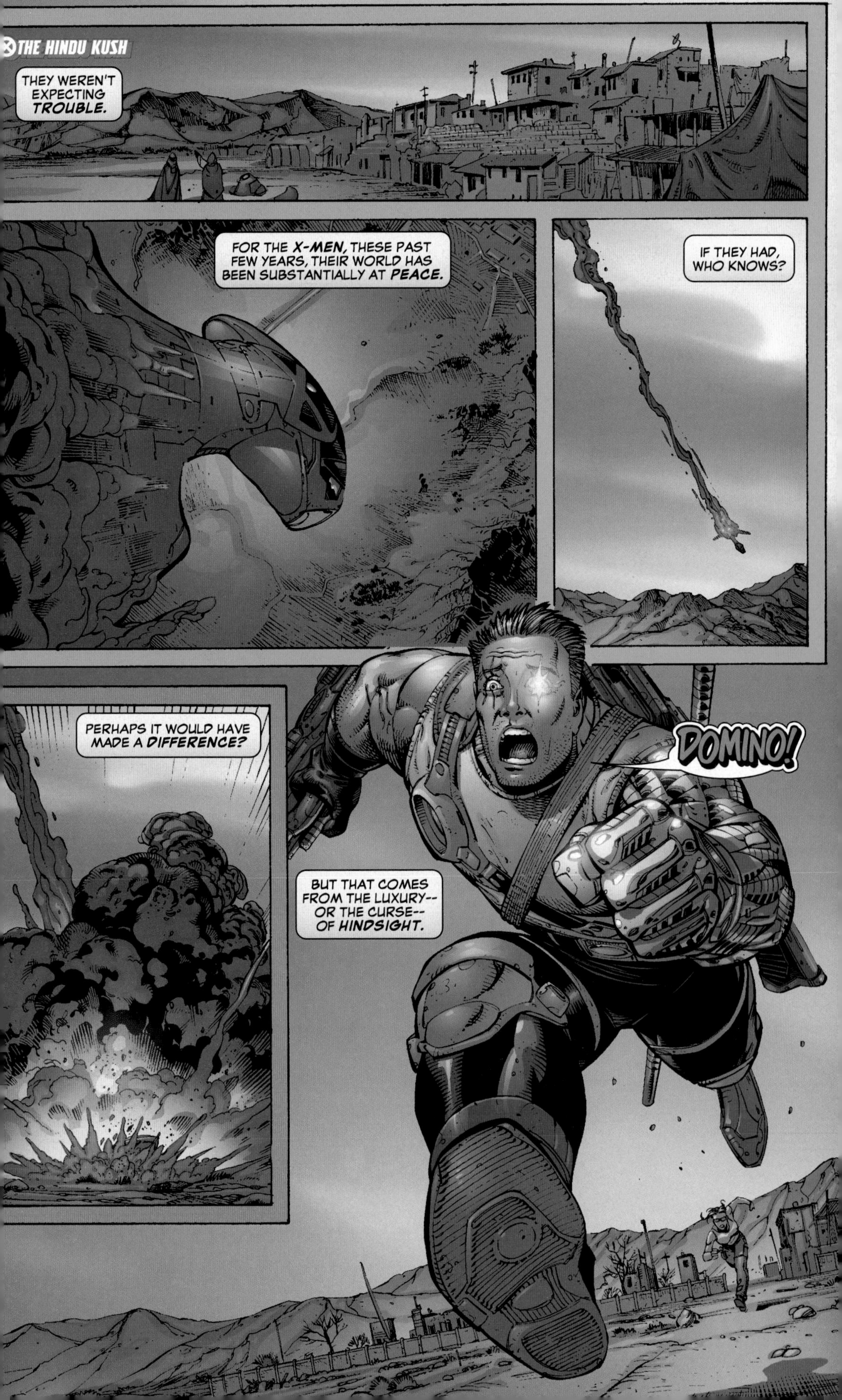

THE HINDU KUSH
THEY WEREN'T EXPECTING TROUBLE.
FOR THE X-MEN, THESE PAST FEW YEARS, THEIR WORLD HAS BEEN SUBSTANTIALLY AT PEACE.
IF THEY HAD, WHO KNOWS?
PERHAPS IT WOULD HAVE MADE A DIFFERENCE?
DOMINO!
BUT THAT COMES FROM THE LUXURY-- OR THE CURSE-- OF HINDSIGHT.

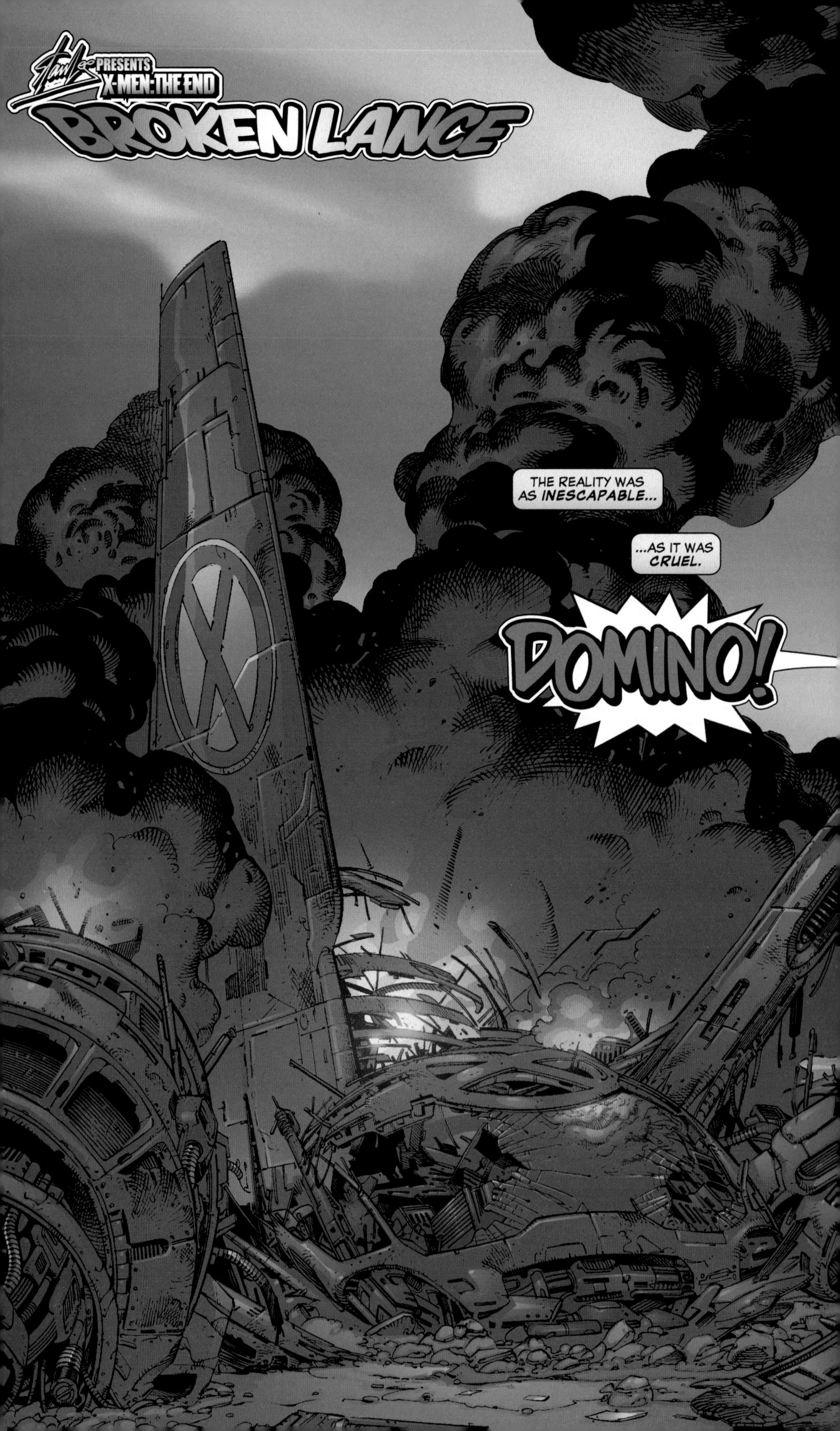
Stan Lee PRESENTS X-MEN: THE END
BROKEN LANCE
THE REALITY WAS AS INESCAPABLE...
...AS IT WAS CRUEL.
DOMINO!

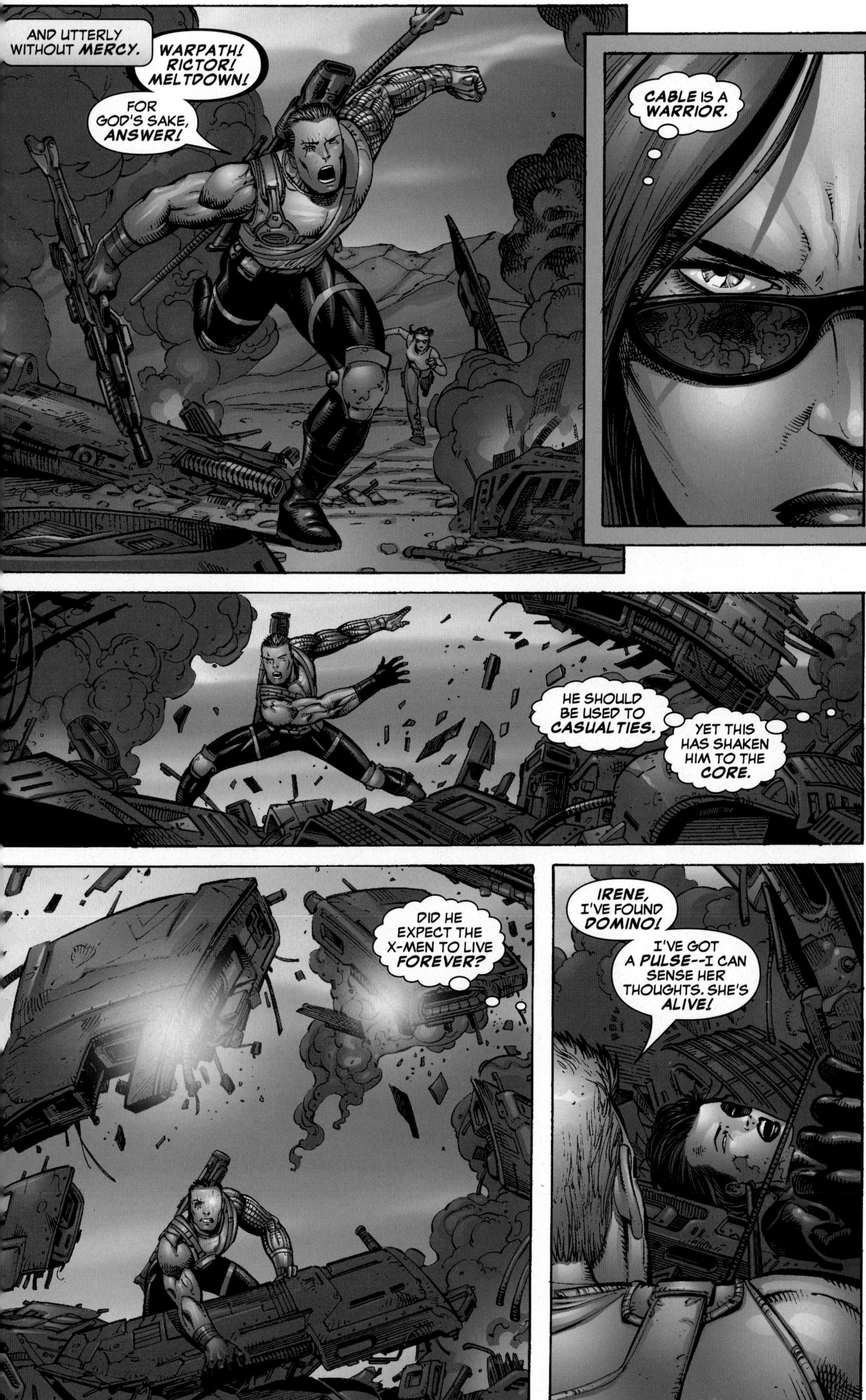
AND UTTERLY WITHOUT MERCY.
WARPATH! RICTOR! MELTDOWN!
FOR GOD'S SAKE, ANSWER!
CABLE IS A WARRIOR.
HE SHOULD BE USED TO CASUALTIES.
YET THIS HAS SHAKEN HIM TO THE CORE.
DID HE EXPECT THE X-MEN TO LIVE FOREVER?
IRENE, I'VE FOUND DOMINO!
I'VE GOT A PULSE--I CAN SENSE HER THOUGHTS. SHE'S ALIVE!

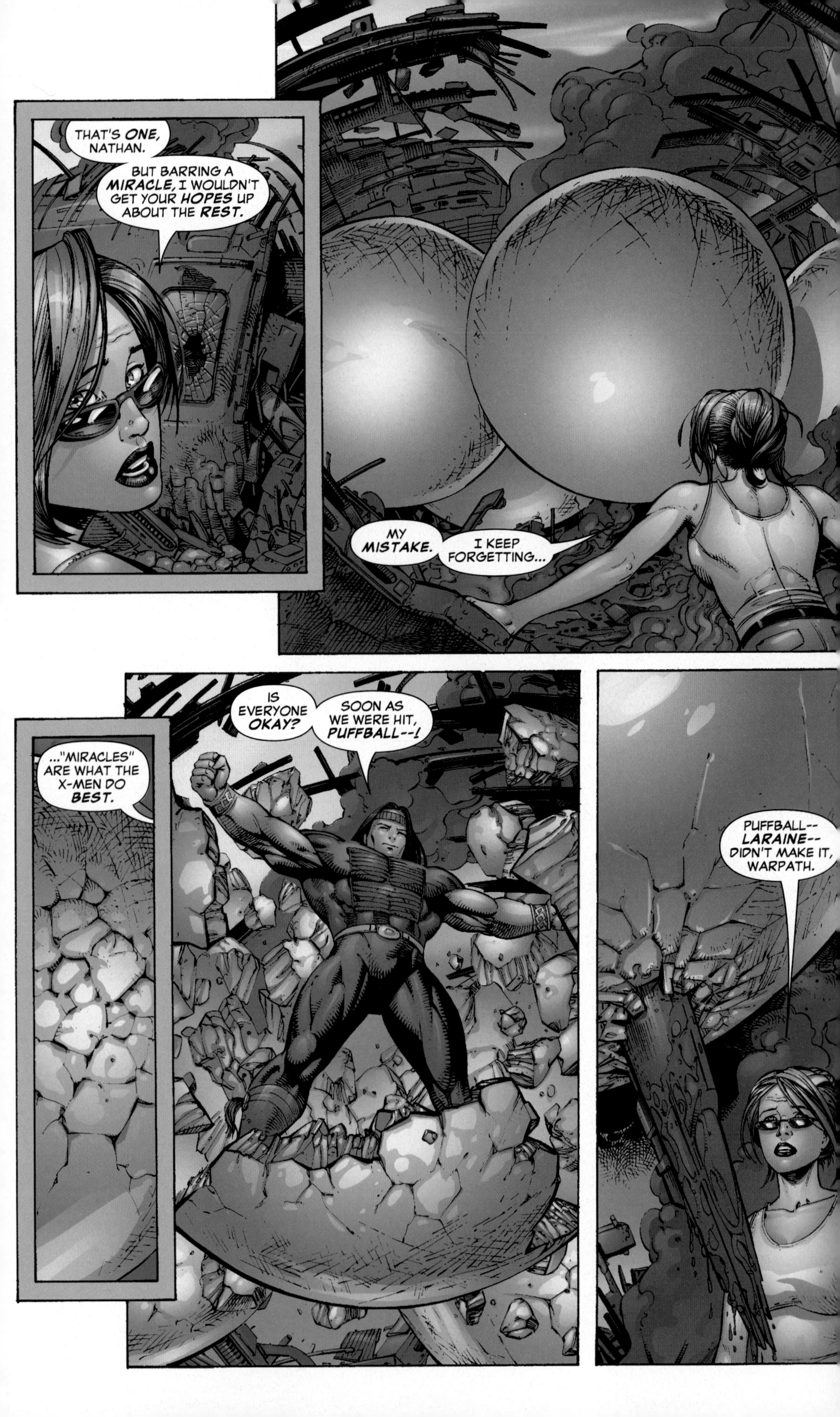
THAT'S ONE, NATHAN.
BUT BARRING A MIRACLE, I WOULDN'T GET YOUR HOPES UP ABOUT THE REST.
MY MISTAKE.
I KEEP FORGETTING...
..."MIRACLES" ARE WHAT THE X-MEN DO BEST.
IS EVERYONE OKAY?
SOON AS WE WERE HIT, PUFFBALL--!
PUFFBALL-- LARAINE-- DIDN'T MAKE IT, WARPATH.

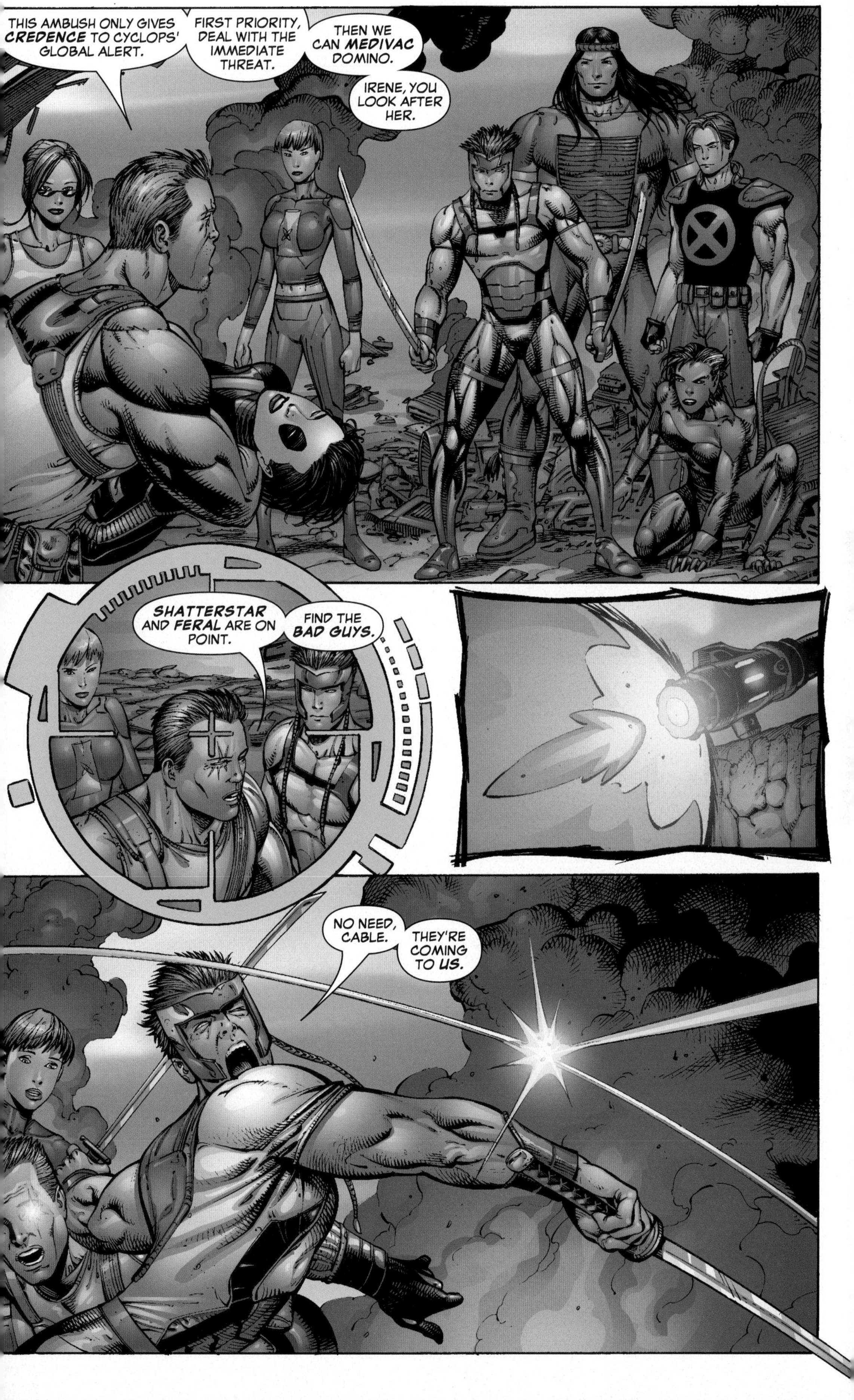

THIS AMBUSH ONLY GIVES CREDENCE TO CYCLOPS' GLOBAL ALERT.
FIRST PRIORITY, DEAL WITH THE IMMEDIATE THREAT.
THEN WE CAN MEDIVAC DOMINO.
IRENE, YOU LOOK AFTER HER.
SHATTERSTAR AND FERAL ARE ON POINT.
FIND THE BAD GUYS.
NO NEED, CABLE.
THEY'RE COMING TO US.

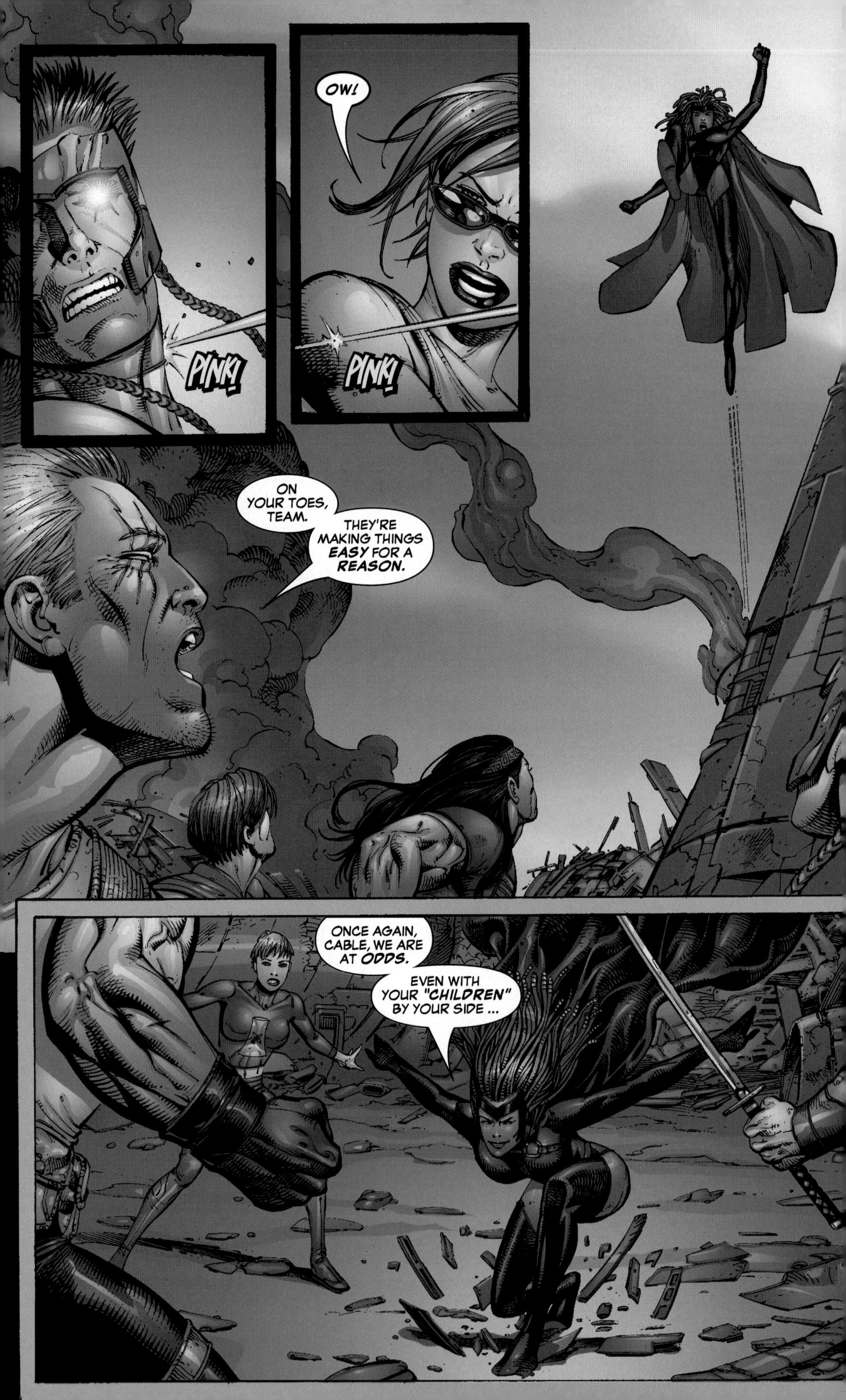
PINK!
OW!
PINK!
ON YOUR TOES, TEAM.
THEY'RE MAKING THINGS EASY FOR A REASON.
ONCE AGAIN, CABLE, WE ARE AT ODDS.
EVEN WITH YOUR "CHILDREN" BY YOUR SIDE ...

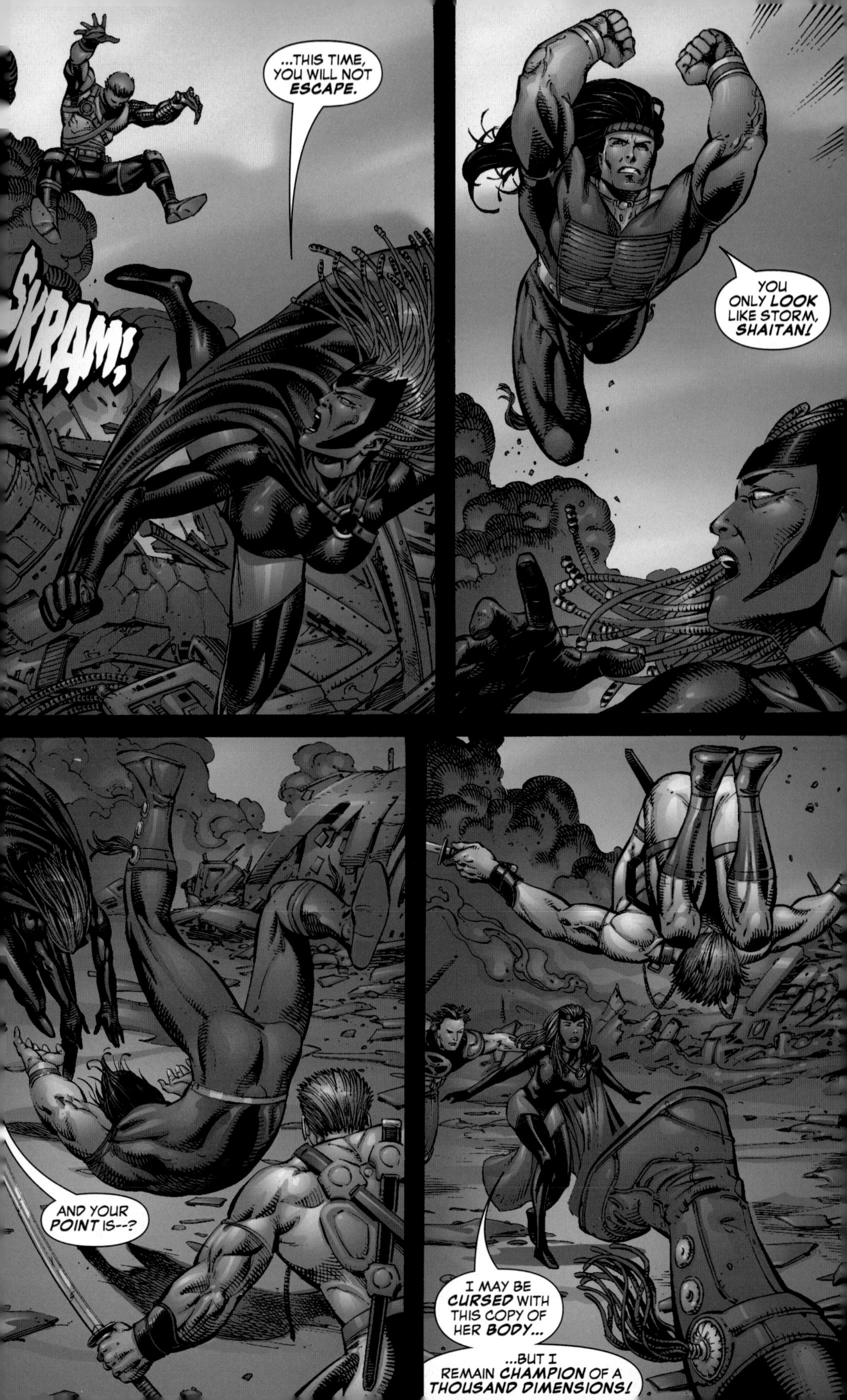
...THIS TIME, YOU WILL NOT ESCAPE.
SKRAM!
YOU ONLY LOOK LIKE STORM, SHAITAN!
AND YOUR POINT IS--?
I MAY BE CURSED WITH THIS COPY OF HER BODY...
...BUT I REMAIN CHAMPION OF A THOUSAND DIMENSIONS!

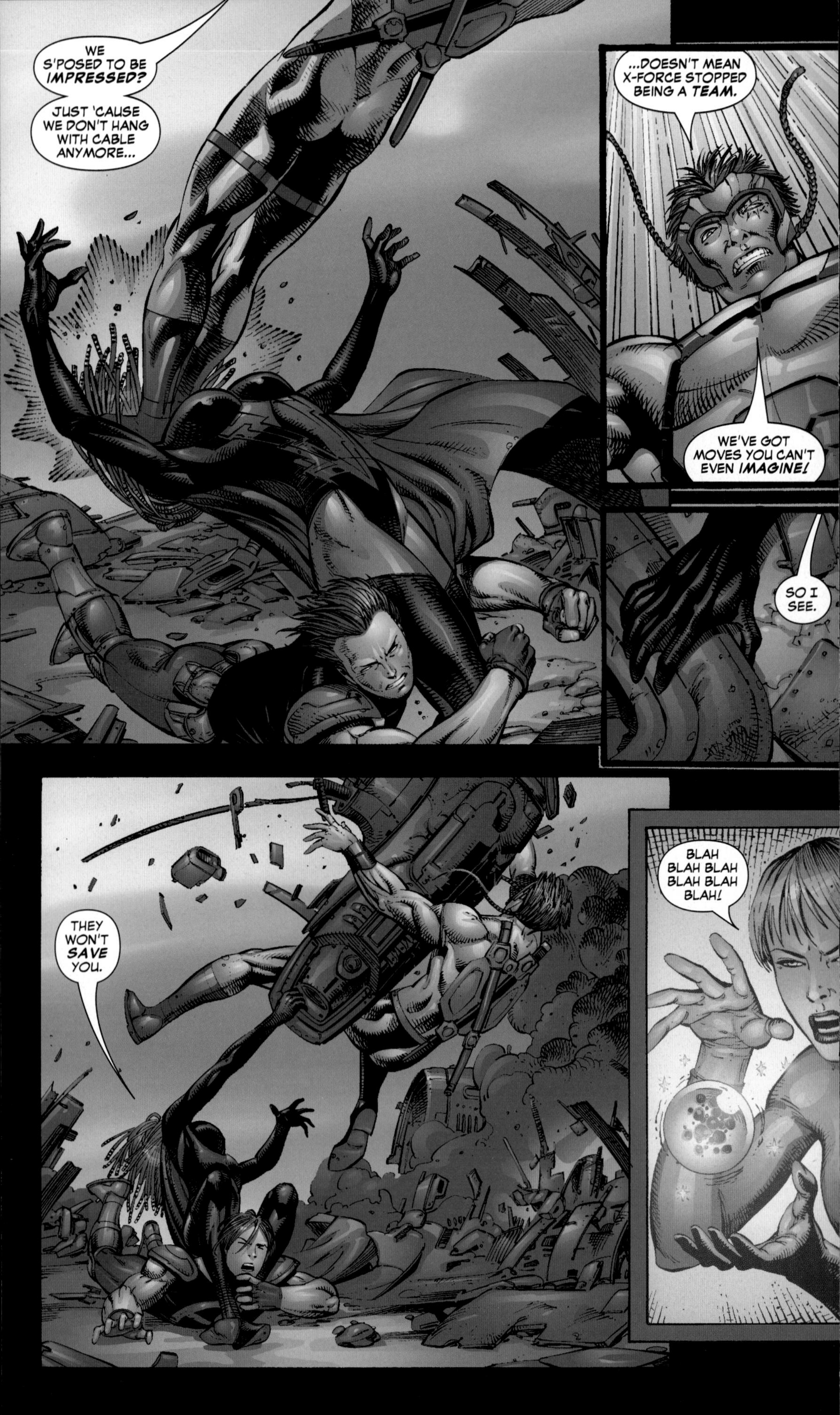
WE S'POSED TO BE IMPRESSED?
JUST 'CAUSE WE DON'T HANG WITH CABLE ANYMORE...
...DOESN'T MEAN X-FORCE STOPPED BEING A TEAM.
WE'VE GOT MOVES YOU CAN'T EVEN IMAGINE!
SO I SEE.
THEY WON'T SAVE YOU.
BLAH BLAH BLAH BLAH BLAH BLAH!

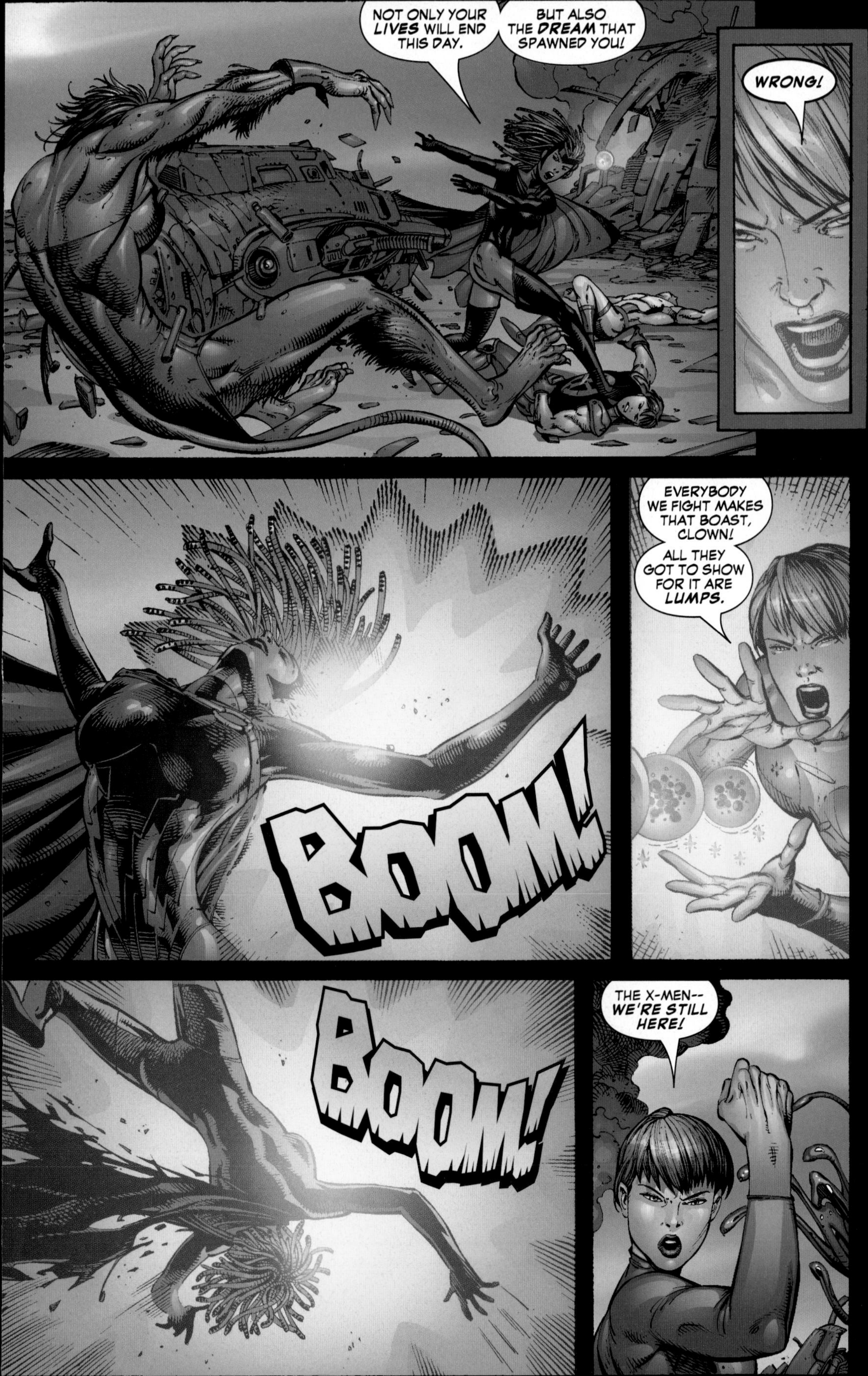
NOT ONLY YOUR *LIVES* WILL END THIS DAY.
BUT ALSO THE *DREAM* THAT SPAWNED YOU!
WRONG!
BOOM!
EVERYBODY WE FIGHT MAKES THAT BOAST, CLOWN!
ALL THEY GOT TO SHOW FOR IT ARE *LUMPS.*
BOOM!
THE X-MEN-- *WE'RE STILL HERE!*

MELTDOWN HITS, MELTDOWN SCORES--!

YEARRRGH!

MELTDOWN IS HISTORY.

TABBY! I'VE GOT TO BLAST DIVINITY CLEAR, BEFORE HE CAN ASSIMILATE HER!

ZAKKAZAKKA

KCHOW!

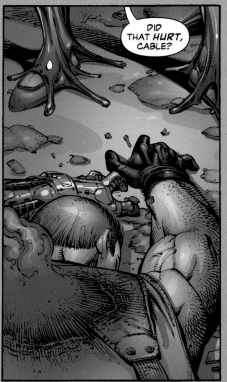

DID THAT HURT, CABLE?

BETCHA THIS HURTS MORE. I'M ALREADY FEASTING ON MELTDOWN'S SOUL.

THE BODY, I'LL KEEP FOR A WHILE.

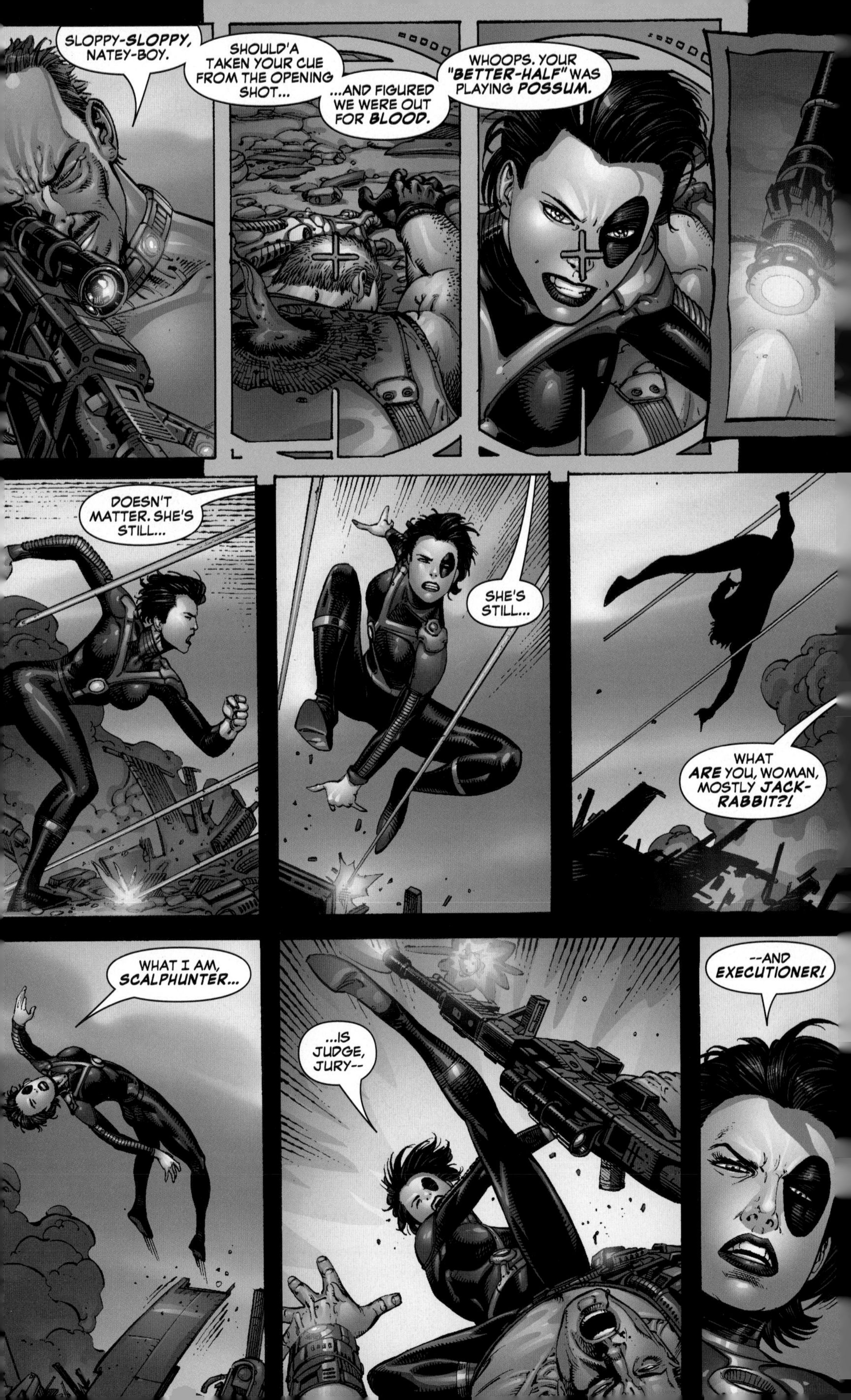
SLOPPY-SLOPPY, NATEY-BOY.
SHOULD'A TAKEN YOUR CUE FROM THE OPENING SHOT...
...AND FIGURED WE WERE OUT FOR BLOOD.
WHOOPS. YOUR "BETTER-HALF" WAS PLAYING POSSUM.
DOESN'T MATTER. SHE'S STILL...
SHE'S STILL...
WHAT ARE YOU, WOMAN, MOSTLY JACK-RABBIT?!
WHAT I AM, SCALPHUNTER...
...IS JUDGE, JURY--
--AND EXECUTIONER!

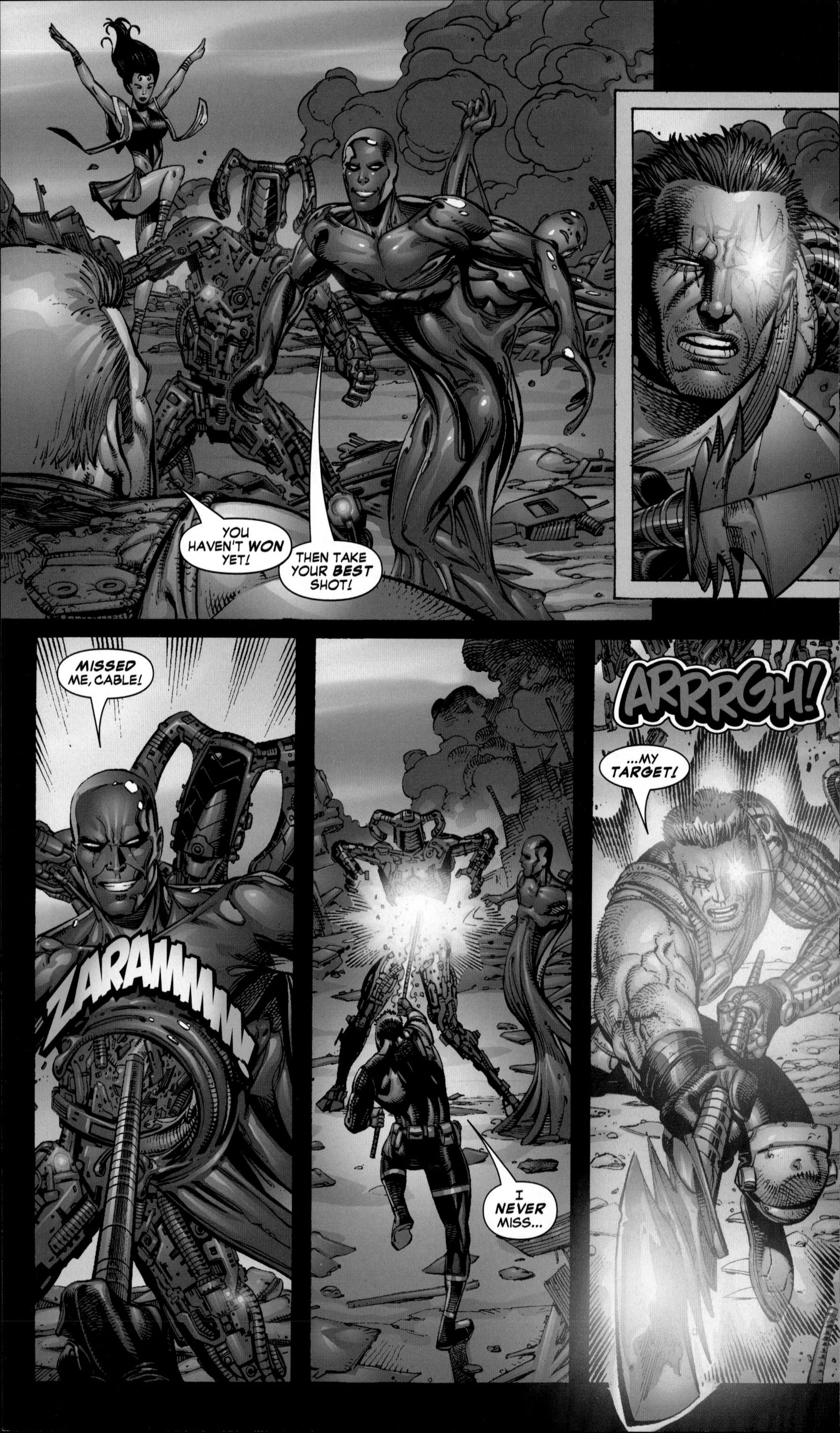
YOU HAVEN'T WON YET!
THEN TAKE YOUR BEST SHOT!
MISSED ME, CABLE!
ZARAMMMM
I NEVER MISS...
ARRRGH!
...MY TARGET!

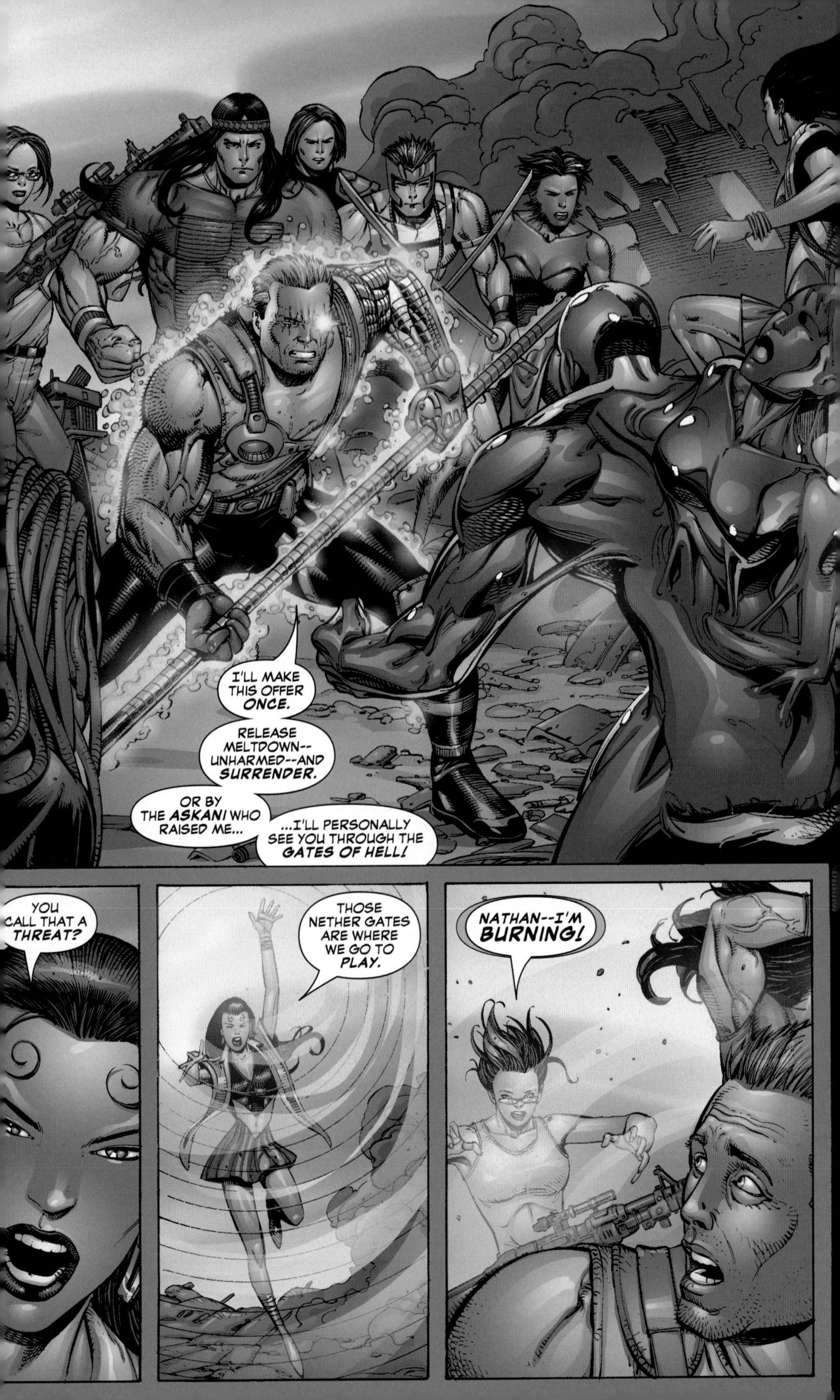
I'LL MAKE THIS OFFER ONCE.
RELEASE MELTDOWN--UNHARMED--AND SURRENDER.
OR BY THE ASKANI WHO RAISED ME...
...I'LL PERSONALLY SEE YOU THROUGH THE GATES OF HELL!
YOU CALL THAT A THREAT?
THOSE NETHER GATES ARE WHERE WE GO TO PLAY.
NATHAN--I'M BURNING!

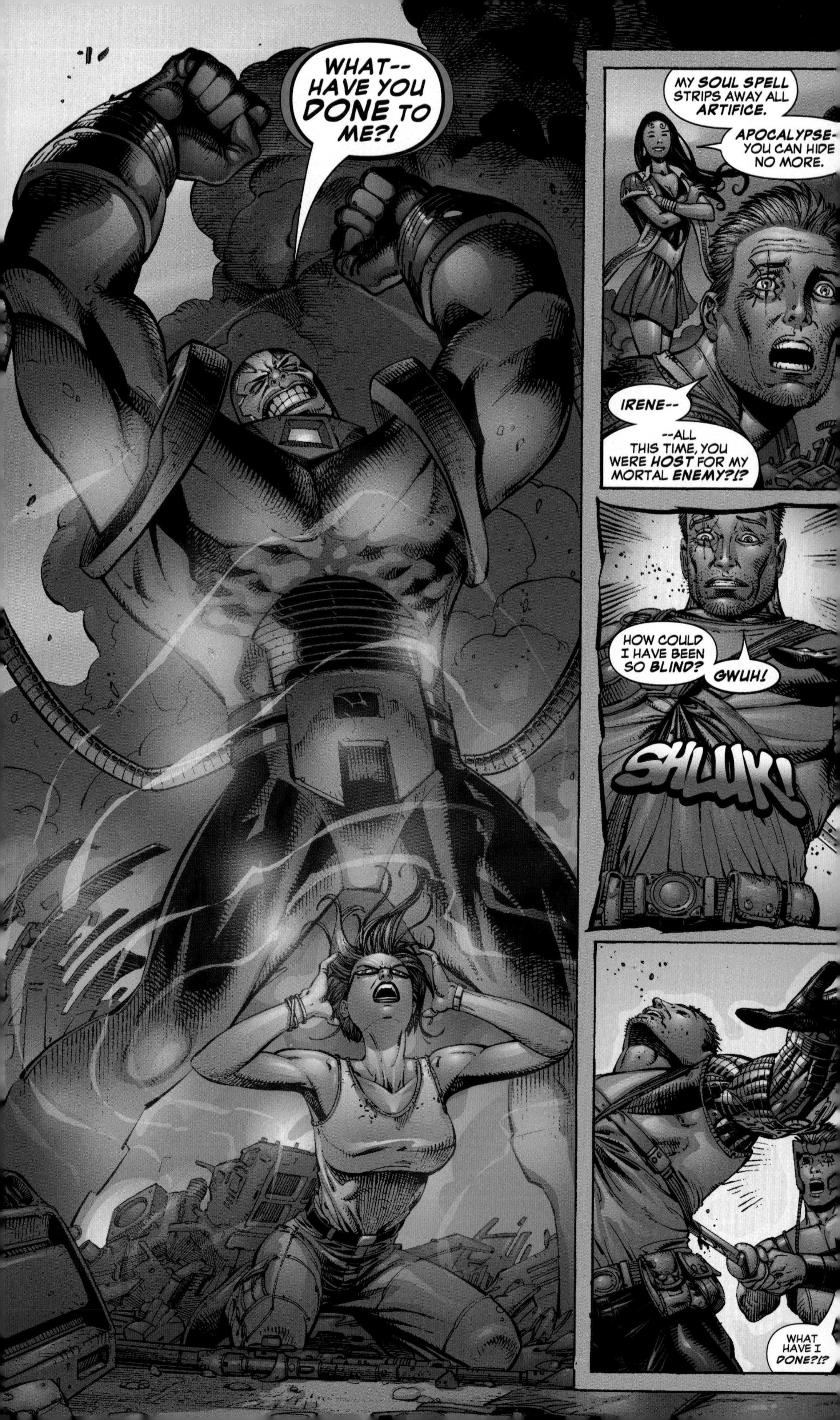
WHAT-- HAVE YOU DONE TO ME?!
MY SOUL SPELL STRIPS AWAY ALL ARTIFICE.
APOCALYPSE-- YOU CAN HIDE NO MORE.
IRENE--
--ALL THIS TIME, YOU WERE HOST FOR MY MORTAL ENEMY?!?
HOW COULD I HAVE BEEN SO BLIND?
GWUH!
SHLUK!
WHAT HAVE I DONE?!?

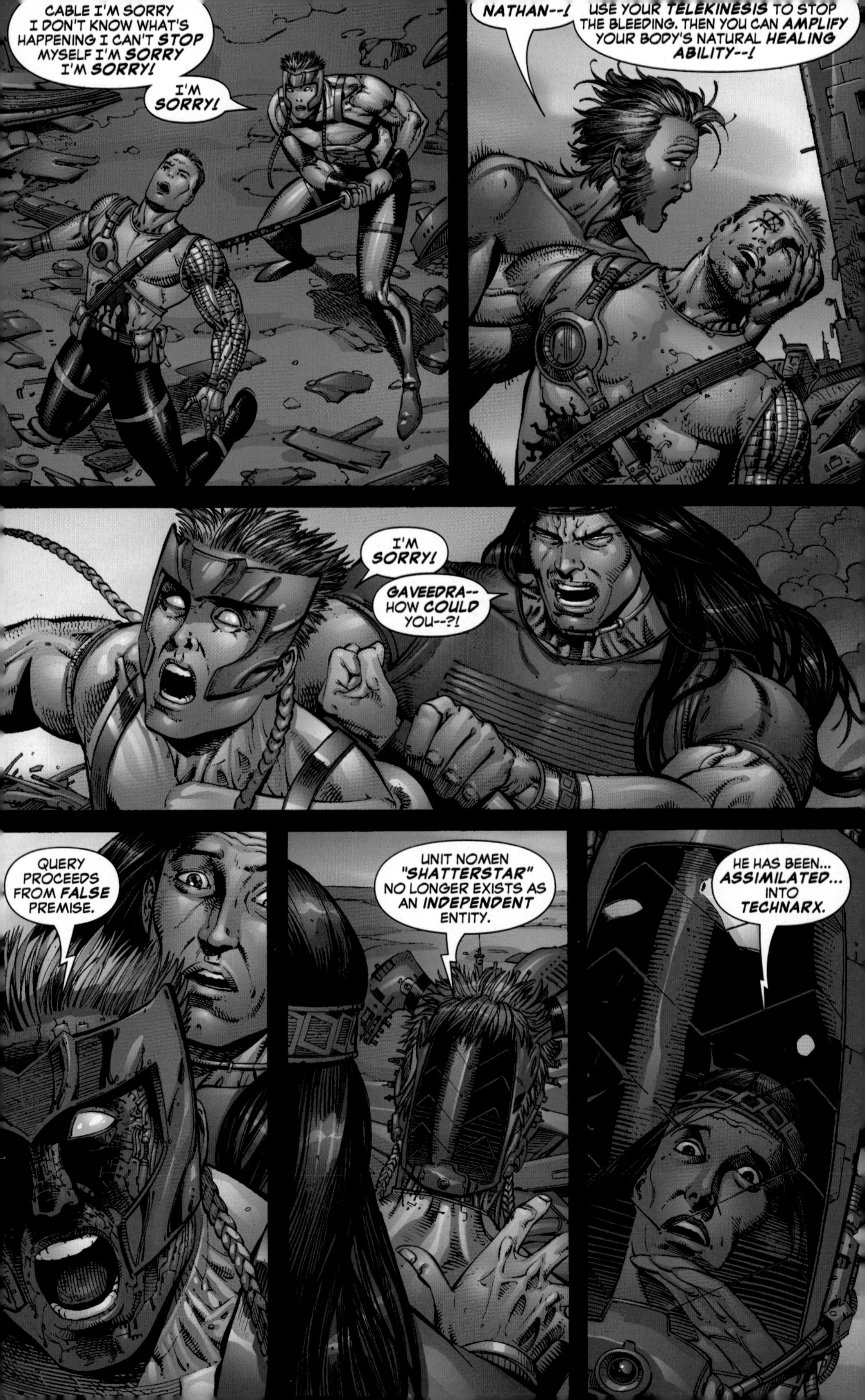
CABLE I'M SORRY I DON'T KNOW WHAT'S HAPPENING I CAN'T STOP MYSELF I'M SORRY I'M SORRY!
I'M SORRY!
NATHAN--!
USE YOUR TELEKINESIS TO STOP THE BLEEDING. THEN YOU CAN AMPLIFY YOUR BODY'S NATURAL HEALING ABILITY--!
I'M SORRY!
GAVEEDRA-- HOW COULD YOU--?!
QUERY PROCEEDS FROM FALSE PREMISE.
UNIT NOMEN "SHATTERSTAR" NO LONGER EXISTS AS AN INDEPENDENT ENTITY.
HE HAS BEEN... ASSIMILATED... INTO TECHNARX.

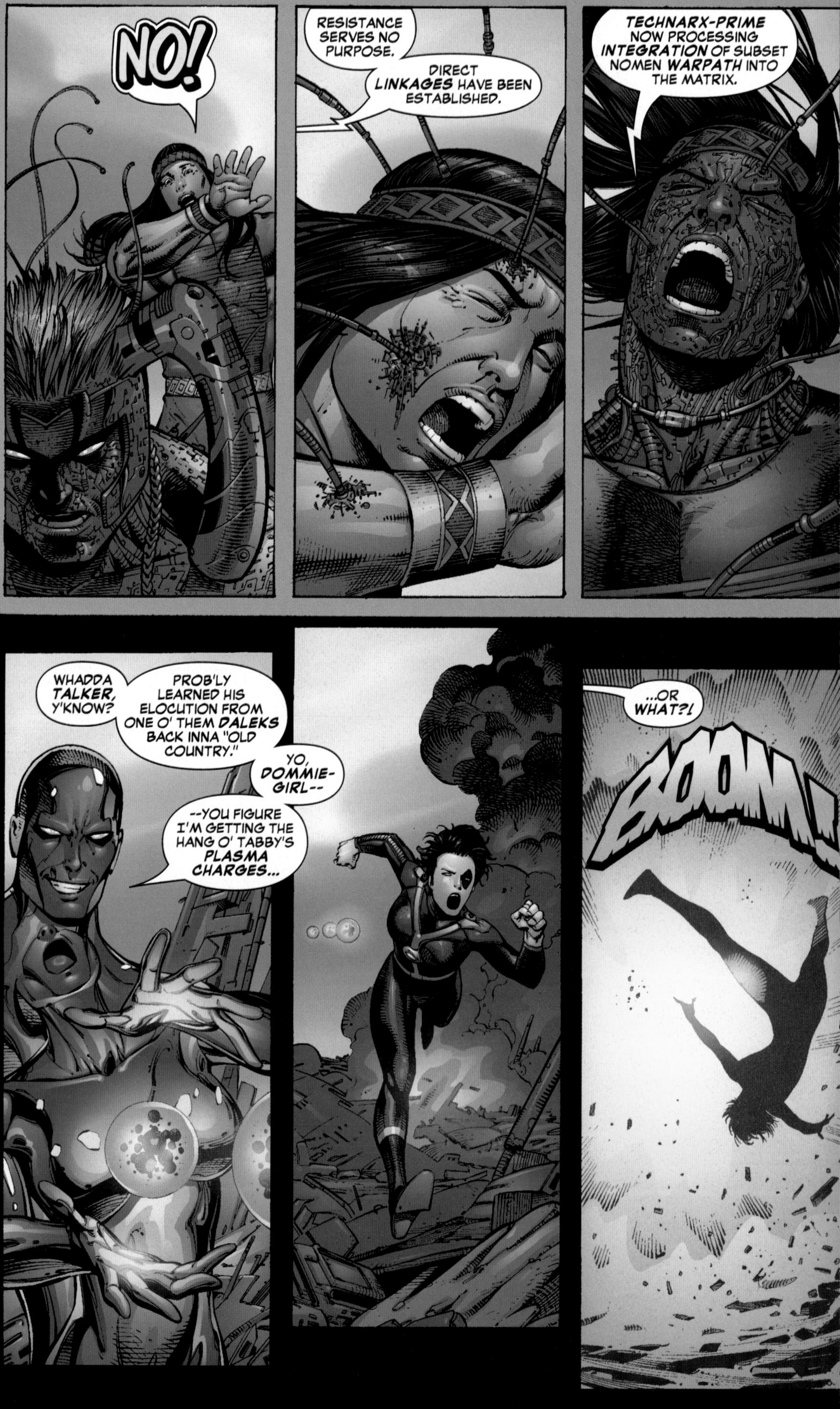
NO!
RESISTANCE SERVES NO PURPOSE.
DIRECT LINKAGES HAVE BEEN ESTABLISHED.
TECHNARX-PRIME NOW PROCESSING INTEGRATION OF SUBSET NOMEN WARPATH INTO THE MATRIX.
WHADDA TALKER, Y'KNOW?
PROB'LY LEARNED HIS ELOCUTION FROM ONE O' THEM DALEKS BACK INNA "OLD COUNTRY."
YO, DOMMIE-GIRL--
--YOU FIGURE I'M GETTING THE HANG O' TABBY'S PLASMA CHARGES...
...OR WHAT?!
BOOM!!

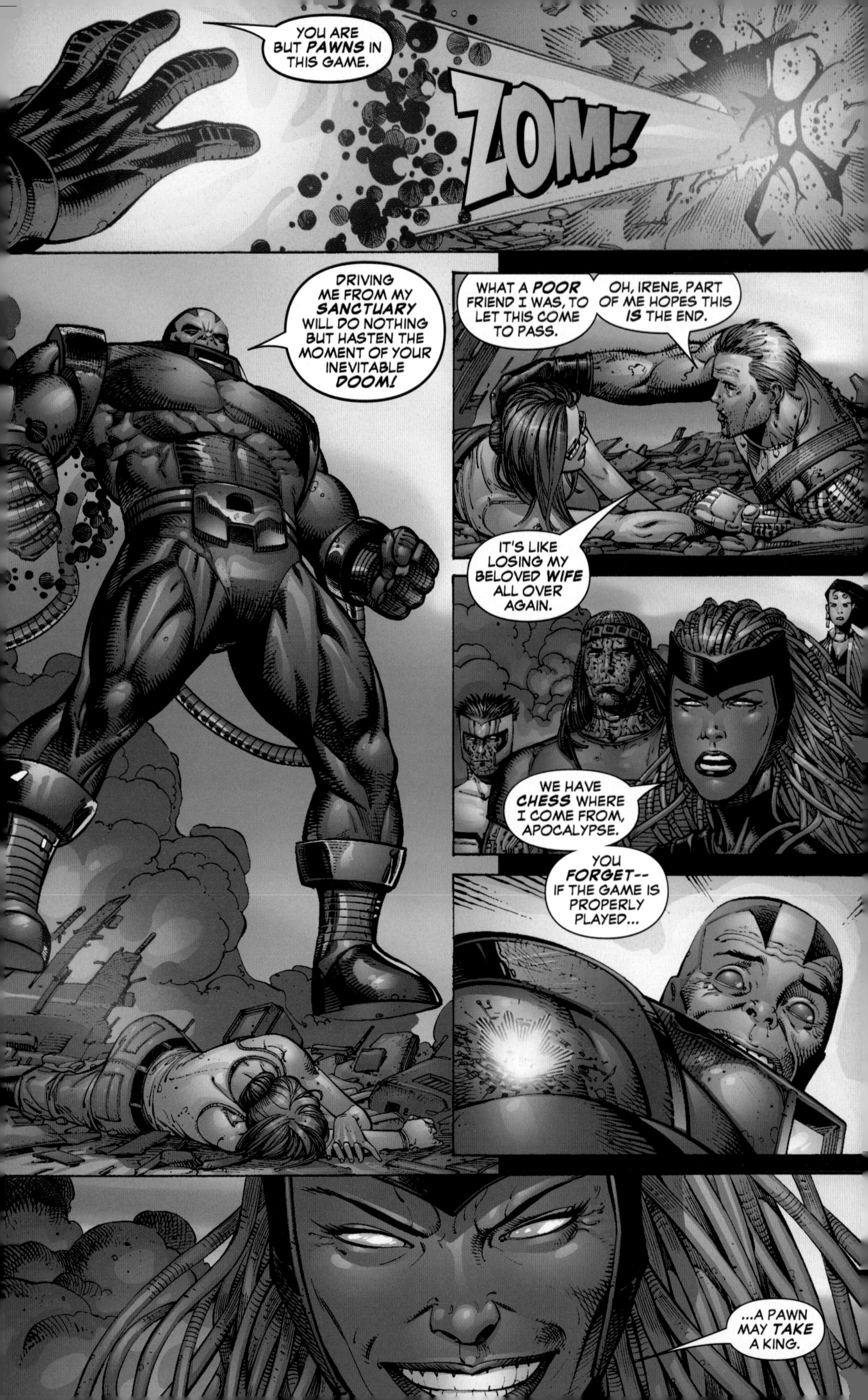
YOU ARE BUT PAWNS IN THIS GAME.
ZOM!
DRIVING ME FROM MY SANCTUARY WILL DO NOTHING BUT HASTEN THE MOMENT OF YOUR INEVITABLE DOOM!
WHAT A POOR FRIEND I WAS, TO LET THIS COME TO PASS.
OH, IRENE, PART OF ME HOPES THIS IS THE END.
IT'S LIKE LOSING MY BELOVED WIFE ALL OVER AGAIN.
WE HAVE CHESS WHERE I COME FROM, APOCALYPSE.
YOU FORGET-- IF THE GAME IS PROPERLY PLAYED...
...A PAWN MAY TAKE A KING.

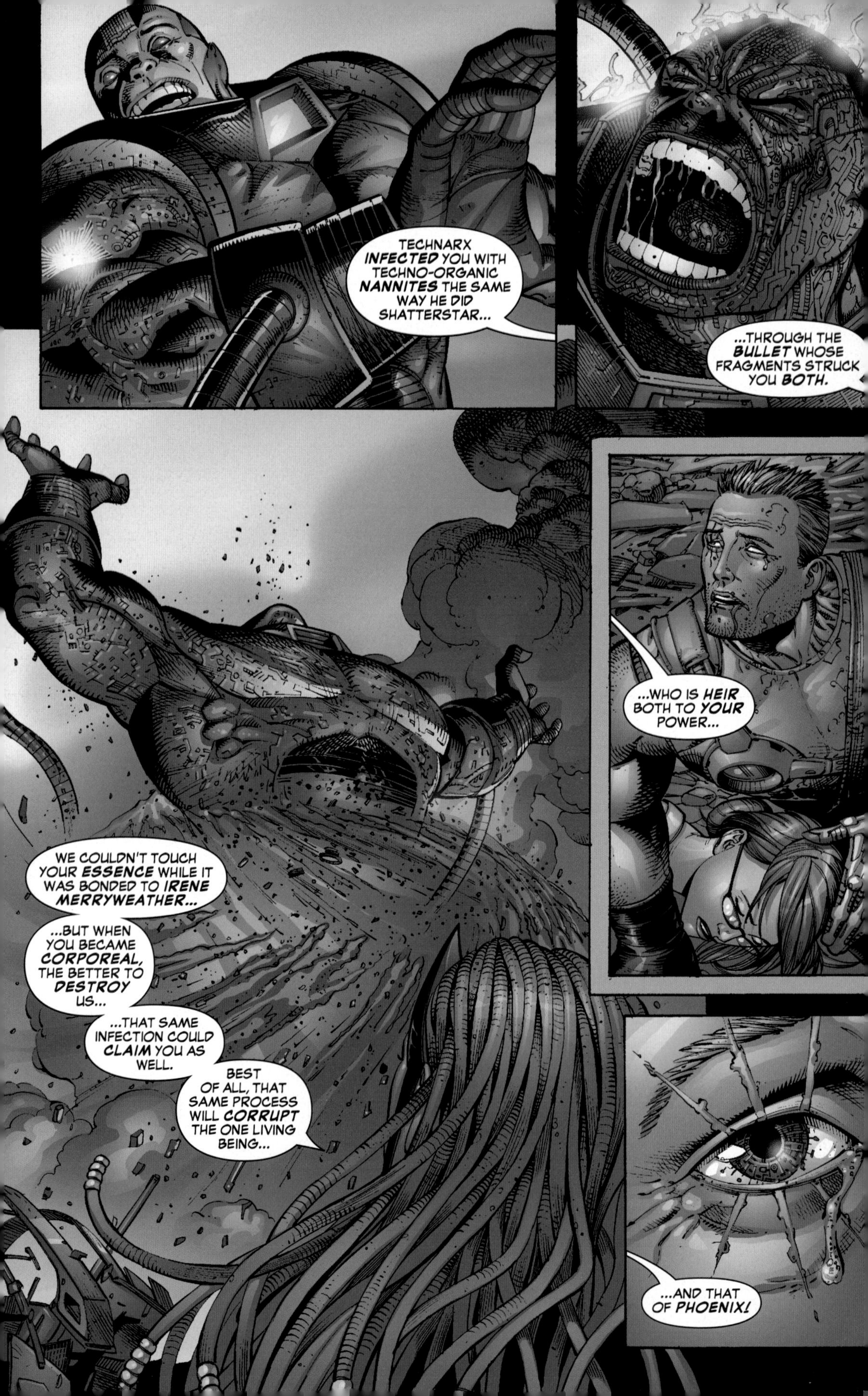
TECHNARX INFECTED YOU WITH TECHNO-ORGANIC NANNITES THE SAME WAY HE DID SHATTERSTAR...
...THROUGH THE BULLET WHOSE FRAGMENTS STRUCK YOU BOTH.
WE COULDN'T TOUCH YOUR ESSENCE WHILE IT WAS BONDED TO IRENE MERRYWEATHER...
...BUT WHEN YOU BECAME CORPOREAL, THE BETTER TO DESTROY US...
...THAT SAME INFECTION COULD CLAIM YOU AS WELL.
BEST OF ALL, THAT SAME PROCESS WILL CORRUPT THE ONE LIVING BEING...
...WHO IS HEIR BOTH TO YOUR POWER...
...AND THAT OF PHOENIX!

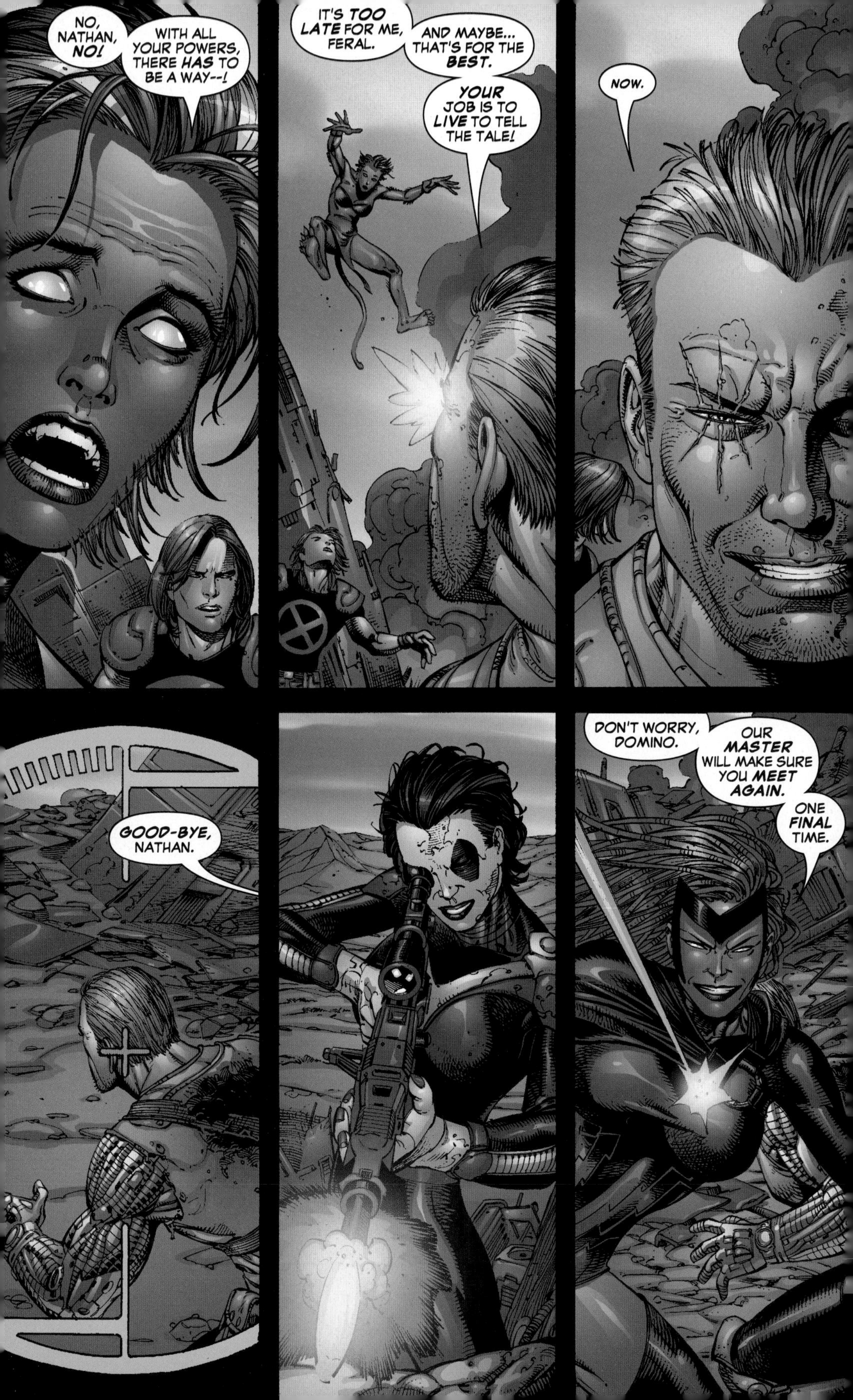
NO, NATHAN, NO!
WITH ALL YOUR POWERS, THERE HAS TO BE A WAY--!
IT'S TOO LATE FOR ME, FERAL.
AND MAYBE... THAT'S FOR THE BEST.
YOUR JOB IS TO LIVE TO TELL THE TALE!
NOW.
GOOD-BYE, NATHAN.
DON'T WORRY, DOMINO.
OUR MASTER WILL MAKE SURE YOU MEET AGAIN.
ONE FINAL TIME.

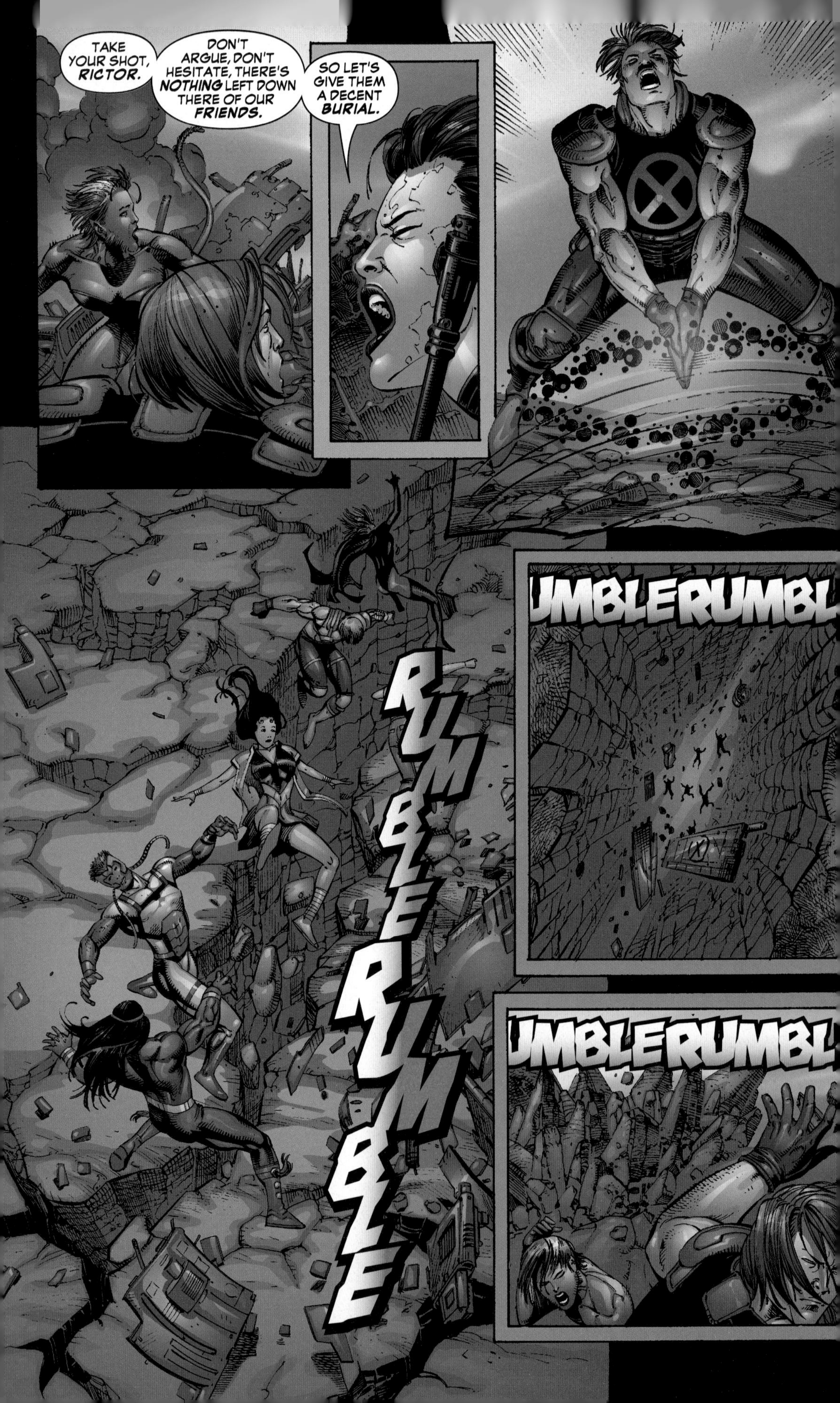
TAKE YOUR SHOT, RICTOR.
DON'T ARGUE, DON'T HESITATE, THERE'S NOTHING LEFT DOWN THERE OF OUR FRIENDS.
SO LET'S GIVE THEM A DECENT BURIAL.
RUMBLE RUMBLE
UMBLERUMBL
UMBLERUMBL

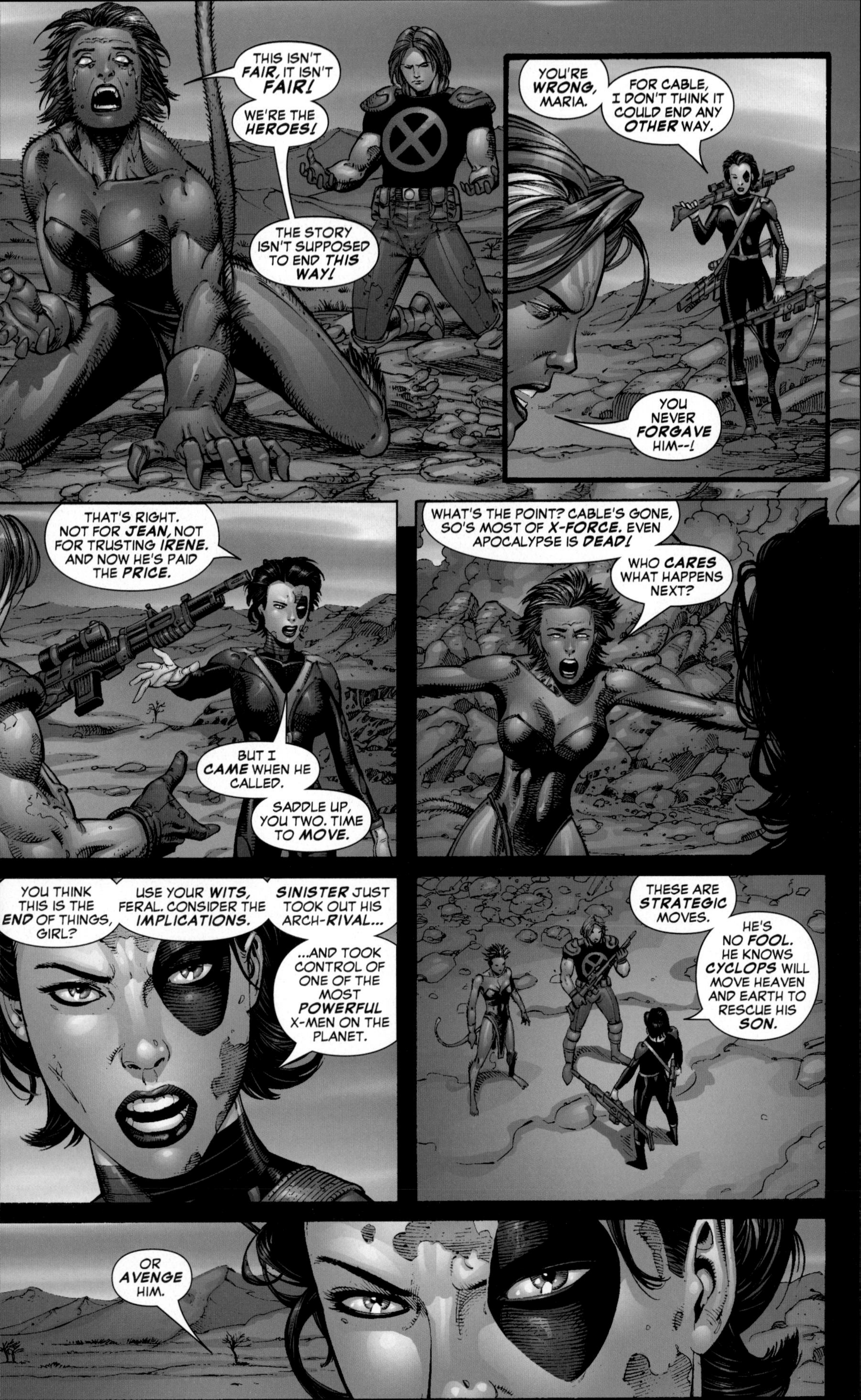
THIS ISN'T FAIR, IT ISN'T FAIR!
WE'RE THE HEROES!
THE STORY ISN'T SUPPOSED TO END THIS WAY!
YOU'RE WRONG, MARIA.
FOR CABLE, I DON'T THINK IT COULD END ANY OTHER WAY.
YOU NEVER FORGAVE HIM--!
THAT'S RIGHT. NOT FOR JEAN, NOT FOR TRUSTING IRENE. AND NOW HE'S PAID THE PRICE.
BUT I CAME WHEN HE CALLED.
SADDLE UP, YOU TWO. TIME TO MOVE.
WHAT'S THE POINT? CABLE'S GONE, SO'S MOST OF X-FORCE. EVEN APOCALYPSE IS DEAD!
WHO CARES WHAT HAPPENS NEXT?
YOU THINK THIS IS THE END OF THINGS, GIRL?
USE YOUR WITS, FERAL. CONSIDER THE IMPLICATIONS.
SINISTER JUST TOOK OUT HIS ARCH-RIVAL...
...AND TOOK CONTROL OF ONE OF THE MOST POWERFUL X-MEN ON THE PLANET.
THESE ARE STRATEGIC MOVES.
HE'S NO FOOL. HE KNOWS CYCLOPS WILL MOVE HEAVEN AND EARTH TO RESCUE HIS SON.
OR AVENGE HIM.

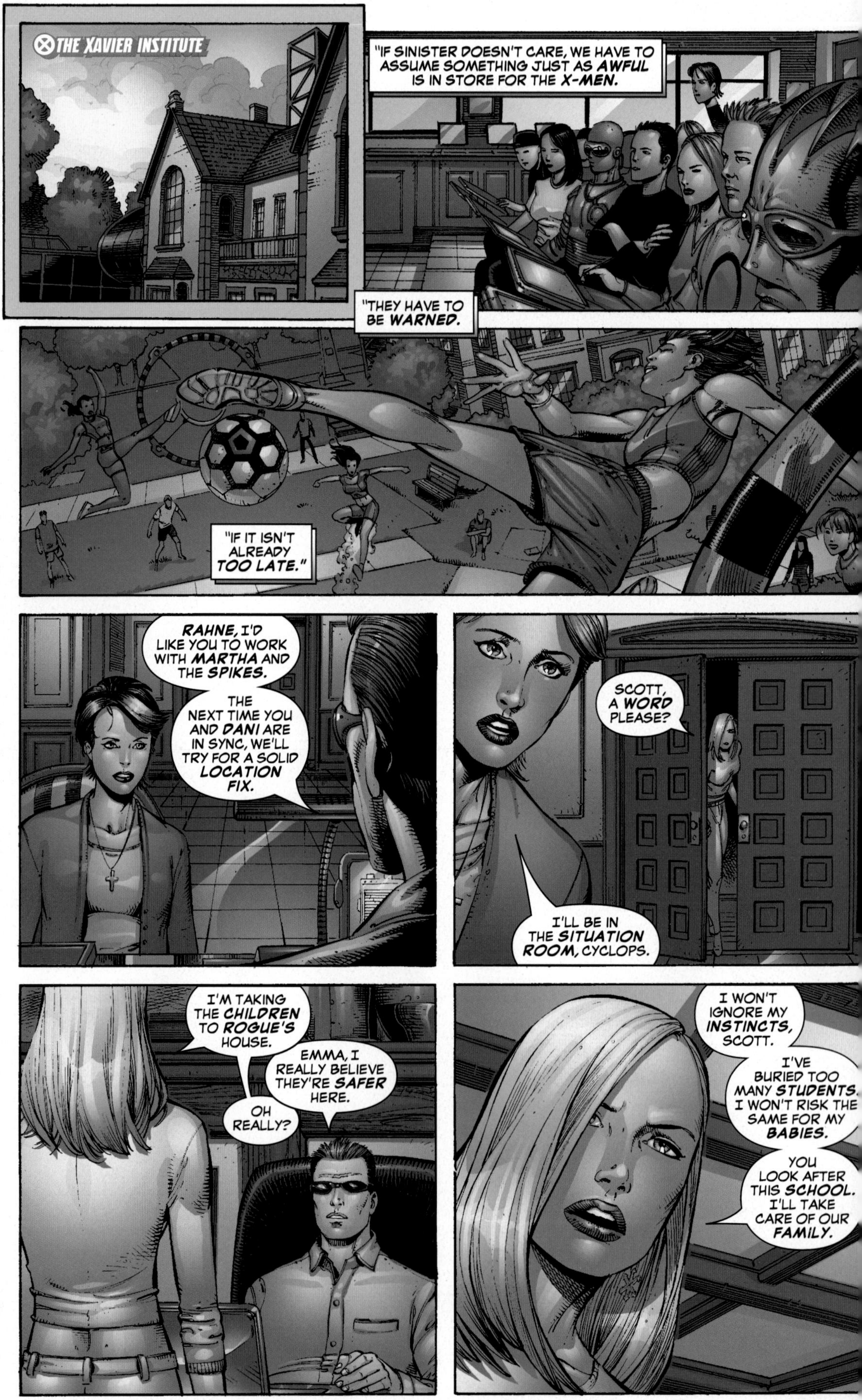
THE XAVIER INSTITUTE
"IF SINISTER DOESN'T CARE, WE HAVE TO ASSUME SOMETHING JUST AS AWFUL IS IN STORE FOR THE X-MEN.
"THEY HAVE TO BE WARNED.
"IF IT ISN'T ALREADY TOO LATE."
RAHNE, I'D LIKE YOU TO WORK WITH MARTHA AND THE SPIKES.
THE NEXT TIME YOU AND DANI ARE IN SYNC, WE'LL TRY FOR A SOLID LOCATION FIX.
SCOTT, A WORD PLEASE?
I'LL BE IN THE SITUATION ROOM, CYCLOPS.
I'M TAKING THE CHILDREN TO ROGUE'S HOUSE.
EMMA, I REALLY BELIEVE THEY'RE SAFER HERE.
OH REALLY?
I WON'T IGNORE MY INSTINCTS, SCOTT.
I'VE BURIED TOO MANY STUDENTS. I WON'T RISK THE SAME FOR MY BABIES.
YOU LOOK AFTER THIS SCHOOL. I'LL TAKE CARE OF OUR FAMILY.

#5

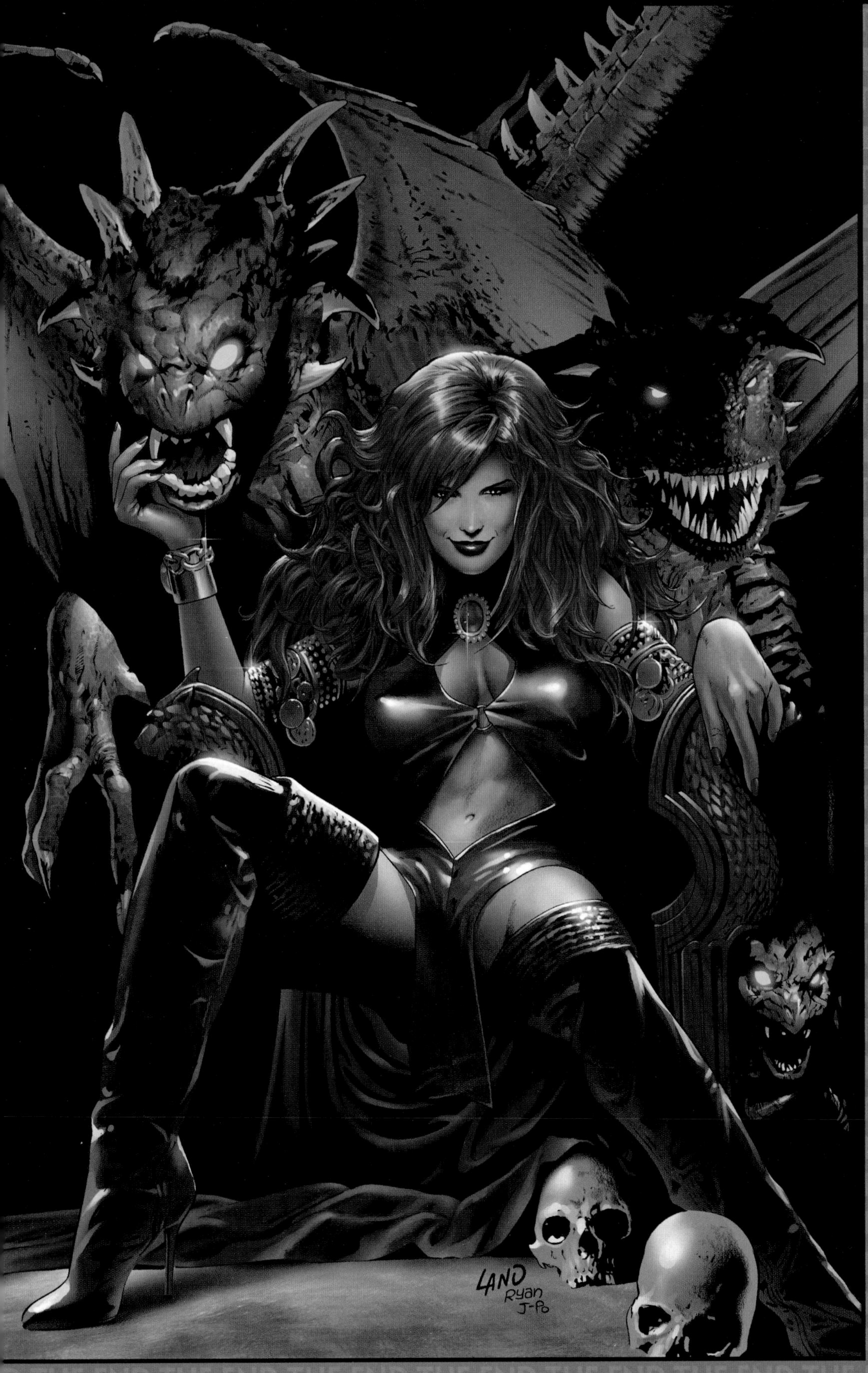
LAND
Ryan
J-Po

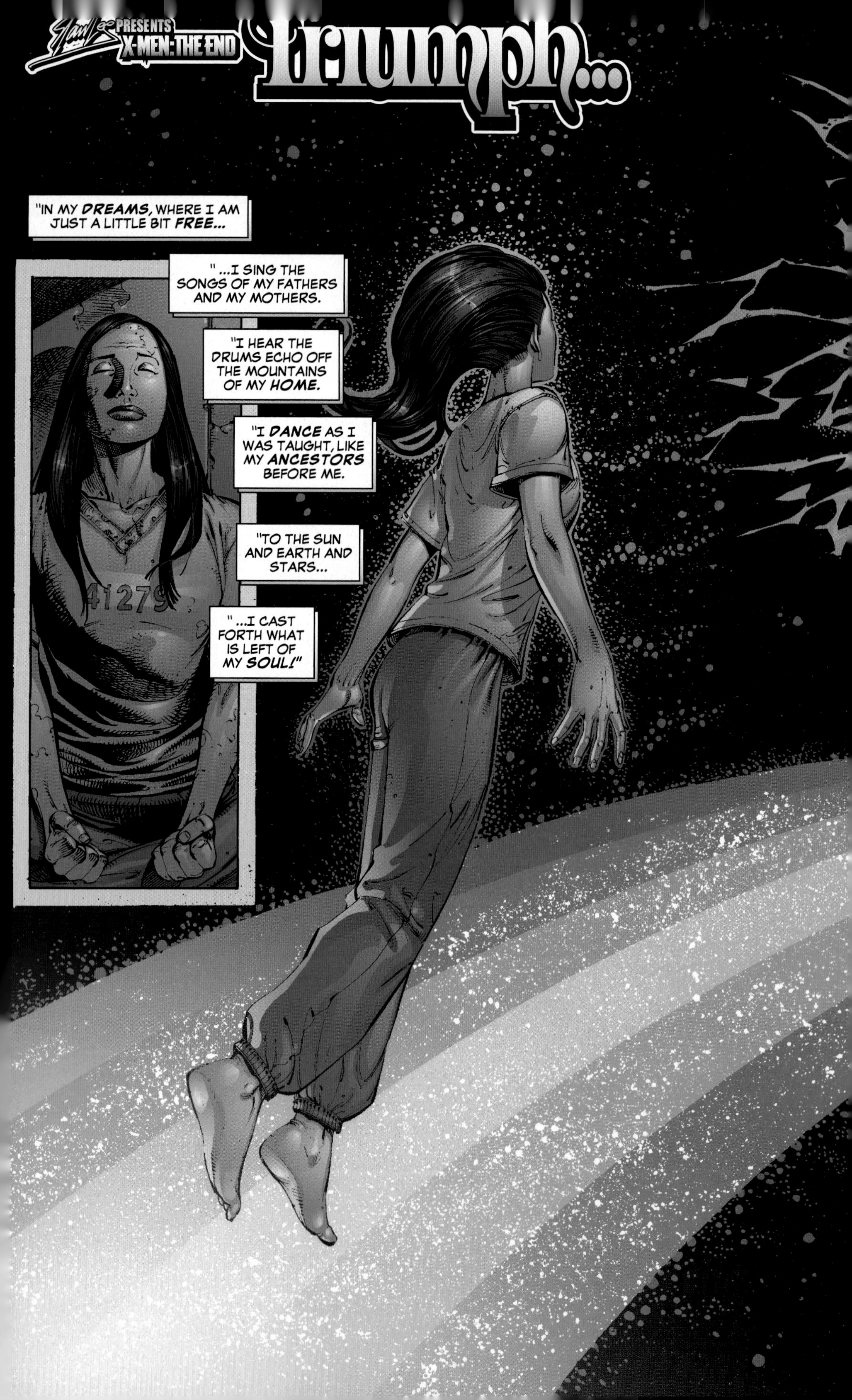
STAN LEE PRESENTS X-MEN: THE END
Triumph...
"IN MY DREAMS, WHERE I AM JUST A LITTLE BIT FREE...
"...I SING THE SONGS OF MY FATHERS AND MY MOTHERS.
"I HEAR THE DRUMS ECHO OFF THE MOUNTAINS OF MY HOME.
"I DANCE AS I WAS TAUGHT, LIKE MY ANCESTORS BEFORE ME.
"TO THE SUN AND EARTH AND STARS...
"...I CAST FORTH WHAT IS LEFT OF MY SOUL!"
41279

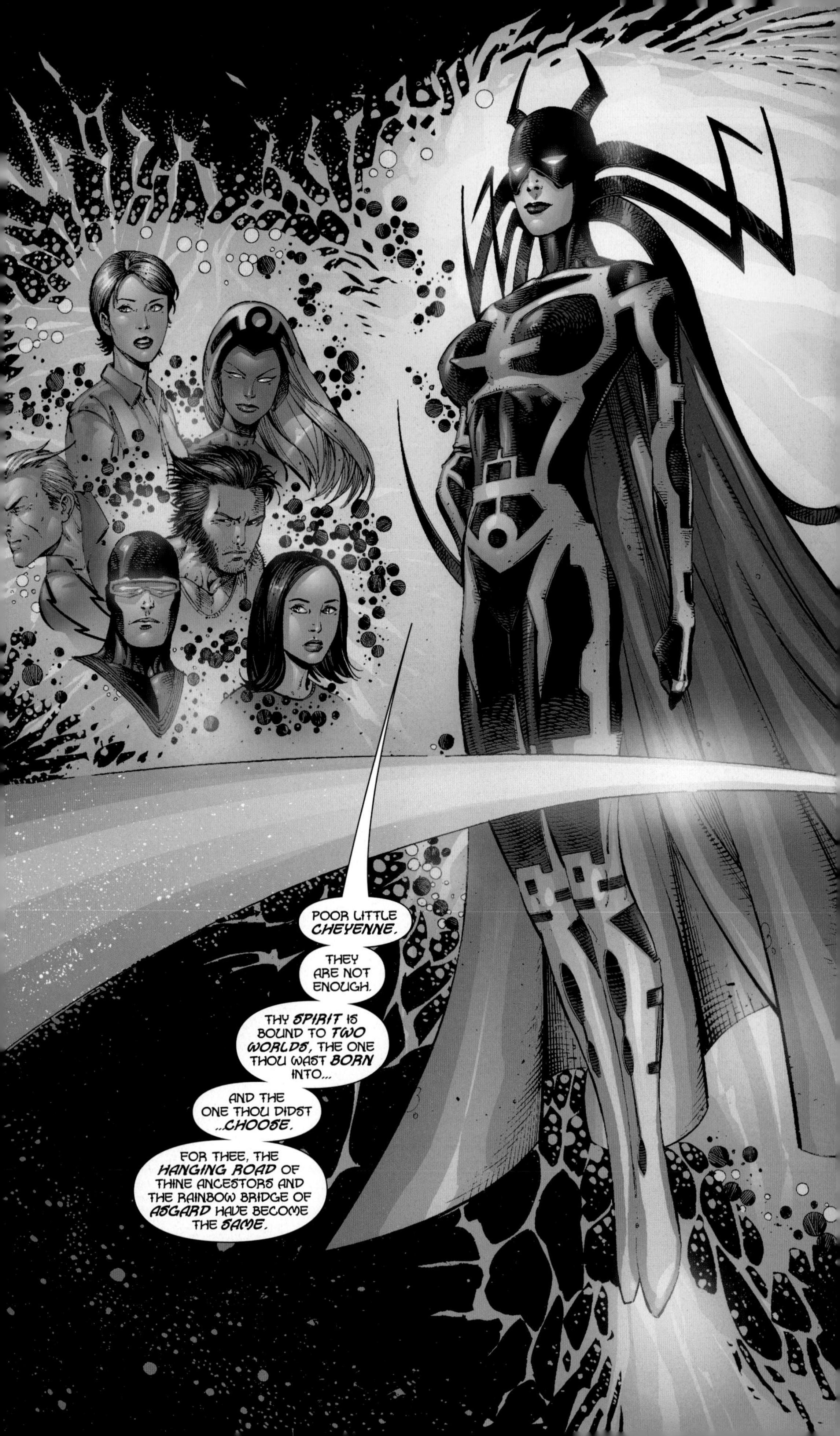
POOR LITTLE CHEYENNE.
THEY ARE NOT ENOUGH.
THY SPIRIT IS BOUND TO TWO WORLDS, THE ONE THOU WAST BORN INTO...
AND THE ONE THOU DIDST ...CHOOSE.
FOR THEE, THE HANGING ROAD OF THINE ANCESTORS AND THE RAINBOW BRIDGE OF ASGARD HAVE BECOME THE SAME.

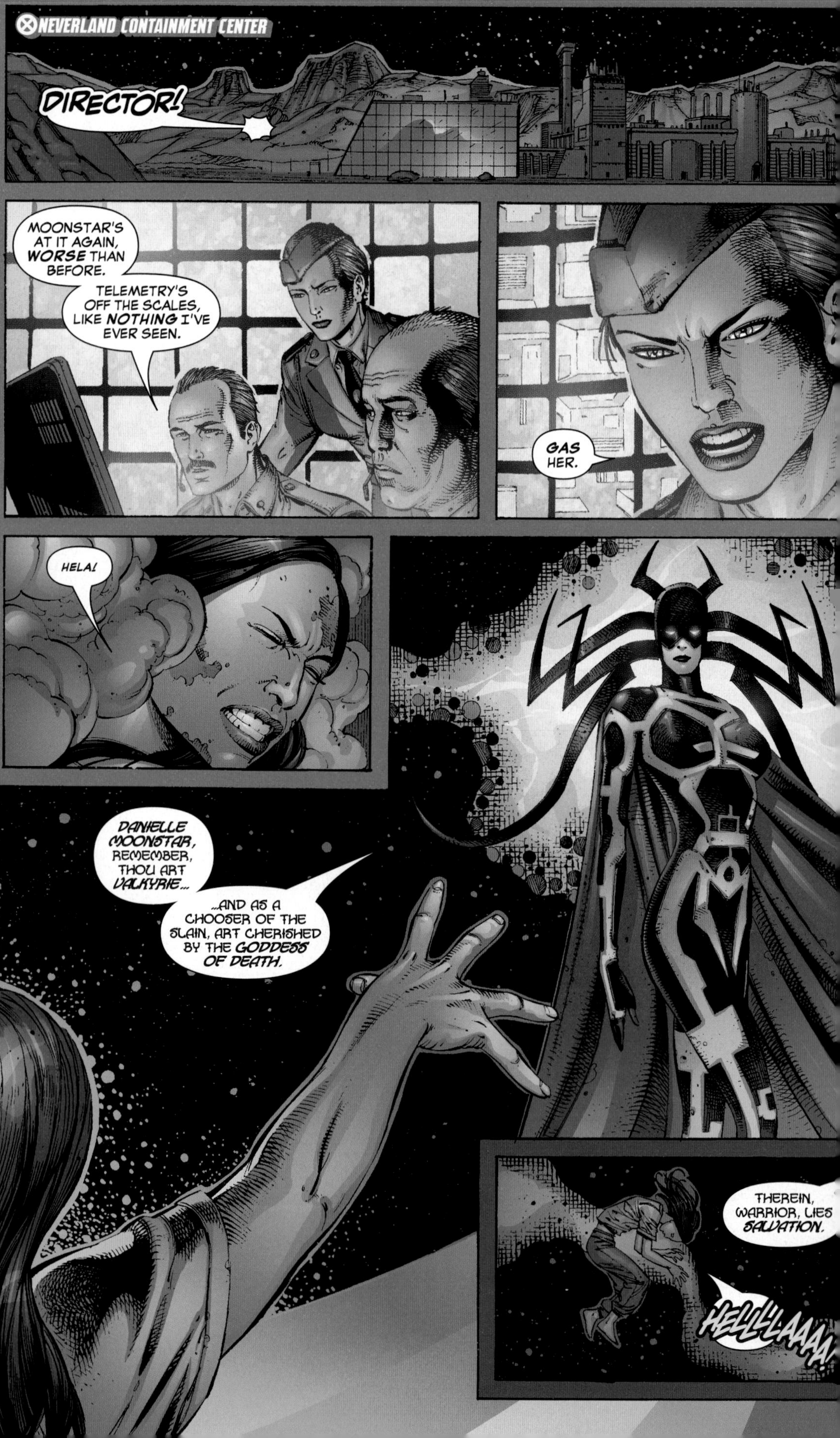
NEVERLAND CONTAINMENT CENTER
DIRECTOR!
MOONSTAR'S AT IT AGAIN, WORSE THAN BEFORE.
TELEMETRY'S OFF THE SCALES, LIKE NOTHING I'VE EVER SEEN.
GAS HER.
HELA!
DANIELLE MOONSTAR, REMEMBER, THOU ART VALKYRIE...
...AND AS A CHOOSER OF THE SLAIN, ART CHERISHED BY THE GODDESS OF DEATH.
THEREIN, WARRIOR, LIES SALVATION.
HELLLLAAAA!

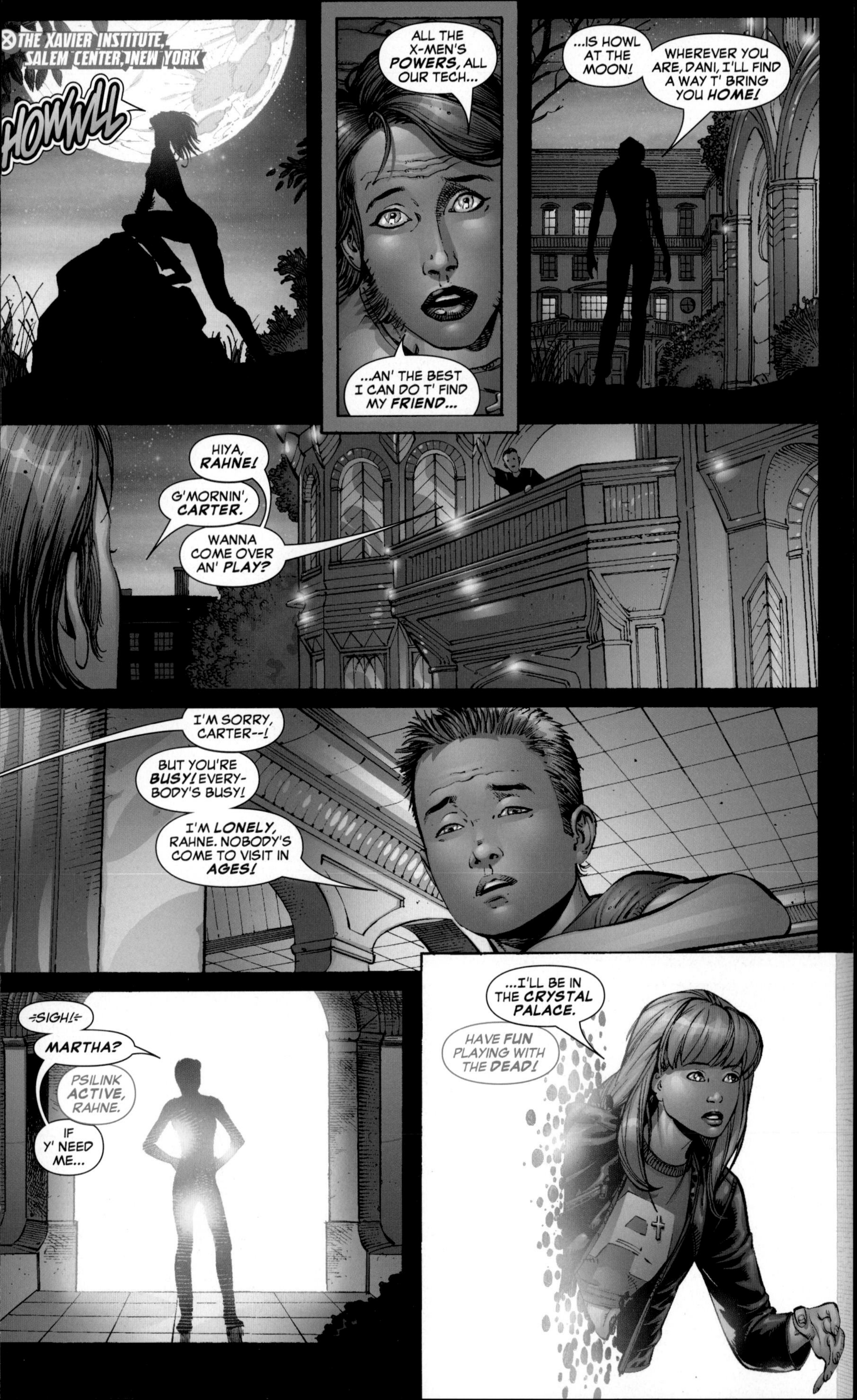

THE XAVIER INSTITUTE, SALEM CENTER, NEW YORK
HOWWLL
ALL THE X-MEN'S POWERS, ALL OUR TECH...
...AN' THE BEST I CAN DO T' FIND MY FRIEND...
...IS HOWL AT THE MOON!
WHEREVER YOU ARE, DANI, I'LL FIND A WAY T' BRING YOU HOME!
HIYA, RAHNE!
G'MORNIN', CARTER.
WANNA COME OVER AN' PLAY?
I'M SORRY, CARTER--!
BUT YOU'RE BUSY! EVERYBODY'S BUSY!
I'M LONELY, RAHNE. NOBODY'S COME TO VISIT IN AGES!
=SIGH!=
MARTHA?
PSILINK ACTIVE, RAHNE.
IF Y' NEED ME...
...I'LL BE IN THE CRYSTAL PALACE.
HAVE FUN PLAYING WITH THE DEAD!

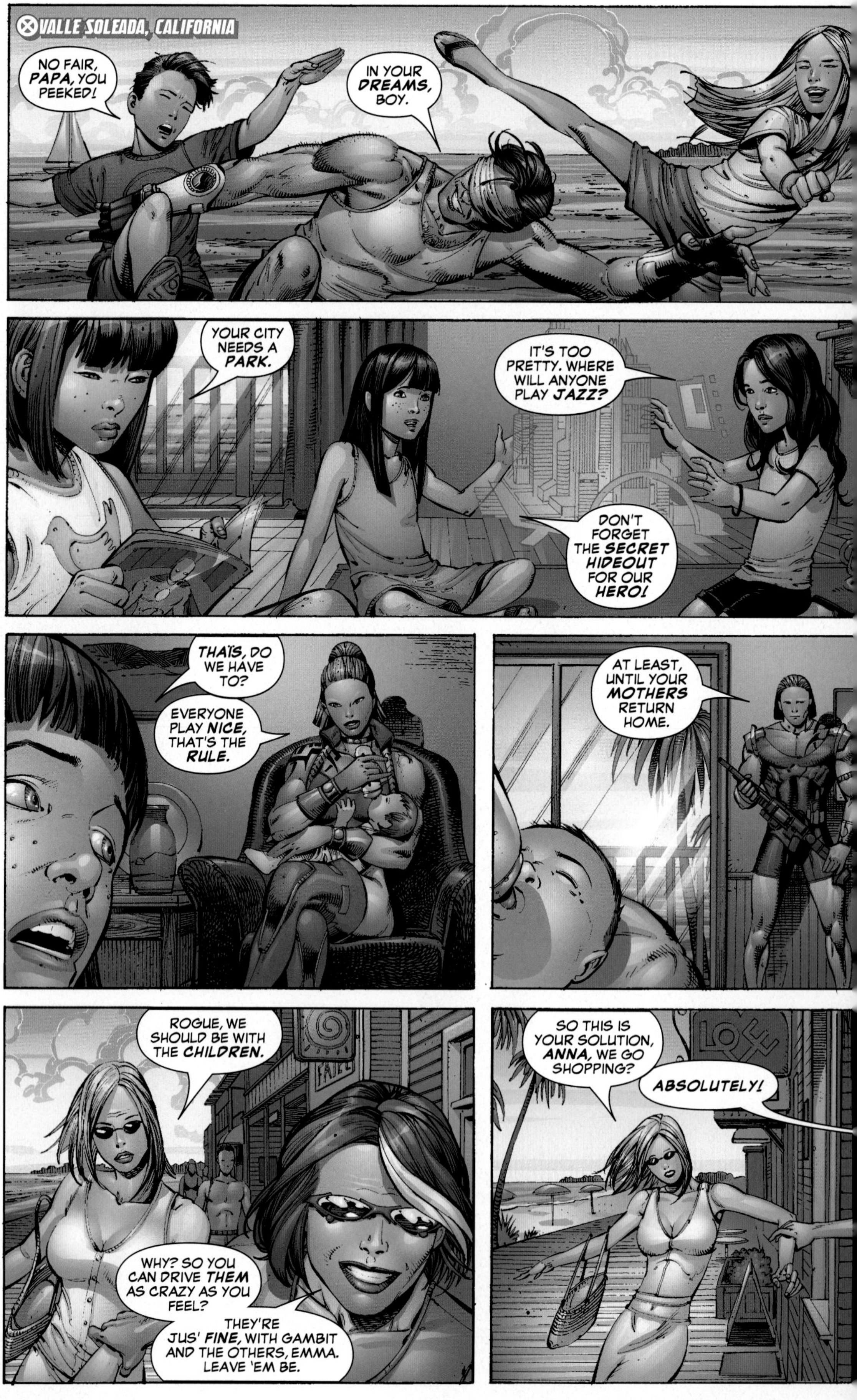
VALLE SOLEADA, CALIFORNIA
NO FAIR, PAPA, YOU PEEKED!
IN YOUR DREAMS, BOY.
YOUR CITY NEEDS A PARK.
IT'S TOO PRETTY. WHERE WILL ANYONE PLAY JAZZ?
DON'T FORGET THE SECRET HIDEOUT FOR OUR HERO!
THAÏS, DO WE HAVE TO?
EVERYONE PLAY NICE, THAT'S THE RULE.
AT LEAST, UNTIL YOUR MOTHERS RETURN HOME.
ROGUE, WE SHOULD BE WITH THE CHILDREN.
WHY? SO YOU CAN DRIVE THEM AS CRAZY AS YOU FEEL?
THEY'RE JUS' FINE, WITH GAMBIT AND THE OTHERS, EMMA. LEAVE 'EM BE.
SO THIS IS YOUR SOLUTION, ANNA, WE GO SHOPPING?
ABSOLUTELY!

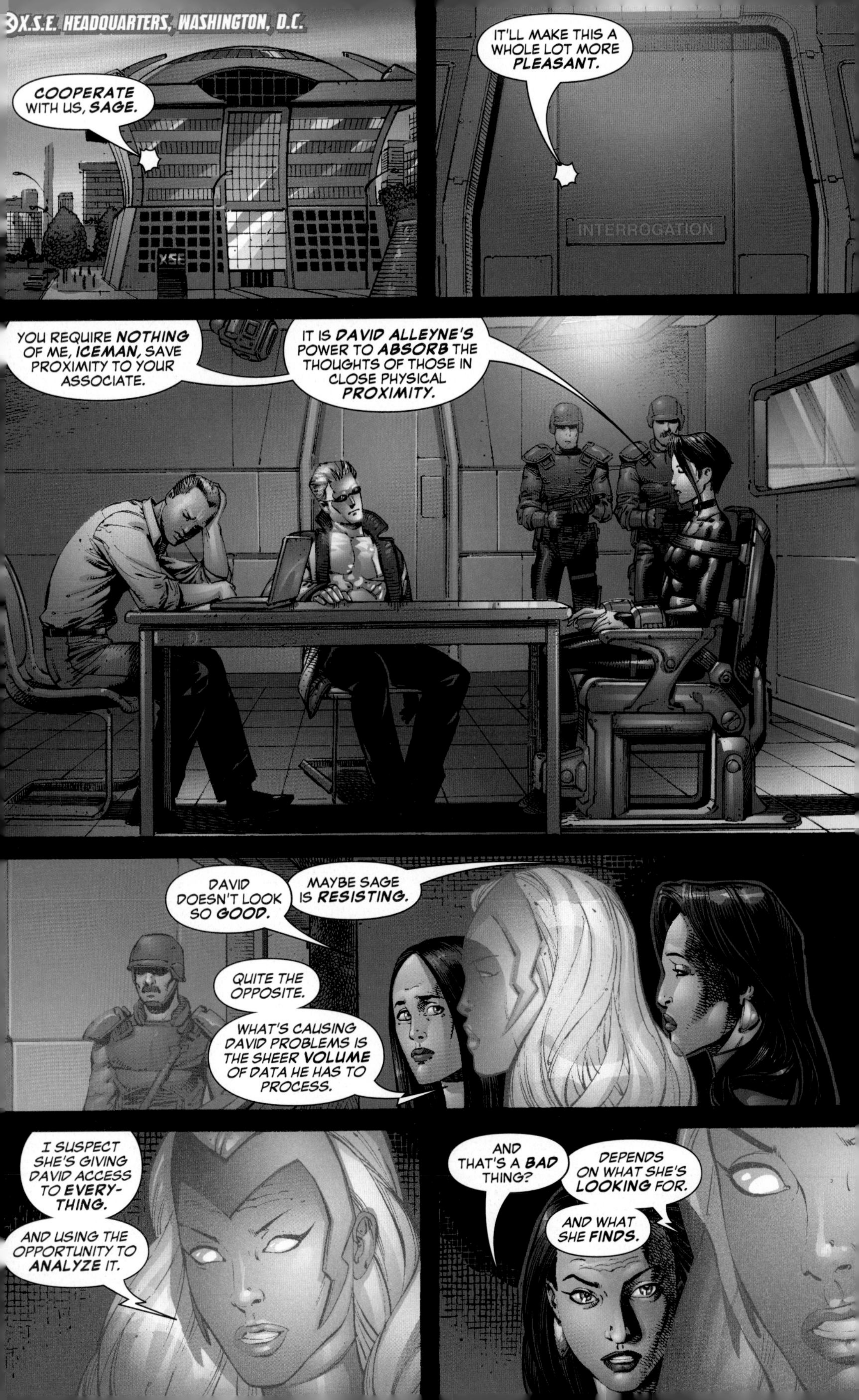
X.S.E. HEADQUARTERS, WASHINGTON, D.C.
COOPERATE WITH US, SAGE.
XSE
IT'LL MAKE THIS A WHOLE LOT MORE PLEASANT.
INTERROGATION
YOU REQUIRE NOTHING OF ME, ICEMAN, SAVE PROXIMITY TO YOUR ASSOCIATE.
IT IS DAVID ALLEYNE'S POWER TO ABSORB THE THOUGHTS OF THOSE IN CLOSE PHYSICAL PROXIMITY.
DAVID DOESN'T LOOK SO GOOD.
MAYBE SAGE IS RESISTING.
QUITE THE OPPOSITE.
WHAT'S CAUSING DAVID PROBLEMS IS THE SHEER VOLUME OF DATA HE HAS TO PROCESS.
I SUSPECT SHE'S GIVING DAVID ACCESS TO EVERY-THING.
AND USING THE OPPORTUNITY TO ANALYZE IT.
AND THAT'S A BAD THING?
DEPENDS ON WHAT SHE'S LOOKING FOR.
AND WHAT SHE FINDS.

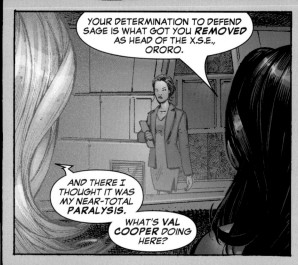

YOUR DETERMINATION TO DEFEND SAGE IS WHAT GOT YOU *REMOVED* AS HEAD OF THE X.S.E., ORORO.

AND THERE I THOUGHT IT WAS MY NEAR-TOTAL PARALYSIS.

WHAT'S VAL COOPER DOING HERE?

DAVID, WHAT HAVE YOU *LEARNED?*

YOU'RE NOT VAL!

GNURRGH!

SHLUKK

WHAT THE--

KROM!

MY TURN?

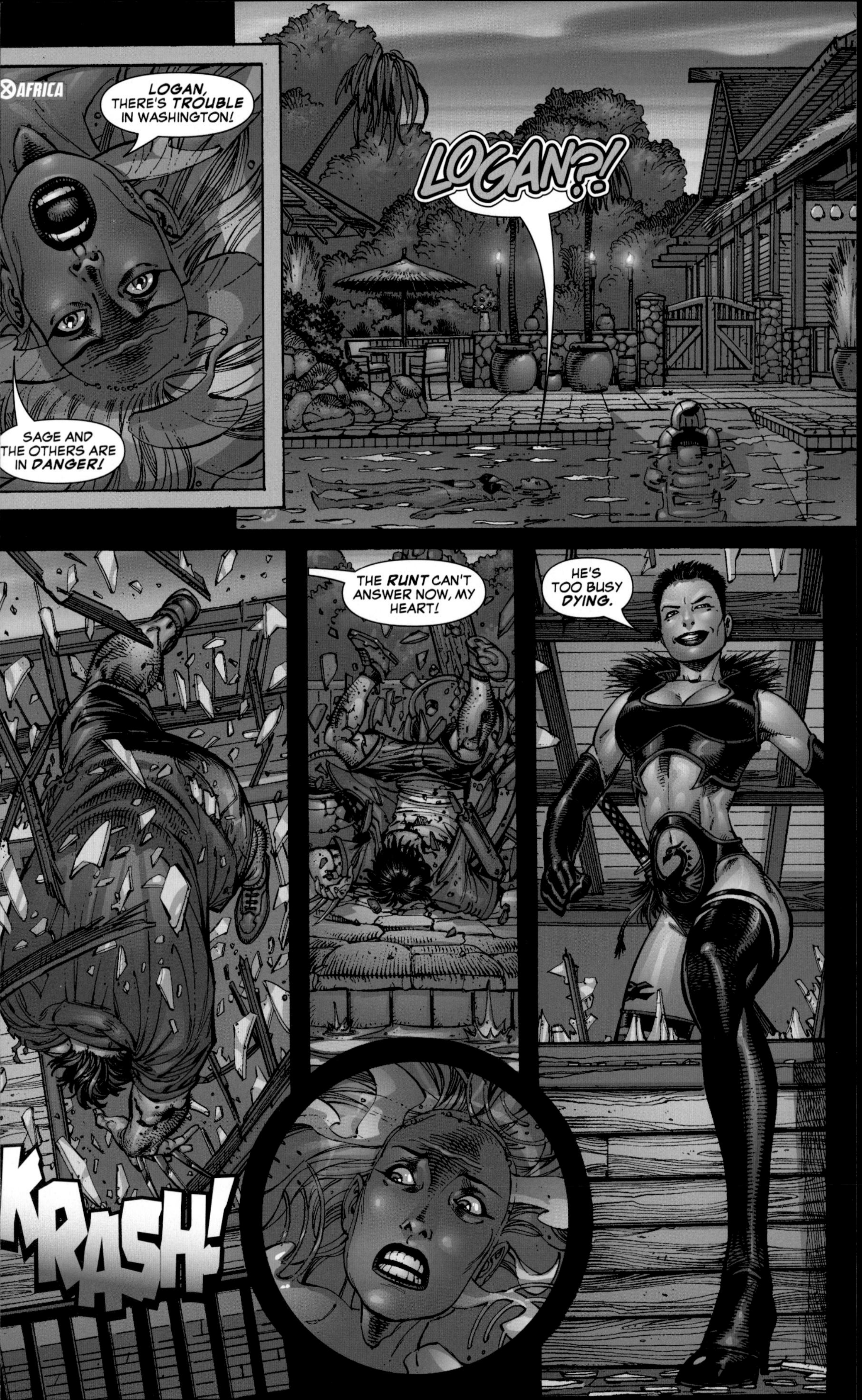
AFRICA
LOGAN, THERE'S TROUBLE IN WASHINGTON!
SAGE AND THE OTHERS ARE IN DANGER!
LOGAN?!
KRASH!
THE RUNT CAN'T ANSWER NOW, MY HEART!
HE'S TOO BUSY DYING.

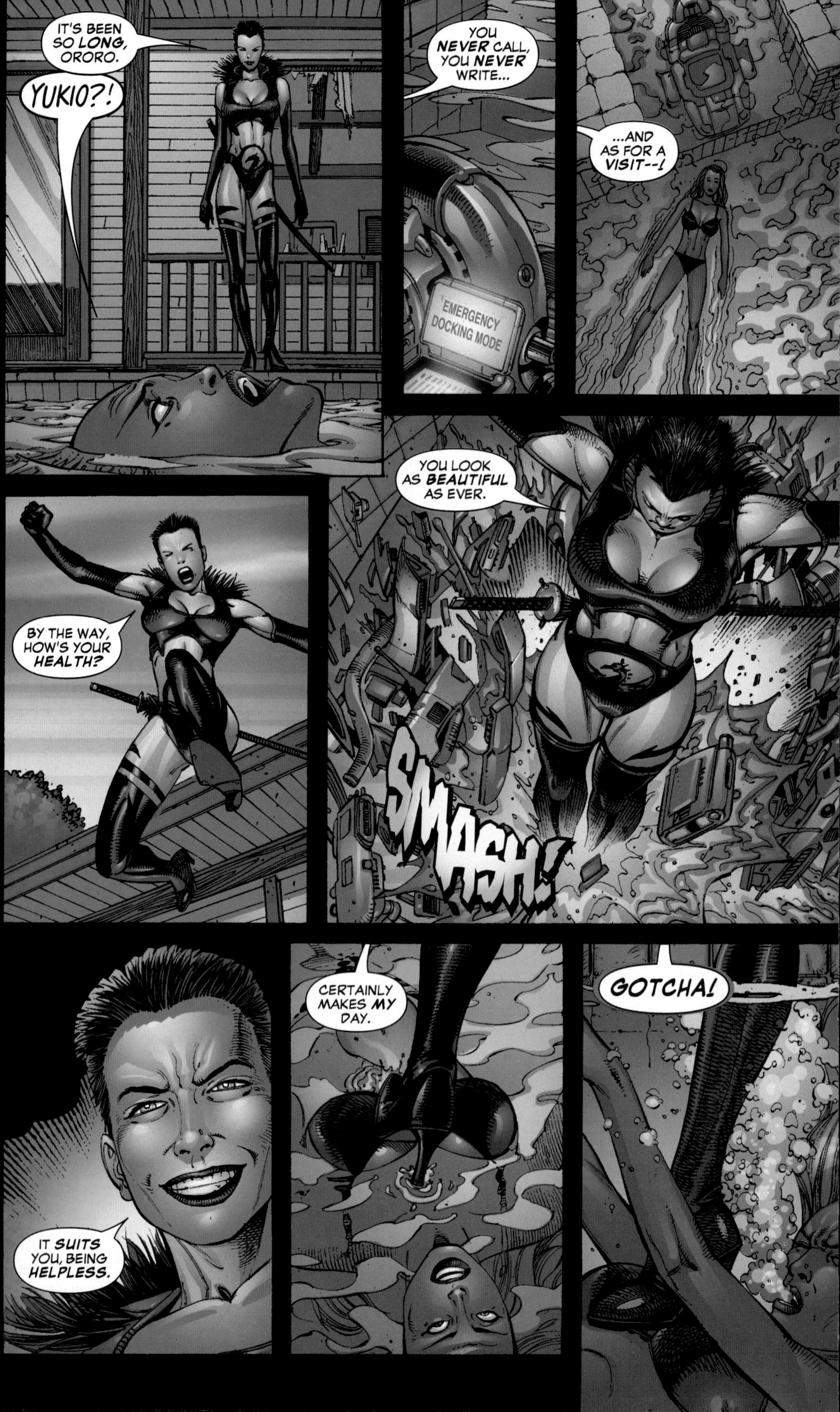

IT'S BEEN SO LONG, ORORO.
YUKIO?!
YOU NEVER CALL, YOU NEVER WRITE...
EMERGENCY DOCKING MODE
...AND AS FOR A VISIT--!
BY THE WAY, HOW'S YOUR HEALTH?
YOU LOOK AS BEAUTIFUL AS EVER.
SMASH!
IT SUITS YOU, BEING HELPLESS.
CERTAINLY MAKES MY DAY.
GOTCHA!

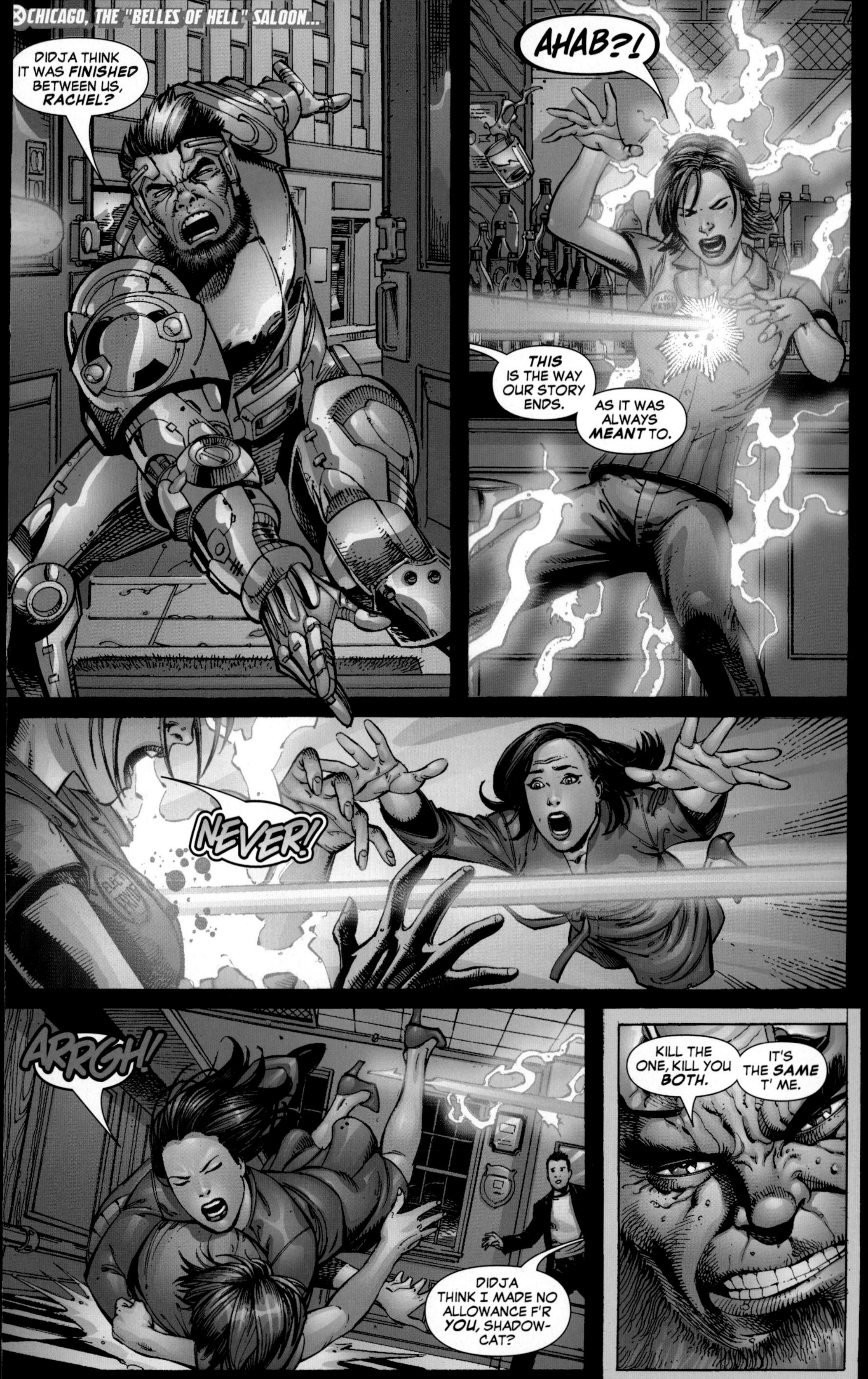

CHICAGO, THE "BELLES OF HELL" SALOON...
DIDJA THINK IT WAS FINISHED BETWEEN US, RACHEL?
AHAB?!
THIS IS THE WAY OUR STORY ENDS.
AS IT WAS ALWAYS MEANT TO.
NEVER!
ARRGH!
DIDJA THINK I MADE NO ALLOWANCE F'R YOU, SHADOW-CAT?
KILL THE ONE, KILL YOU BOTH.
IT'S THE SAME T' ME.

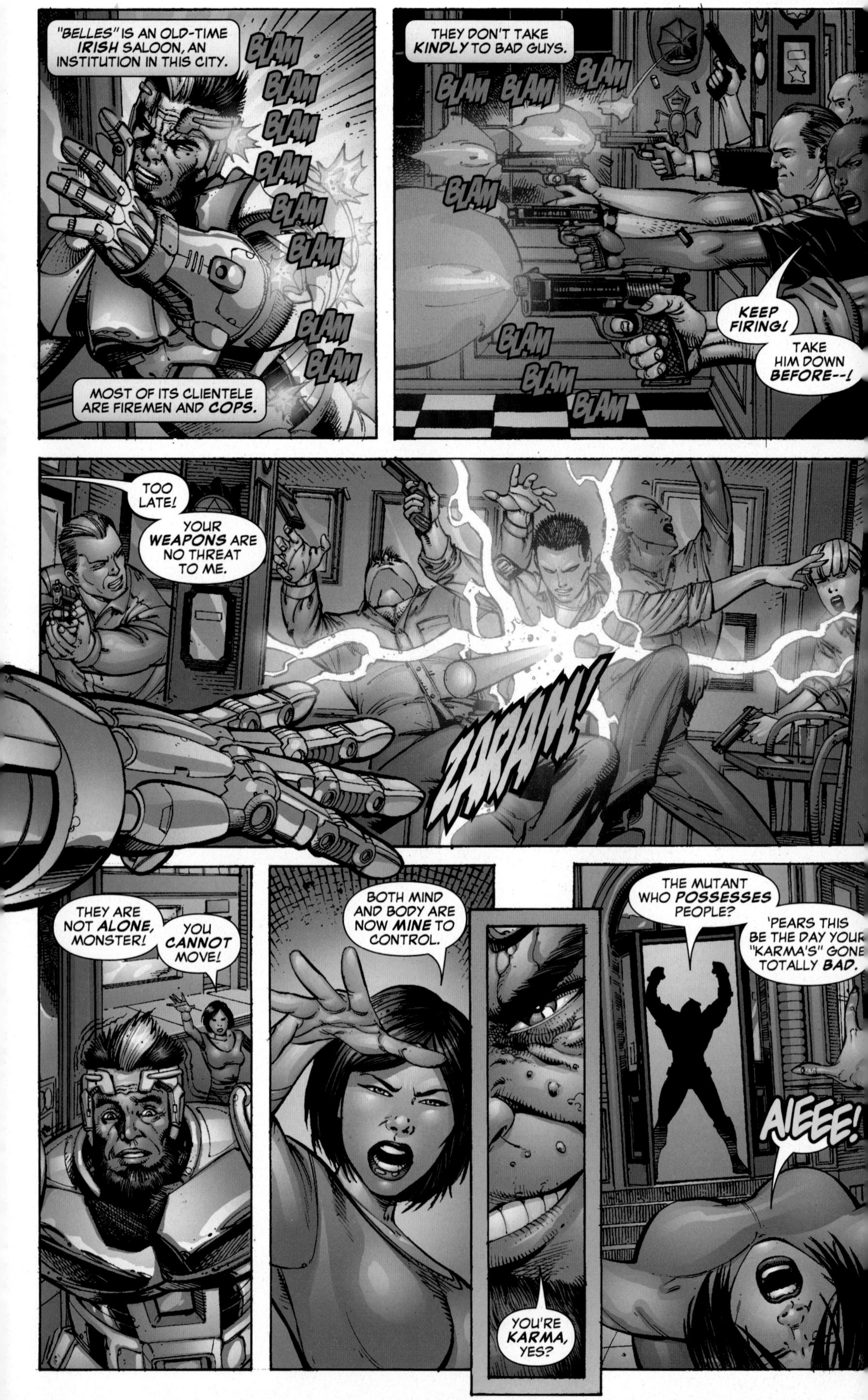
"BELLES" IS AN OLD-TIME IRISH SALOON, AN INSTITUTION IN THIS CITY.
BLAM BLAM BLAM BLAM BLAM BLAM
BLAM BLAM
MOST OF ITS CLIENTELE ARE FIREMEN AND COPS.
THEY DON'T TAKE KINDLY TO BAD GUYS.
BLAM BLAM BLAM
BLAM
BLAM BLAM BLAM
KEEP FIRING!
TAKE HIM DOWN BEFORE--!
TOO LATE!
YOUR WEAPONS ARE NO THREAT TO ME.
ZARAM!
THEY ARE NOT ALONE, MONSTER!
YOU CANNOT MOVE!
BOTH MIND AND BODY ARE NOW MINE TO CONTROL.
YOU'RE KARMA, YES?
THE MUTANT WHO POSSESSES PEOPLE?
'PEARS THIS BE THE DAY YOUR "KARMA'S" GONE TOTALLY BAD.
AIEEE!

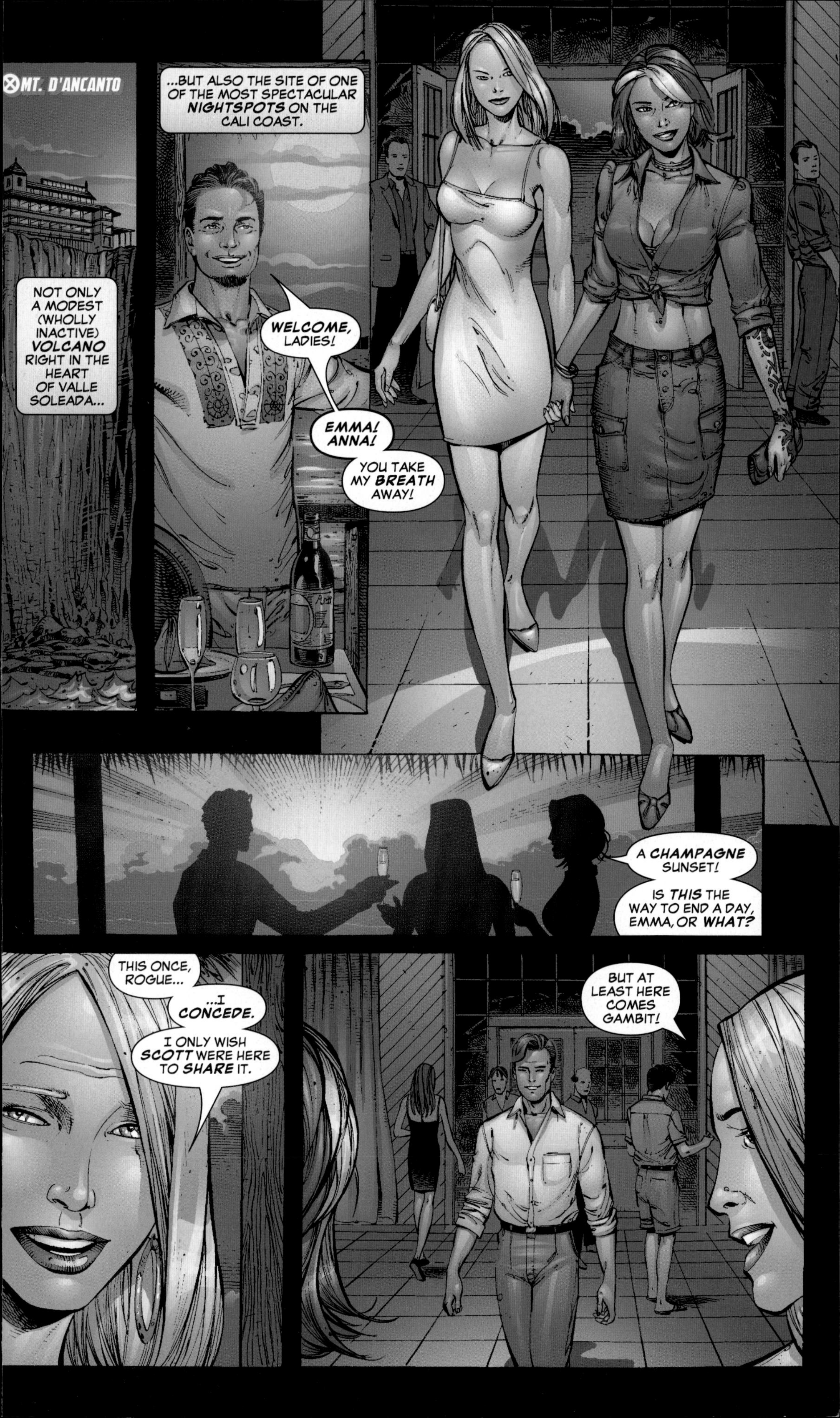
MT. D'ANCANTO
NOT ONLY A MODEST (WHOLLY INACTIVE) VOLCANO RIGHT IN THE HEART OF VALLE SOLEADA...
...BUT ALSO THE SITE OF ONE OF THE MOST SPECTACULAR NIGHTSPOTS ON THE CALI COAST.
WELCOME, LADIES!
EMMA! ANNA!
YOU TAKE MY BREATH AWAY!
A CHAMPAGNE SUNSET!
IS THIS THE WAY TO END A DAY, EMMA, OR WHAT?
THIS ONCE, ROGUE...
...I CONCEDE.
I ONLY WISH SCOTT WERE HERE TO SHARE IT.
BUT AT LEAST HERE COMES GAMBIT!

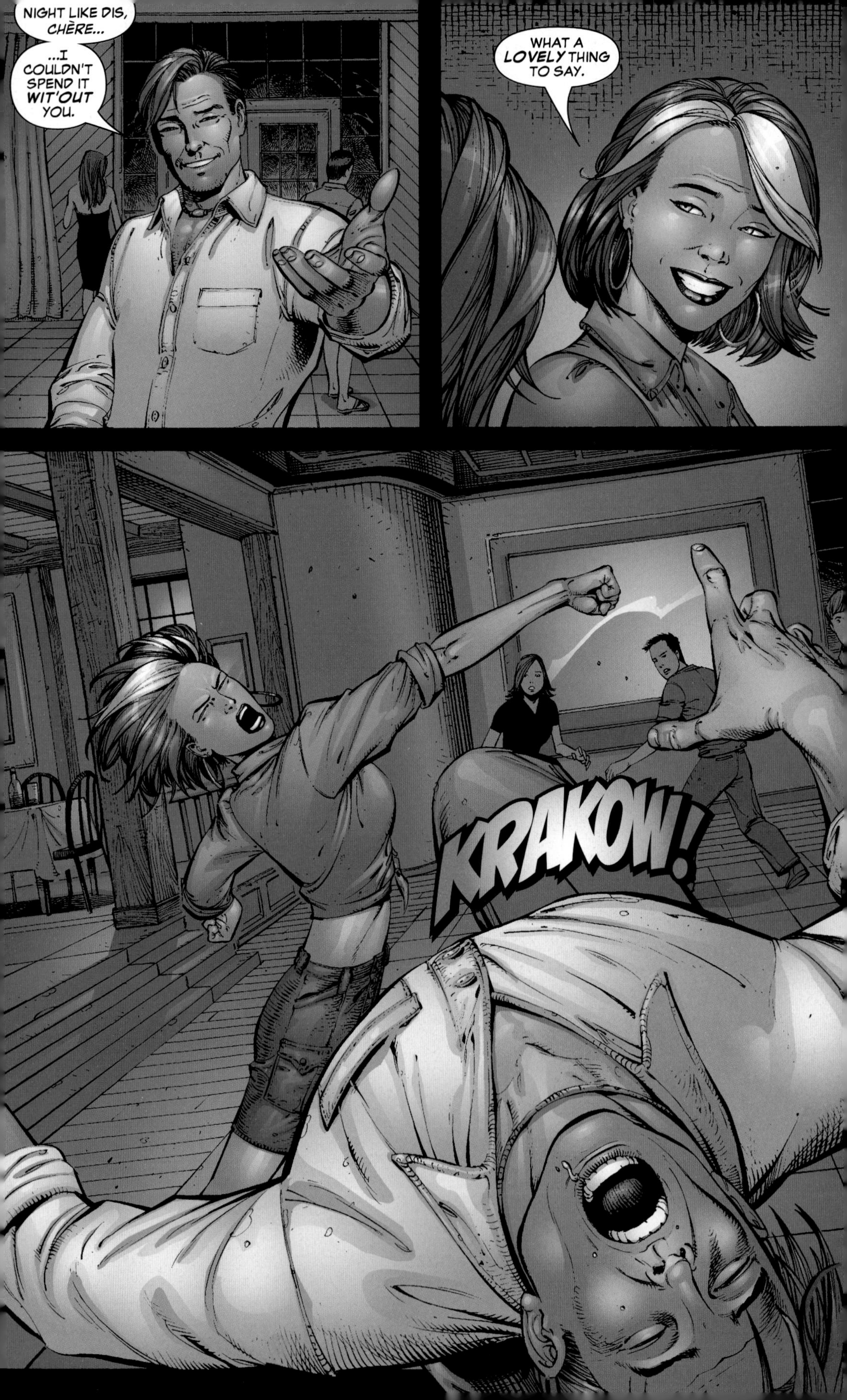
NIGHT LIKE DIS, CHÈRE...
...I COULDN'T SPEND IT WIT'OUT YOU.
WHAT A LOVELY THING TO SAY.
KRAKOW!

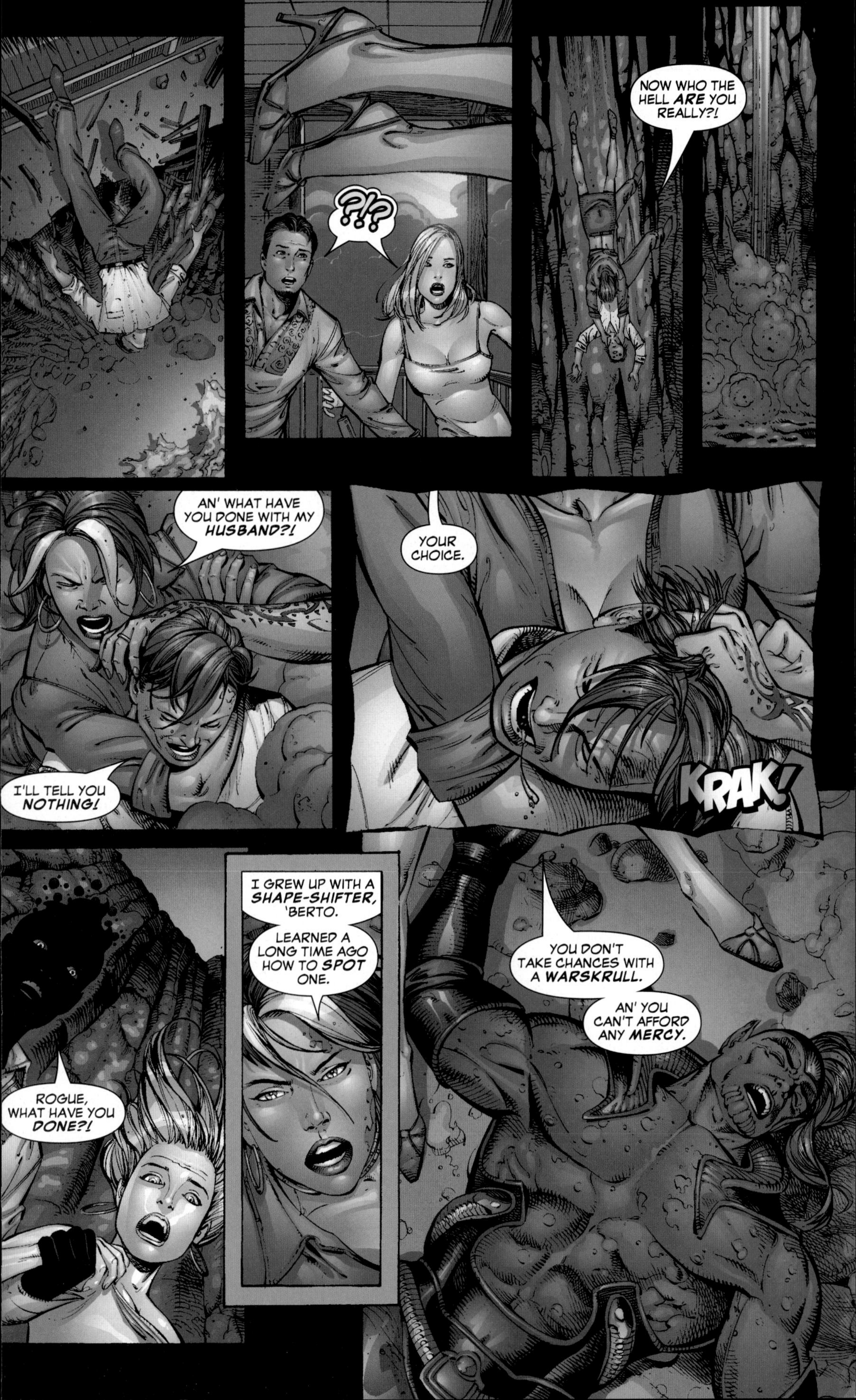
?!?
NOW WHO THE HELL ARE YOU REALLY?!
AN' WHAT HAVE YOU DONE WITH MY HUSBAND?!
I'LL TELL YOU NOTHING!
YOUR CHOICE.
KRAK!
ROGUE, WHAT HAVE YOU DONE?!
I GREW UP WITH A SHAPE-SHIFTER, 'BERTO.
LEARNED A LONG TIME AGO HOW TO SPOT ONE.
YOU DON'T TAKE CHANCES WITH A WARSKRULL.
AN' YOU CAN'T AFFORD ANY MERCY.

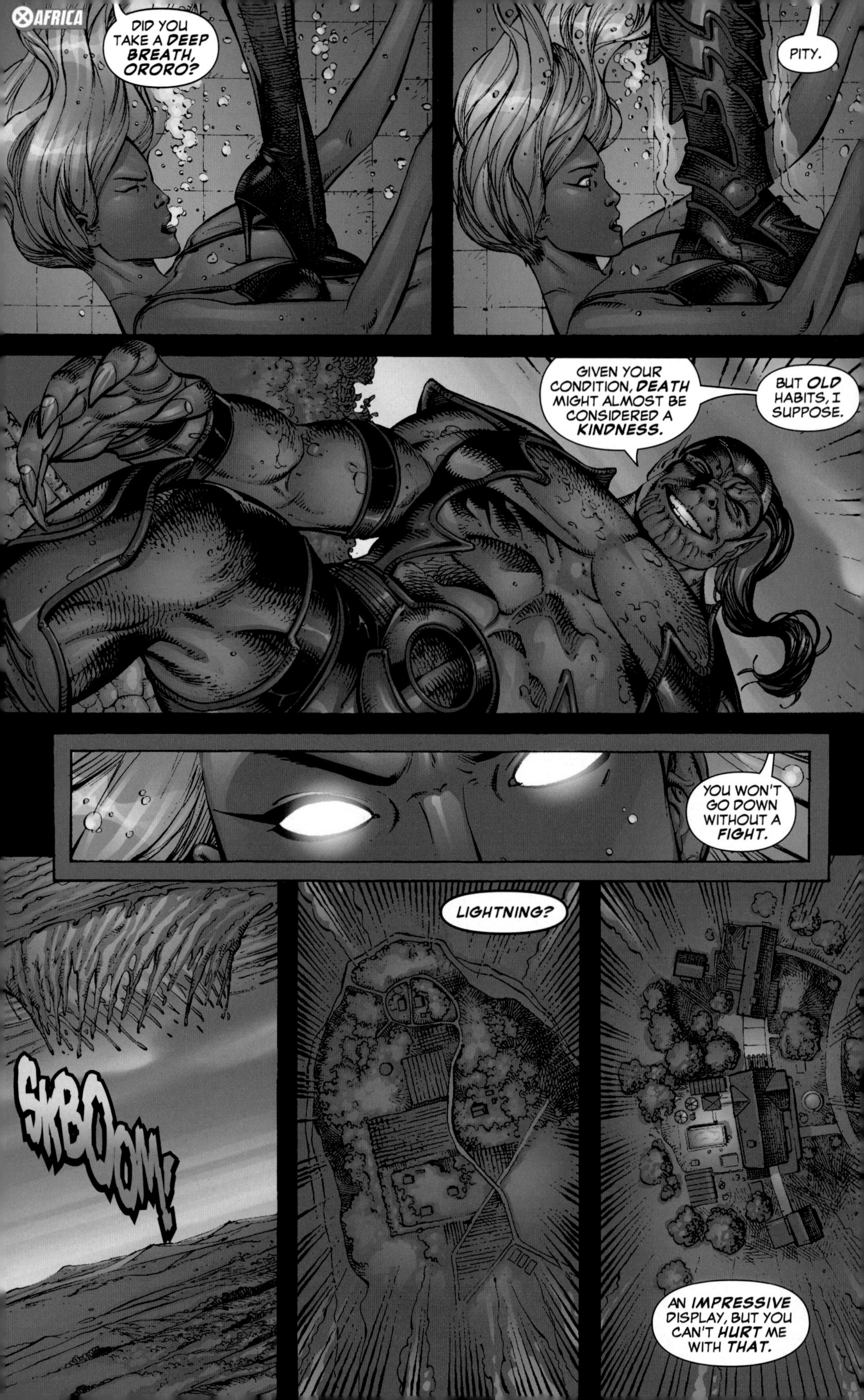
DID YOU TAKE A DEEP BREATH, ORORO?
PITY.
GIVEN YOUR CONDITION, DEATH MIGHT ALMOST BE CONSIDERED A KINDNESS.
BUT OLD HABITS, I SUPPOSE.
YOU WON'T GO DOWN WITHOUT A FIGHT.
SKBOOM!
LIGHTNING?
AN IMPRESSIVE DISPLAY, BUT YOU CAN'T HURT ME WITH THAT.

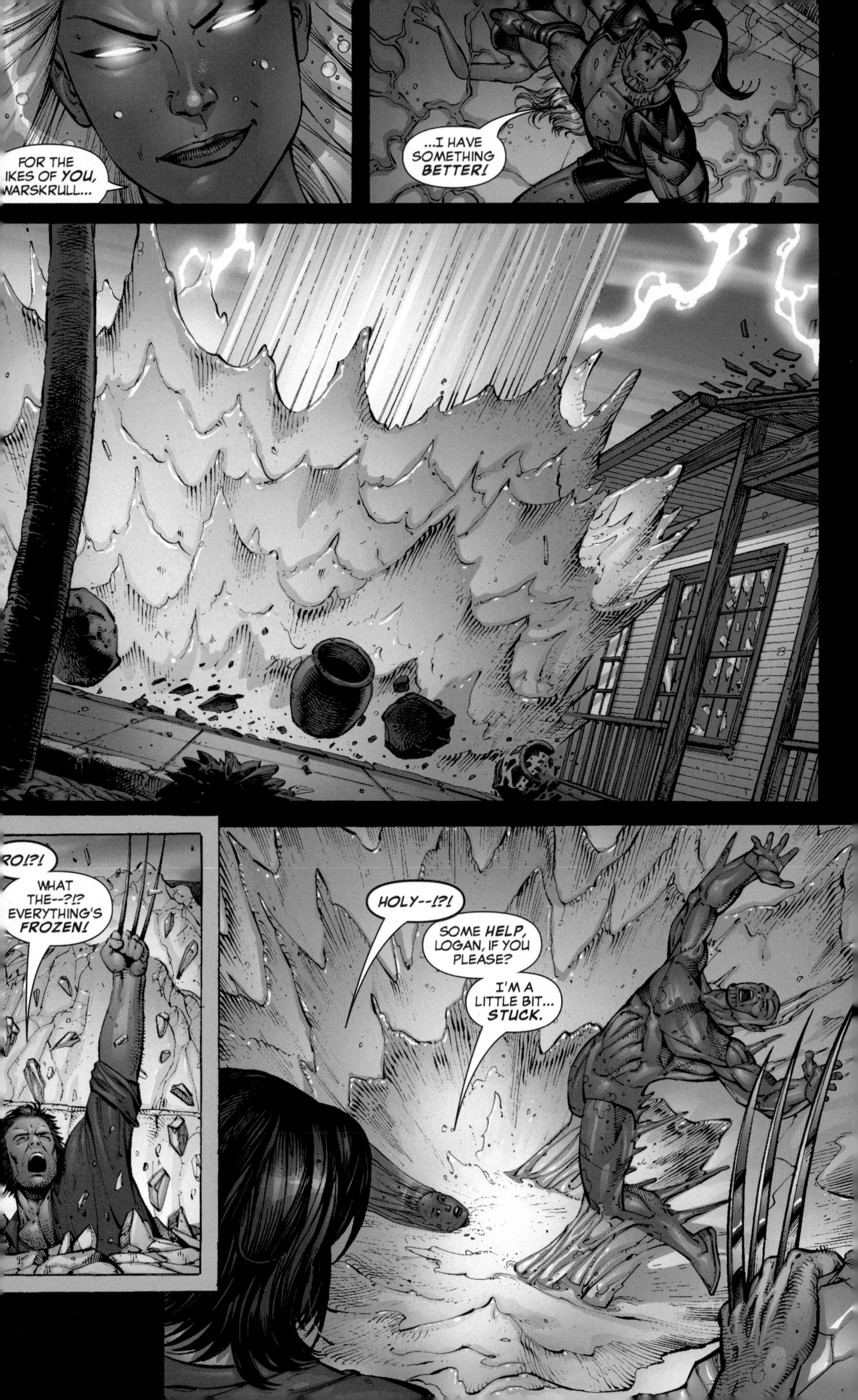
FOR THE
IKES OF YOU,
WARSKRULL...
...I HAVE SOMETHING BETTER!
RO!?!
WHAT THE--?!? EVERYTHING'S FROZEN!
HOLY--!?!
SOME HELP, LOGAN, IF YOU PLEASE?
I'M A LITTLE BIT... STUCK.

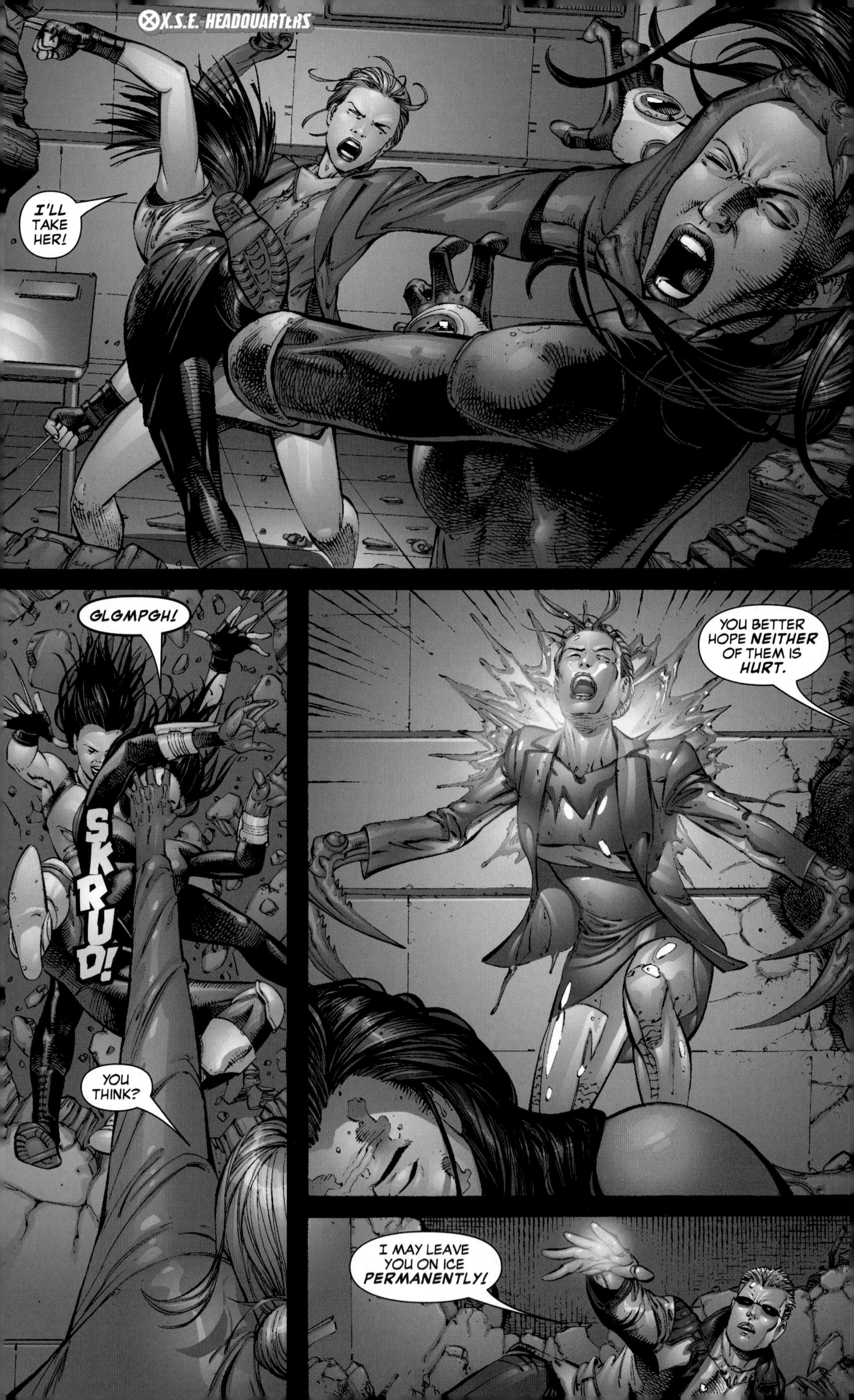
X.S.E. HEADQUARTERS
I'LL TAKE HER!
GLGMPGH!
SKRUD!
YOU THINK?
YOU BETTER HOPE NEITHER OF THEM IS HURT.
I MAY LEAVE YOU ON ICE PERMANENTLY!

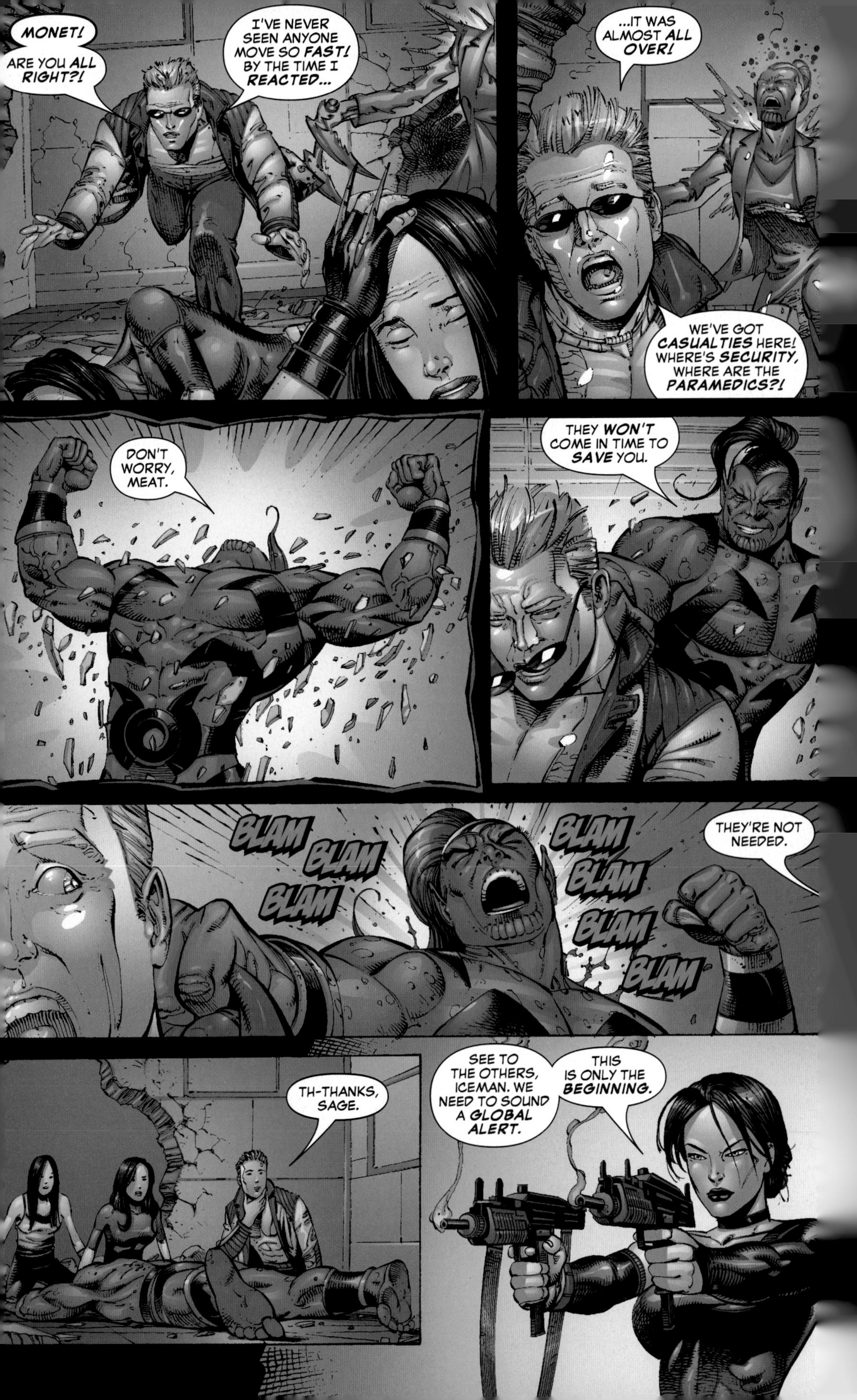
MONET!
ARE YOU ALL RIGHT?!
I'VE NEVER SEEN ANYONE MOVE SO FAST! BY THE TIME I REACTED...
...IT WAS ALMOST ALL OVER!
WE'VE GOT CASUALTIES HERE! WHERE'S SECURITY, WHERE ARE THE PARAMEDICS?!
DON'T WORRY, MEAT.
THEY WON'T COME IN TIME TO SAVE YOU.
BLAM
BLAM
BLAM
BLAM
BLAM
BLAM
BLAM
THEY'RE NOT NEEDED.
TH-THANKS, SAGE.
SEE TO THE OTHERS, ICEMAN. WE NEED TO SOUND A GLOBAL ALERT.
THIS IS ONLY THE BEGINNING.

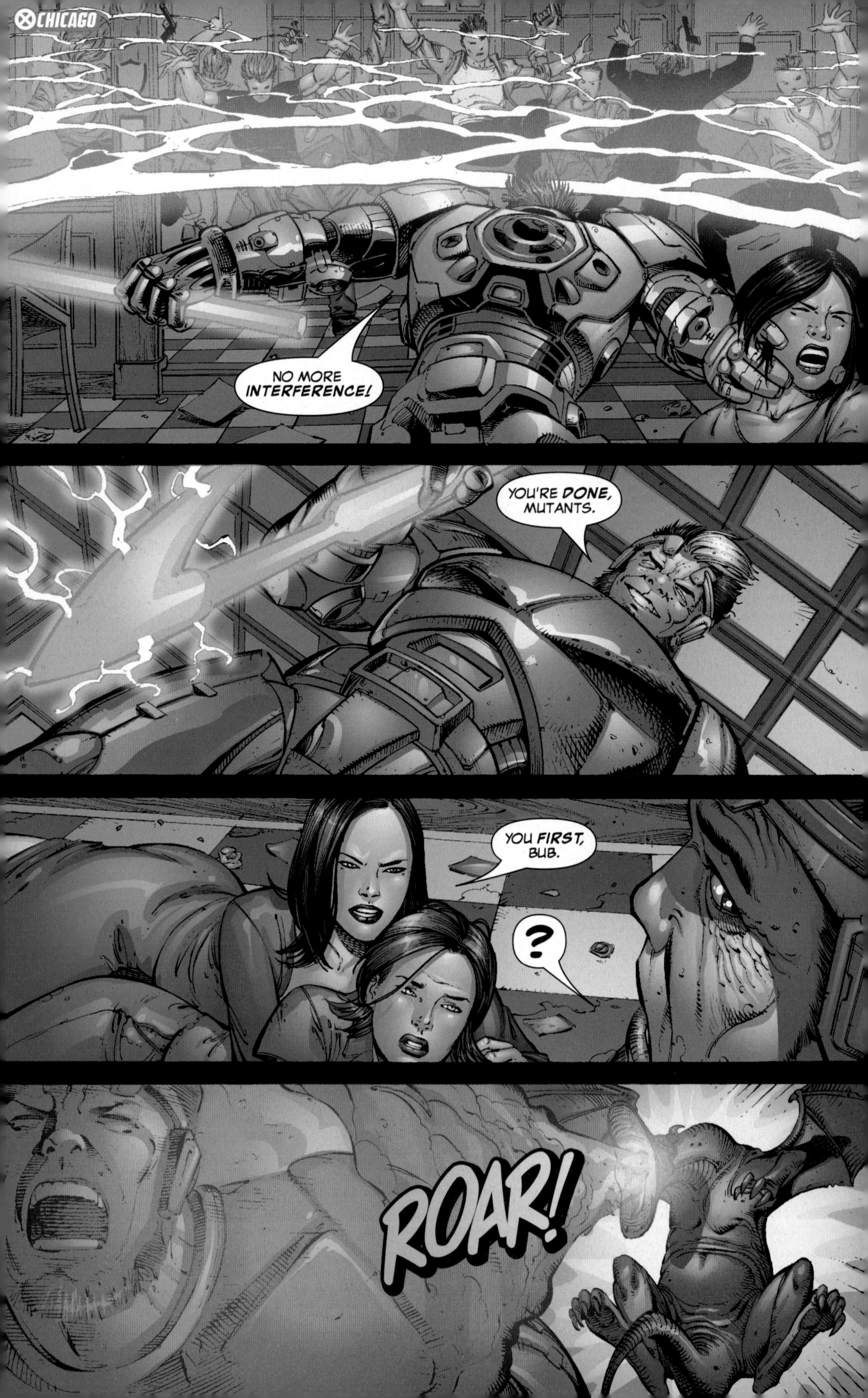

CHICAGO
NO MORE INTERFERENCE!
YOU'RE DONE, MUTANTS.
YOU FIRST, BUB.
?
ROAR!

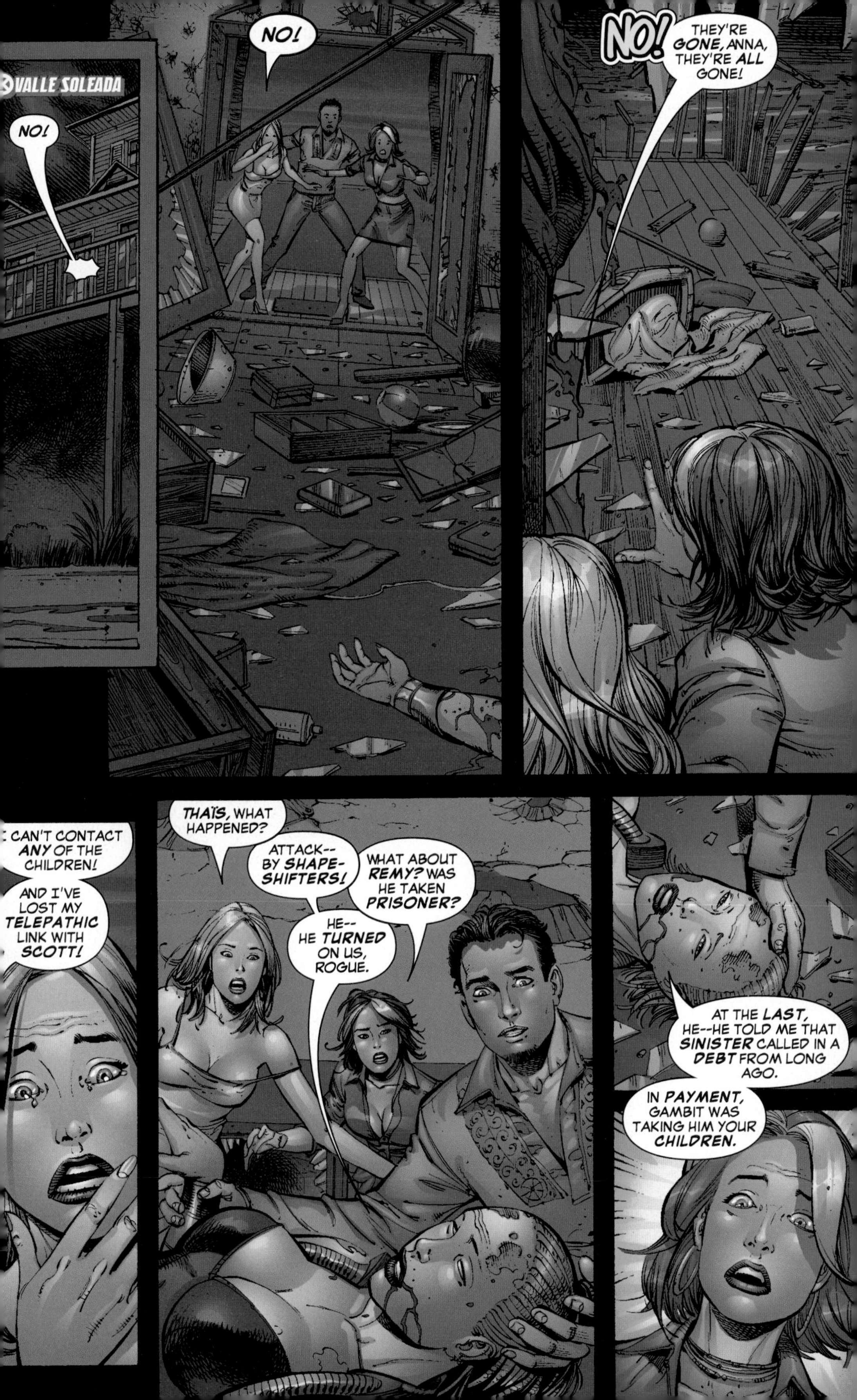
VALLE SOLEADA
NO!
NO!
NO!
THEY'RE GONE, ANNA, THEY'RE ALL GONE!
CAN'T CONTACT ANY OF THE CHILDREN!
AND I'VE LOST MY TELEPATHIC LINK WITH SCOTT!
THAÏS, WHAT HAPPENED?
ATTACK-- BY SHAPE-SHIFTERS!
WHAT ABOUT REMY? WAS HE TAKEN PRISONER?
HE-- HE TURNED ON US, ROGUE.
AT THE LAST, HE--HE TOLD ME THAT SINISTER CALLED IN A DEBT FROM LONG AGO.
IN PAYMENT, GAMBIT WAS TAKING HIM YOUR CHILDREN.

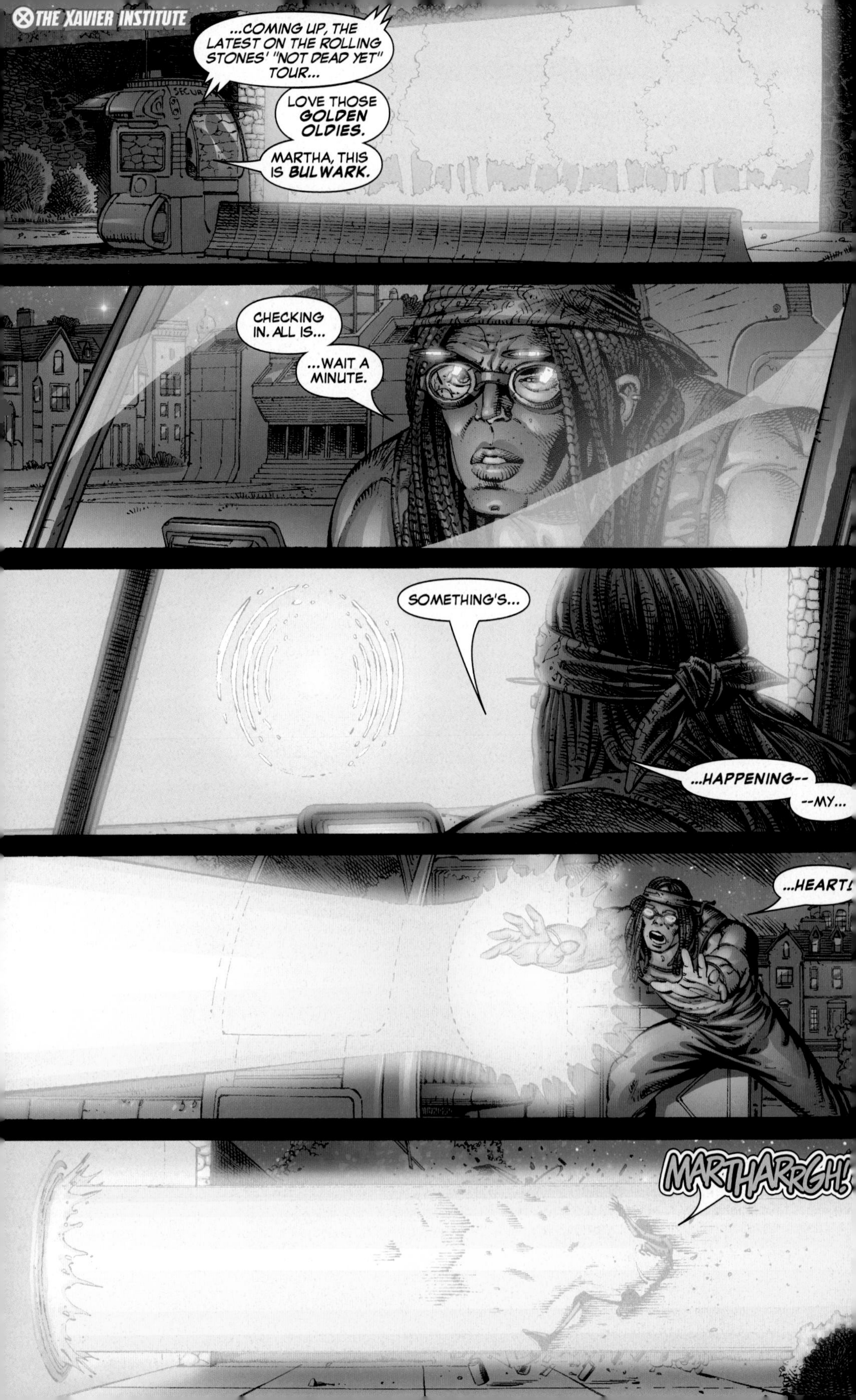
THE XAVIER INSTITUTE
...COMING UP, THE LATEST ON THE ROLLING STONES' "NOT DEAD YET" TOUR...
LOVE THOSE GOLDEN OLDIES.
MARTHA, THIS IS BULWARK.
CHECKING IN. ALL IS...
...WAIT A MINUTE.
SOMETHING'S...
...HAPPENING--
--MY...
...HEART!
MARTHARRGH!

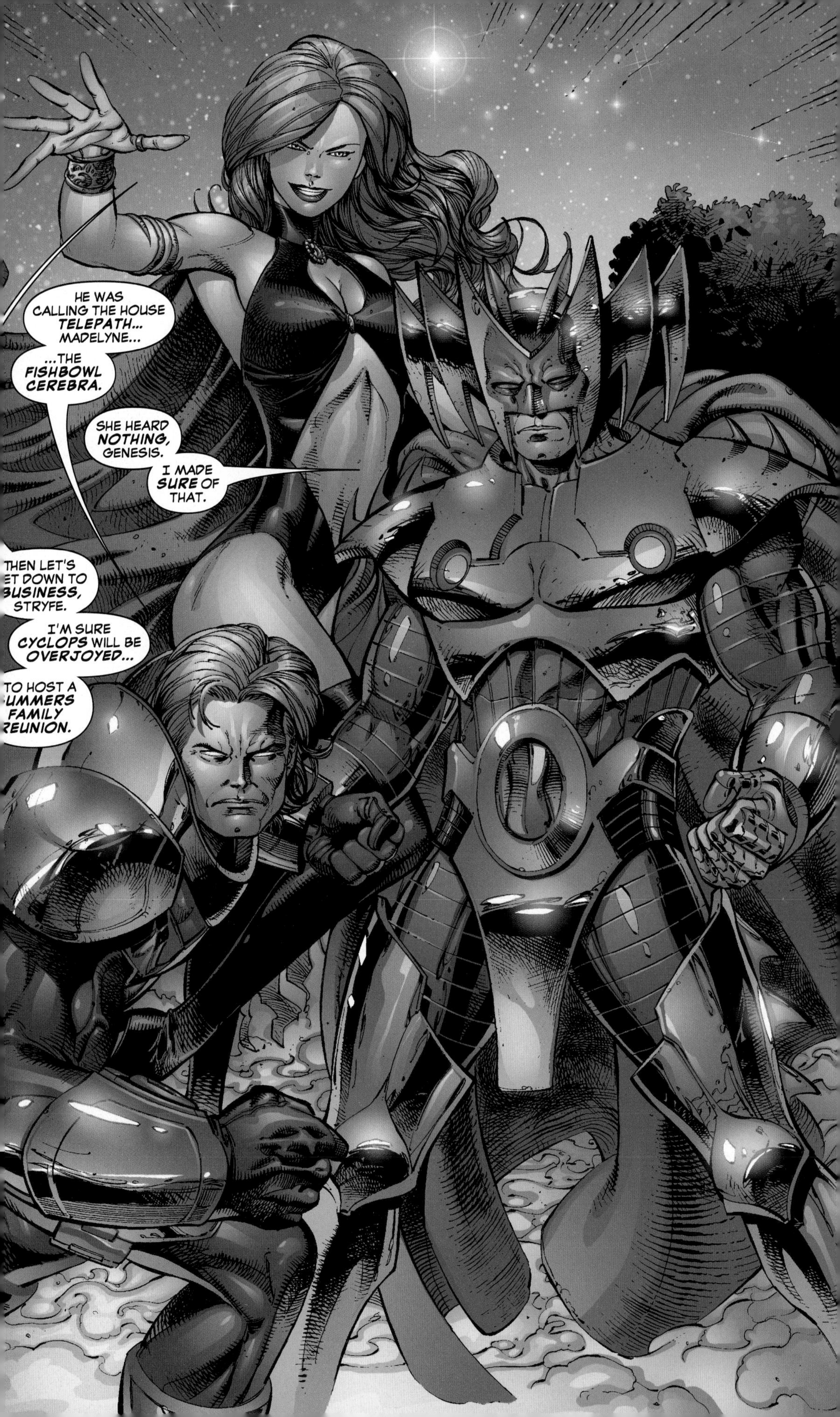
HE WAS CALLING THE HOUSE TELEPATH... MADELYNE...
...THE FISHBOWL CEREBRA.
SHE HEARD NOTHING, GENESIS.
I MADE SURE OF THAT.
THEN LET'S ET DOWN TO BUSINESS, STRYFE.
I'M SURE CYCLOPS WILL BE OVERJOYED...
TO HOST A UMMERS FAMILY EUNION.

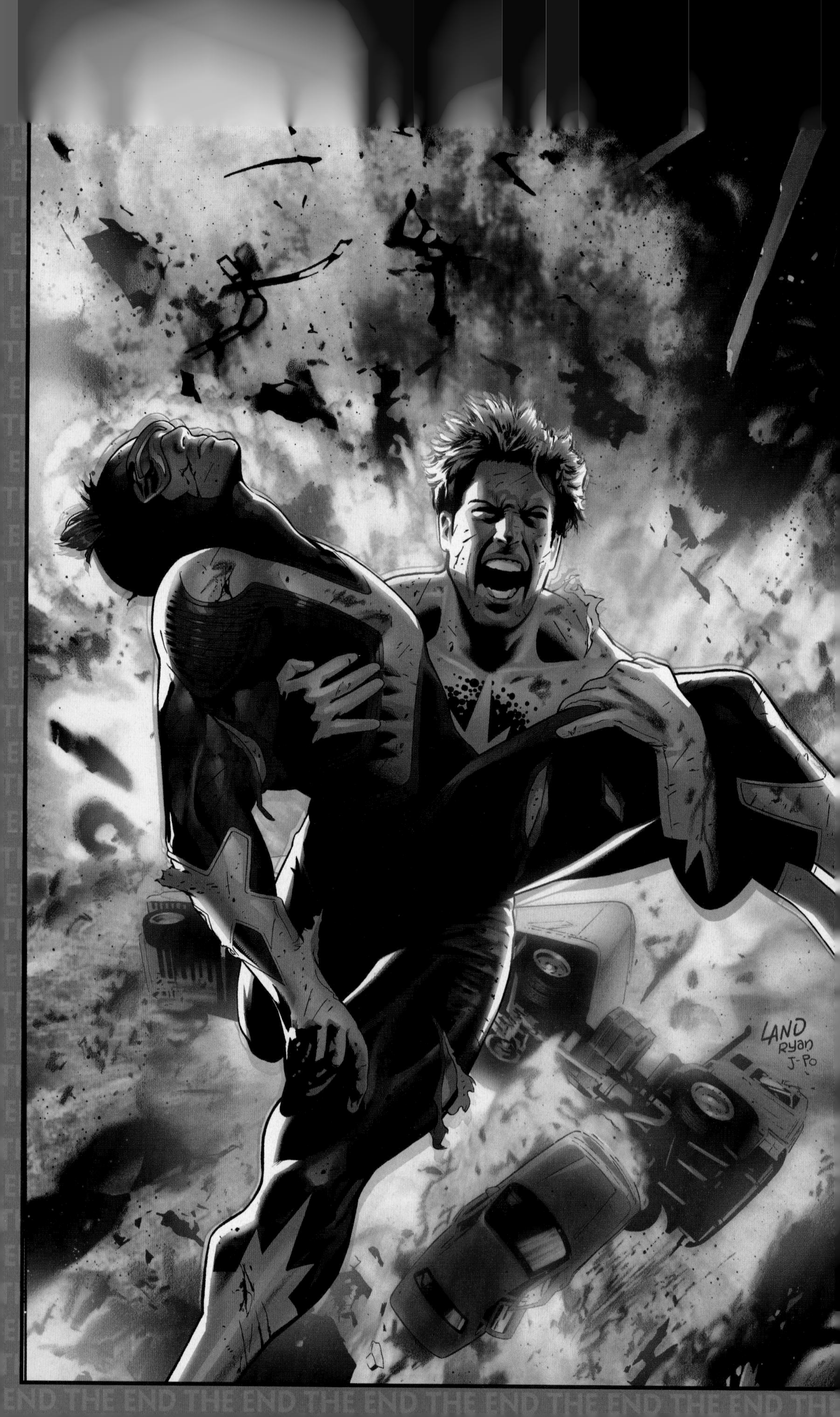
LAND
Ryan
J-Po
THE END

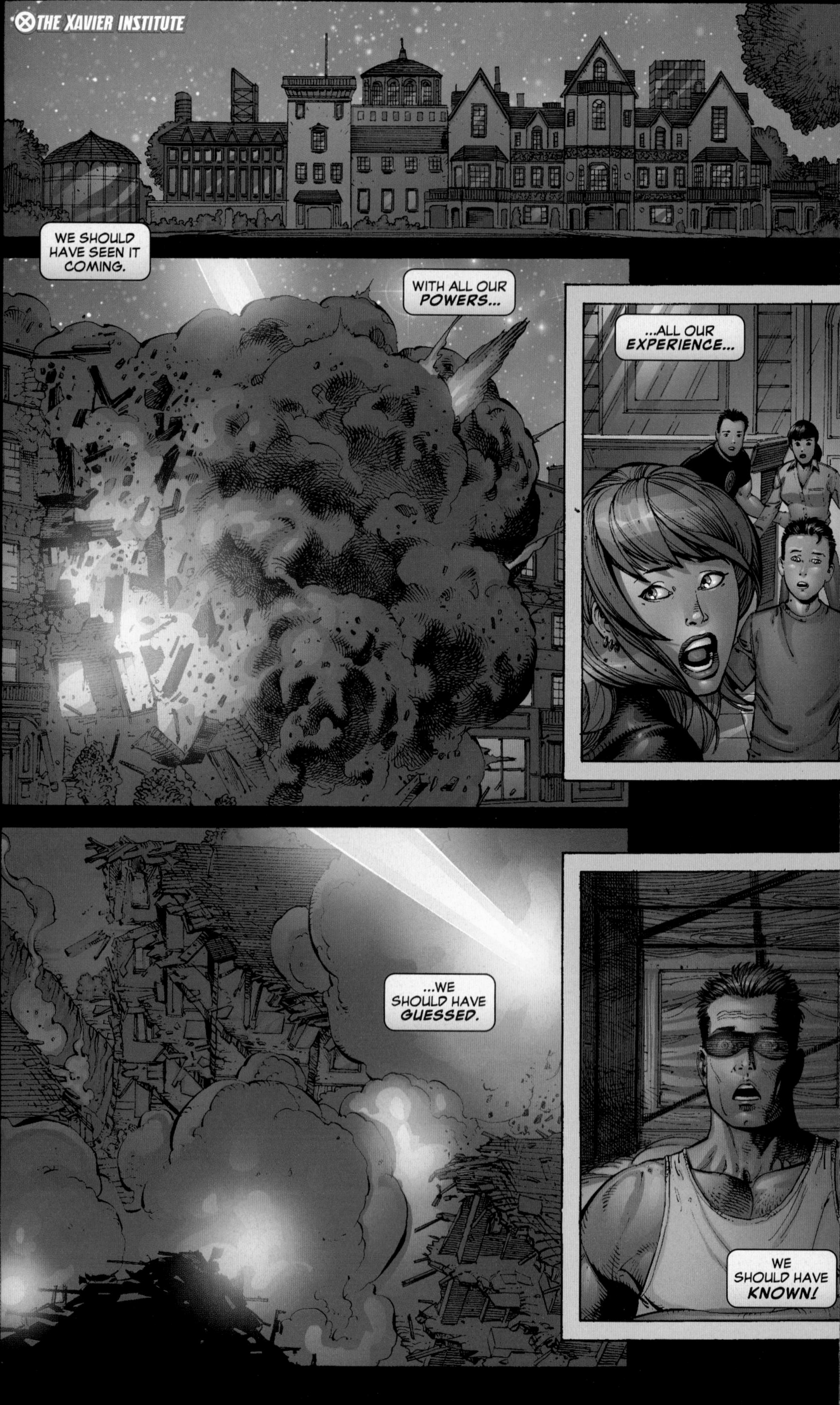
THE XAVIER INSTITUTE
WE SHOULD HAVE SEEN IT COMING.
WITH ALL OUR POWERS...
...ALL OUR EXPERIENCE...
...WE SHOULD HAVE GUESSED.
WE SHOULD HAVE KNOWN!

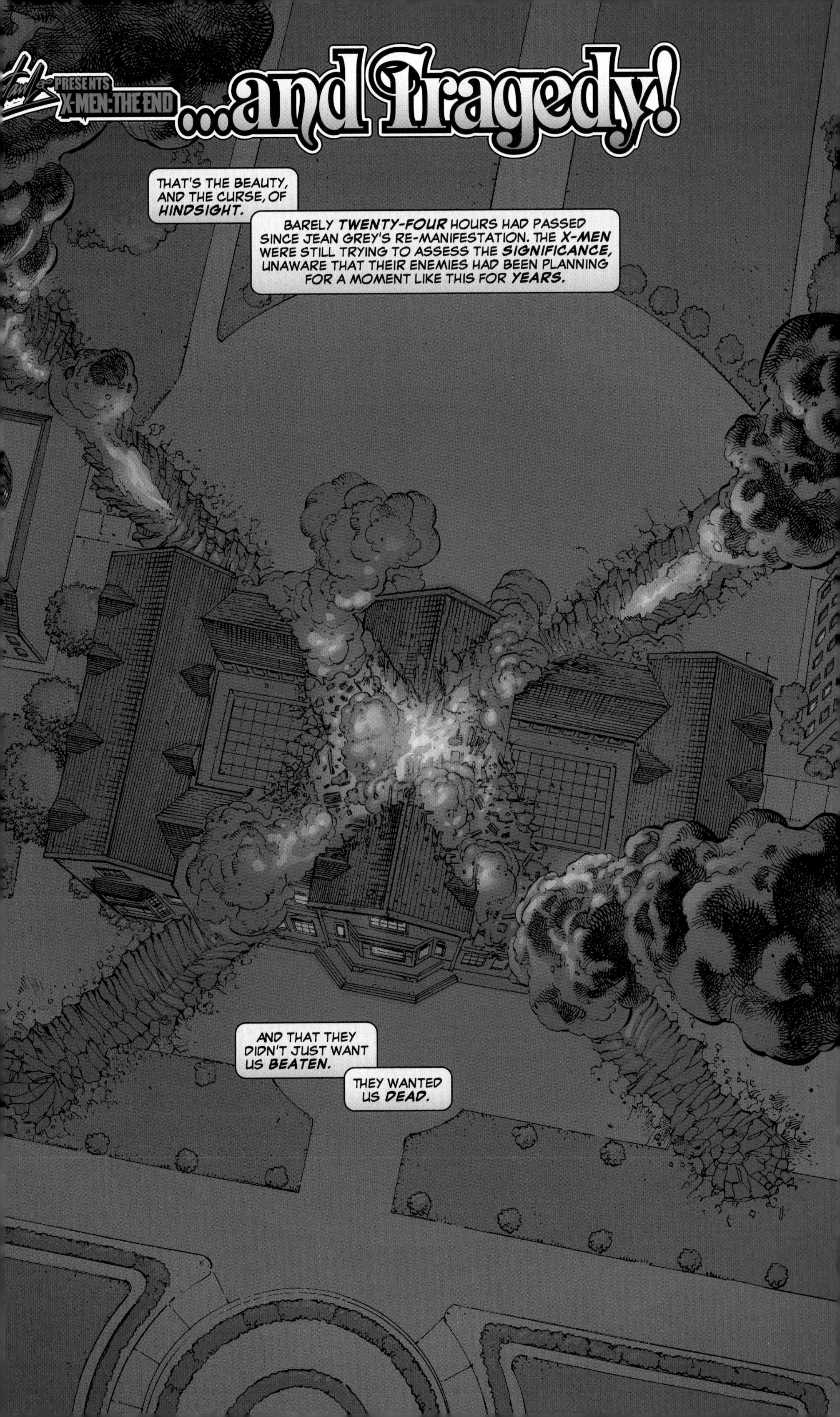
STAN LEE PRESENTS X-MEN: THE END
...and Tragedy!
THAT'S THE BEAUTY, AND THE CURSE, OF HINDSIGHT.
BARELY TWENTY-FOUR HOURS HAD PASSED SINCE JEAN GREY'S RE-MANIFESTATION. THE X-MEN WERE STILL TRYING TO ASSESS THE SIGNIFICANCE, UNAWARE THAT THEIR ENEMIES HAD BEEN PLANNING FOR A MOMENT LIKE THIS FOR YEARS.
AND THAT THEY DIDN'T JUST WANT US BEATEN.
THEY WANTED US DEAD.

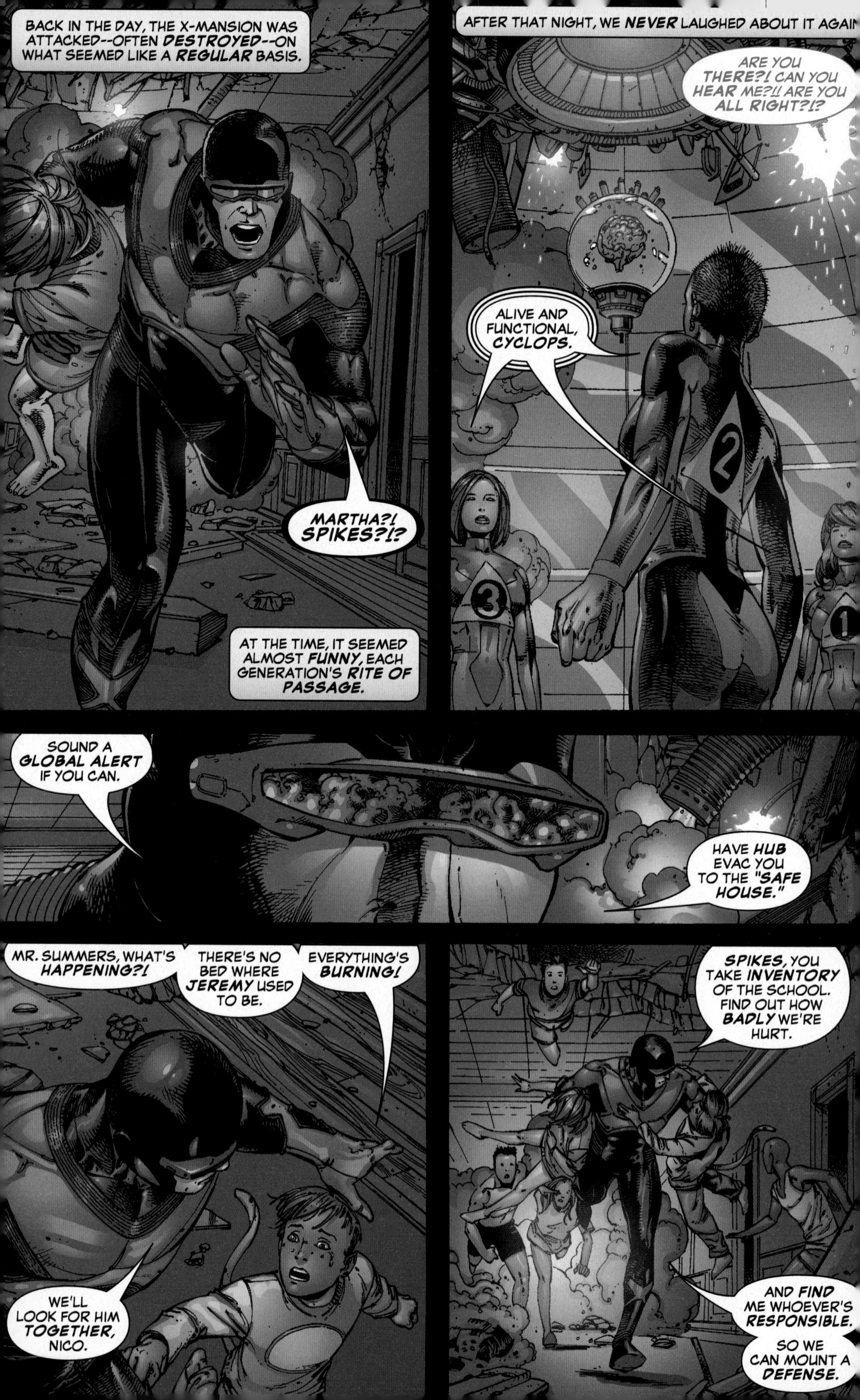
BACK IN THE DAY, THE X-MANSION WAS ATTACKED--OFTEN DESTROYED--ON WHAT SEEMED LIKE A REGULAR BASIS.
MARTHA?! SPIKES?!?
AT THE TIME, IT SEEMED ALMOST FUNNY, EACH GENERATION'S RITE OF PASSAGE.
AFTER THAT NIGHT, WE NEVER LAUGHED ABOUT IT AGAIN
ARE YOU THERE?! CAN YOU HEAR ME?!! ARE YOU ALL RIGHT?!?
ALIVE AND FUNCTIONAL, CYCLOPS.
SOUND A GLOBAL ALERT IF YOU CAN.
HAVE HUB EVAC YOU TO THE "SAFE HOUSE."
MR. SUMMERS, WHAT'S HAPPENING?!
THERE'S NO BED WHERE JEREMY USED TO BE.
EVERYTHING'S BURNING!
WE'LL LOOK FOR HIM TOGETHER, NICO.
SPIKES, YOU TAKE INVENTORY OF THE SCHOOL. FIND OUT HOW BADLY WE'RE HURT.
AND FIND ME WHOEVER'S RESPONSIBLE.
SO WE CAN MOUNT A DEFENSE.

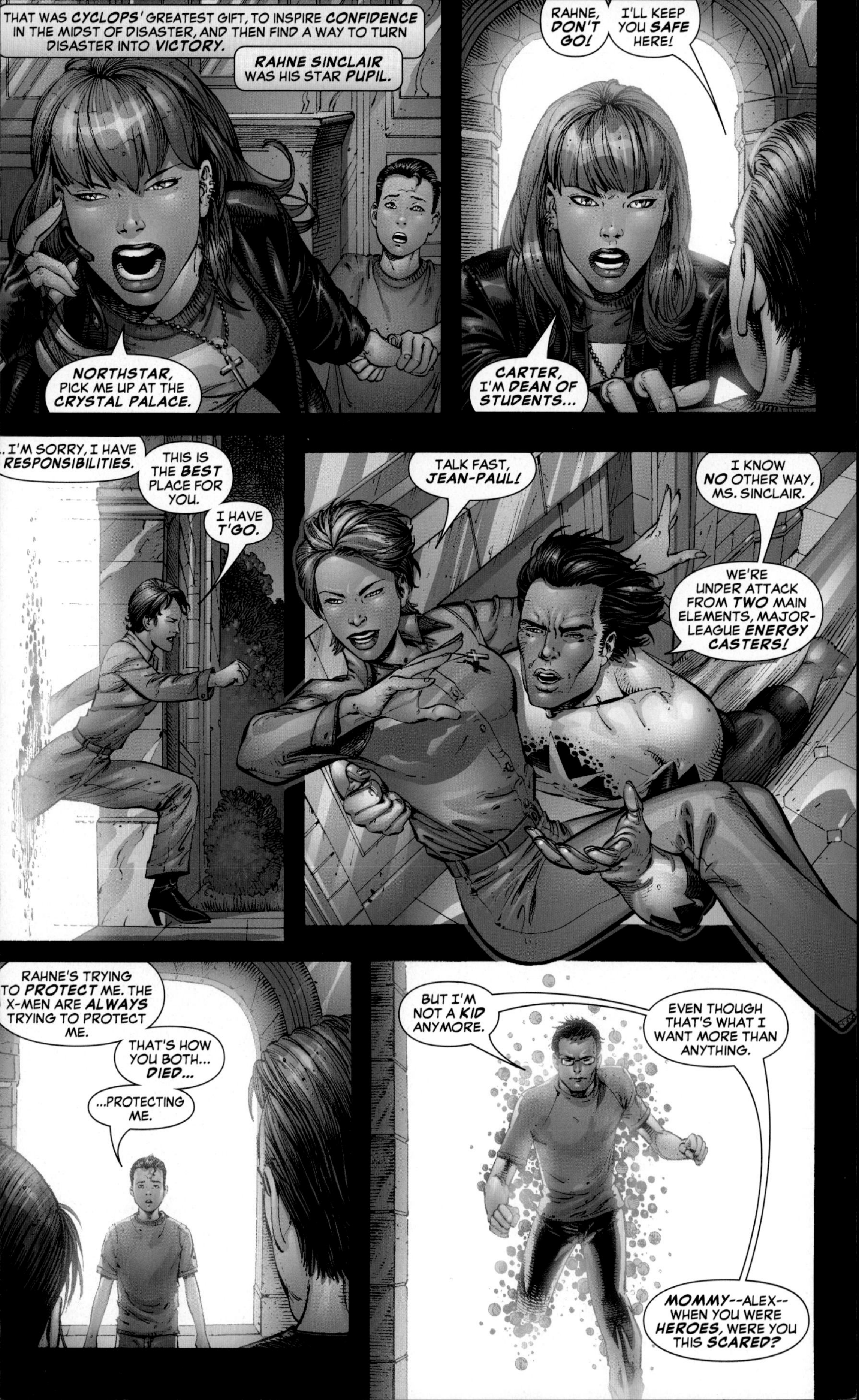
THAT WAS CYCLOPS' GREATEST GIFT, TO INSPIRE CONFIDENCE IN THE MIDST OF DISASTER, AND THEN FIND A WAY TO TURN DISASTER INTO VICTORY.
RAHNE SINCLAIR WAS HIS STAR PUPIL.
NORTHSTAR, PICK ME UP AT THE CRYSTAL PALACE.
RAHNE, DON'T GO!
I'LL KEEP YOU SAFE HERE!
CARTER, I'M DEAN OF STUDENTS...
...I'M SORRY, I HAVE RESPONSIBILITIES.
THIS IS THE BEST PLACE FOR YOU.
I HAVE T'GO.
TALK FAST, JEAN-PAUL!
I KNOW NO OTHER WAY, MS. SINCLAIR.
WE'RE UNDER ATTACK FROM TWO MAIN ELEMENTS, MAJOR-LEAGUE ENERGY CASTERS!
RAHNE'S TRYING TO PROTECT ME. THE X-MEN ARE ALWAYS TRYING TO PROTECT ME.
THAT'S HOW YOU BOTH... DIED...
...PROTECTING ME.
BUT I'M NOT A KID ANYMORE.
EVEN THOUGH THAT'S WHAT I WANT MORE THAN ANYTHING.
MOMMY--ALEX--WHEN YOU WERE HEROES, WERE YOU THIS SCARED?

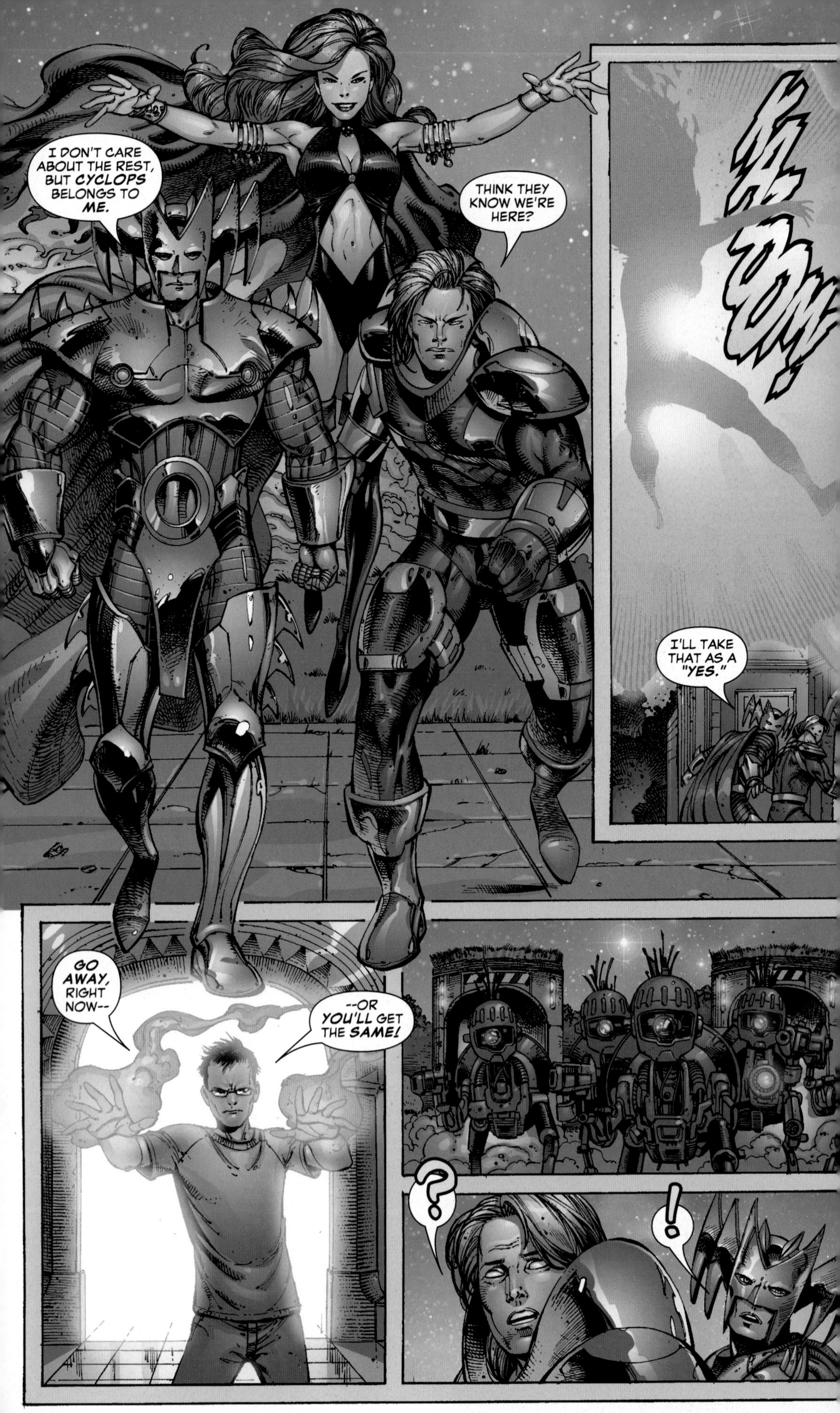
I DON'T CARE ABOUT THE REST, BUT CYCLOPS BELONGS TO ME.
THINK THEY KNOW WE'RE HERE?
I'LL TAKE THAT AS A "YES."
GO AWAY, RIGHT NOW--
--OR YOU'LL GET THE SAME!
?
!

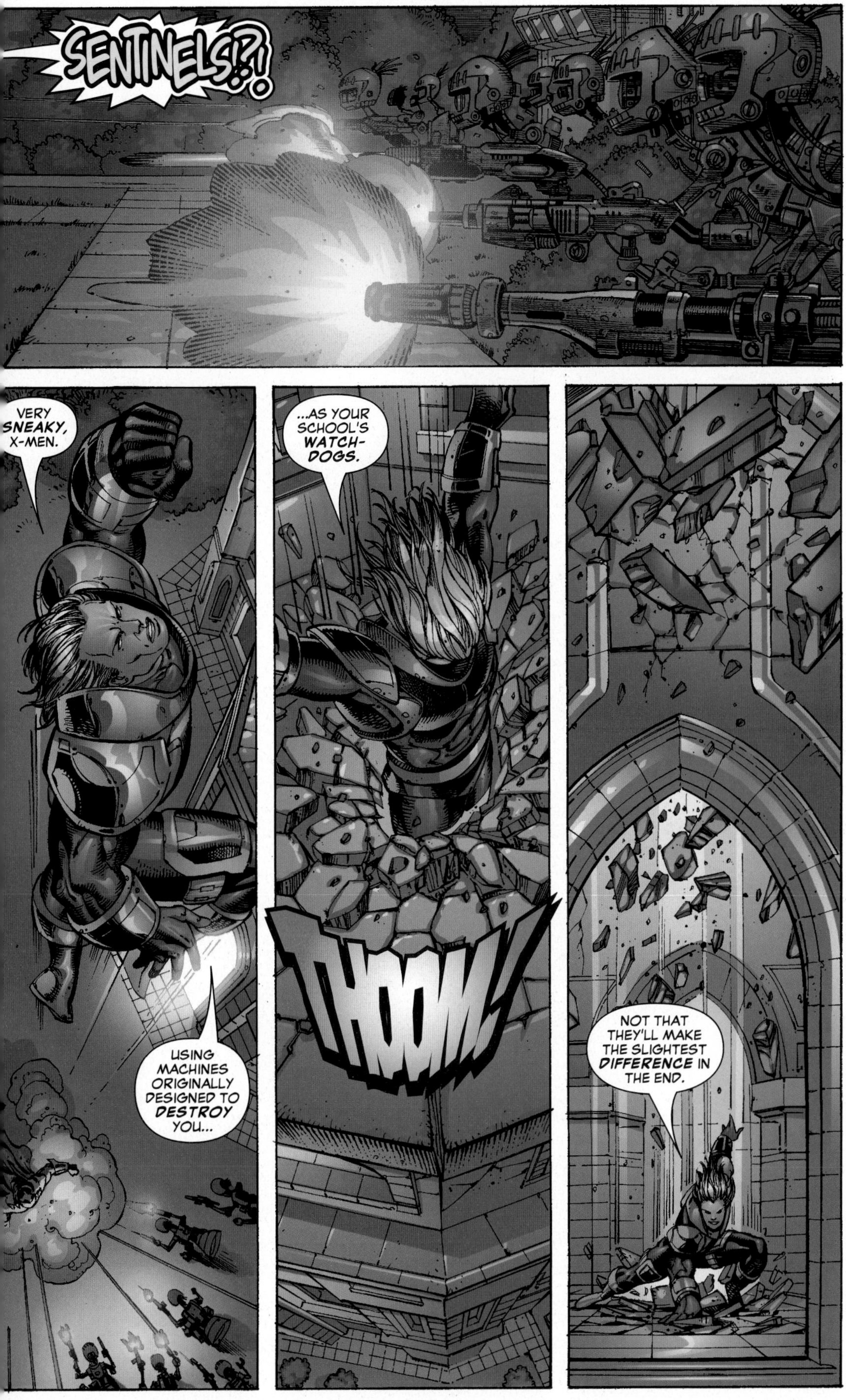
SENTINELS!?!
VERY SNEAKY, X-MEN.
USING MACHINES ORIGINALLY DESIGNED TO DESTROY YOU...
...AS YOUR SCHOOL'S WATCH-DOGS.
THOOM!
NOT THAT THEY'LL MAKE THE SLIGHTEST DIFFERENCE IN THE END.

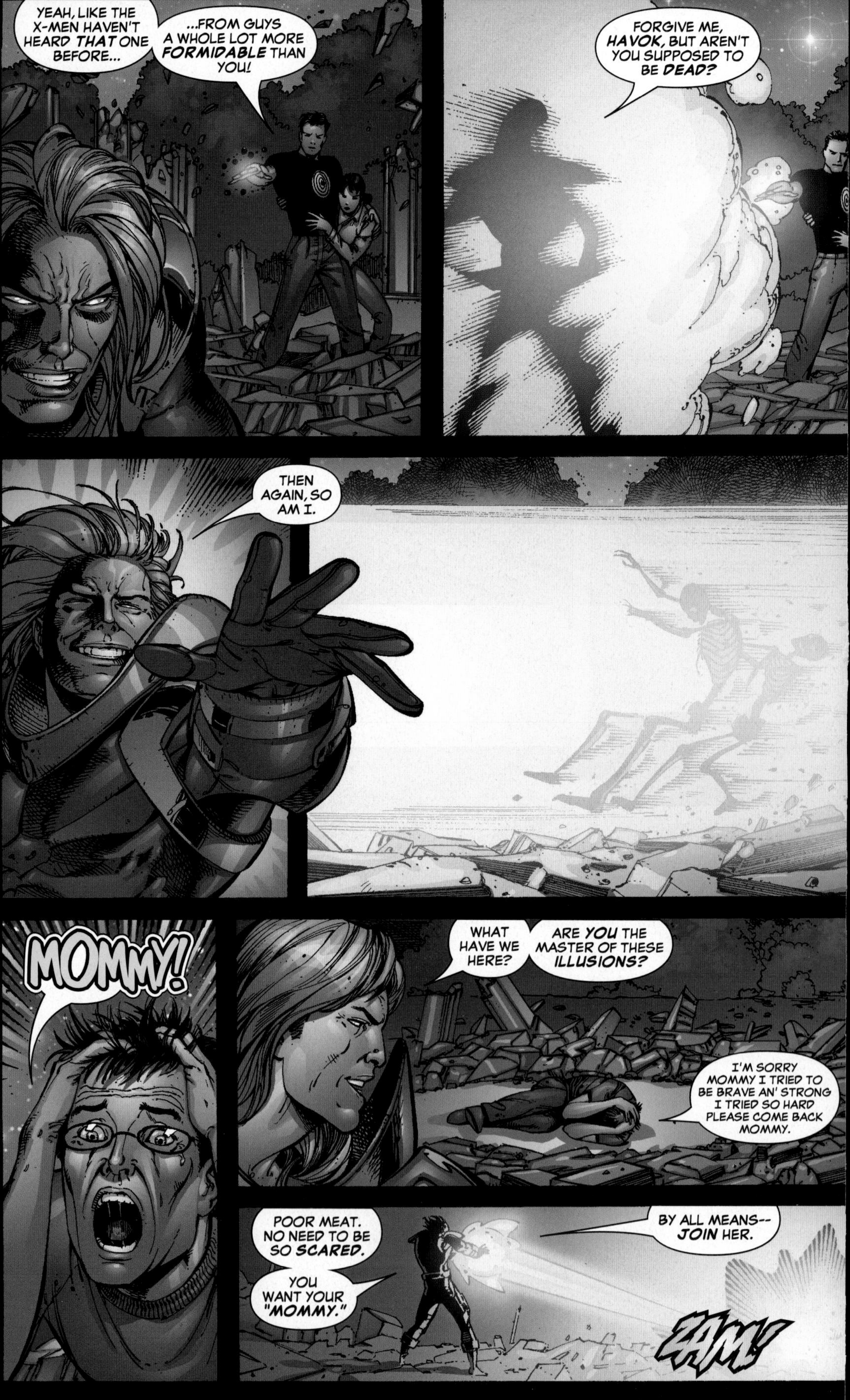
YEAH, LIKE THE X-MEN HAVEN'T HEARD THAT ONE BEFORE...
...FROM GUYS A WHOLE LOT MORE FORMIDABLE THAN YOU!
FORGIVE ME, HAVOK, BUT AREN'T YOU SUPPOSED TO BE DEAD?
THEN AGAIN, SO AM I.
MOMMY!
WHAT HAVE WE HERE?
ARE YOU THE MASTER OF THESE ILLUSIONS?
I'M SORRY MOMMY I TRIED TO BE BRAVE AN' STRONG I TRIED SO HARD PLEASE COME BACK MOMMY.
POOR MEAT. NO NEED TO BE SO SCARED.
YOU WANT YOUR "MOMMY."
BY ALL MEANS-- JOIN HER.
ZAM!

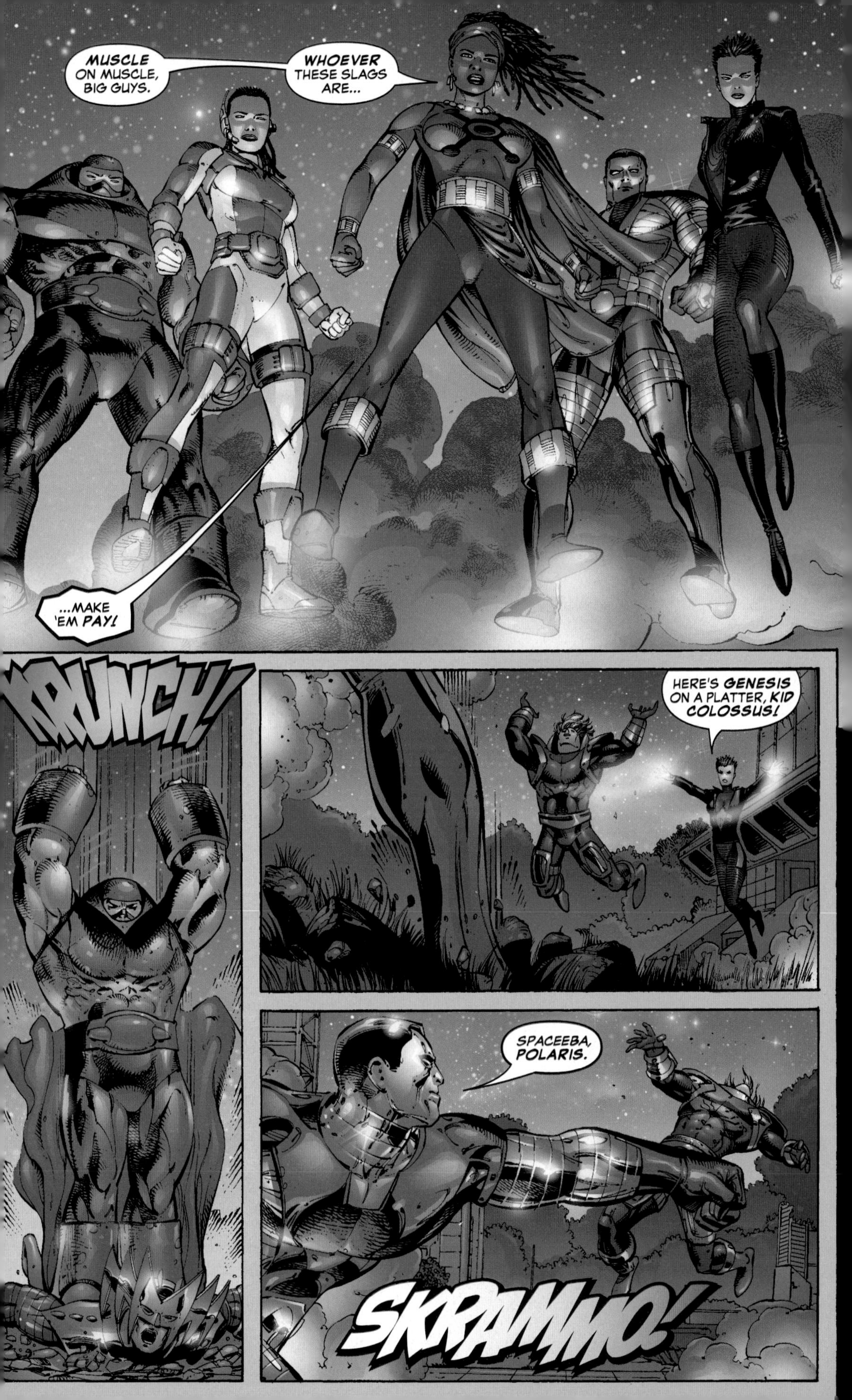
MUSCLE ON MUSCLE, BIG GUYS.
WHOEVER THESE SLAGS ARE...
...MAKE 'EM PAY!
KRUNCH!
HERE'S GENESIS ON A PLATTER, KID COLOSSUS!
SPACEEBA, POLARIS.
SKRAMMO!

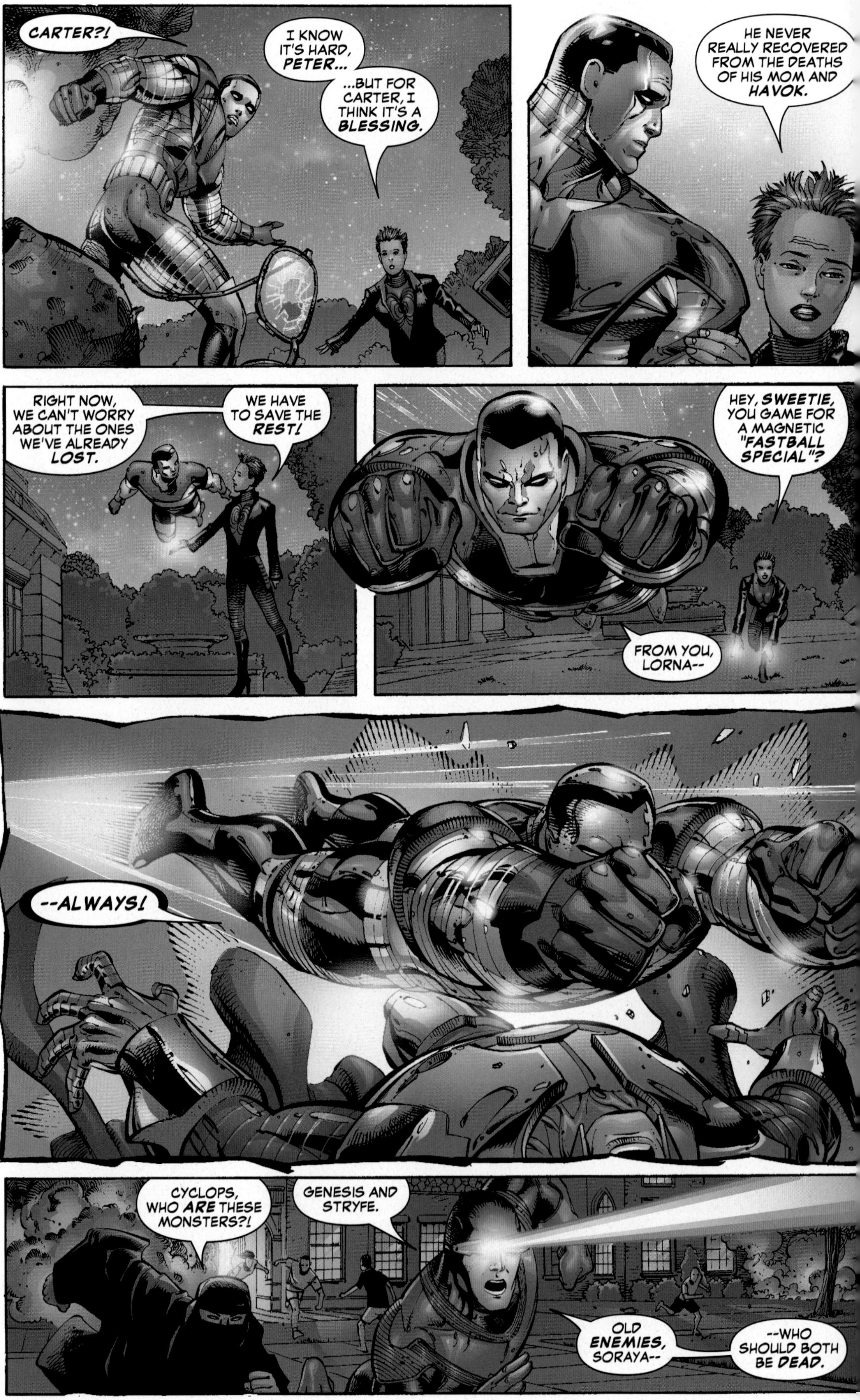
CARTER?!
I KNOW IT'S HARD, PETER...
...BUT FOR CARTER, I THINK IT'S A BLESSING.
HE NEVER REALLY RECOVERED FROM THE DEATHS OF HIS MOM AND HAVOK.
RIGHT NOW, WE CAN'T WORRY ABOUT THE ONES WE'VE ALREADY LOST.
WE HAVE TO SAVE THE REST!
HEY, SWEETIE, YOU GAME FOR A MAGNETIC "FASTBALL SPECIAL"?
FROM YOU, LORNA--
--ALWAYS!
CYCLOPS, WHO ARE THESE MONSTERS?!
GENESIS AND STRYFE.
OLD ENEMIES, SORAYA--
--WHO SHOULD BOTH BE DEAD.

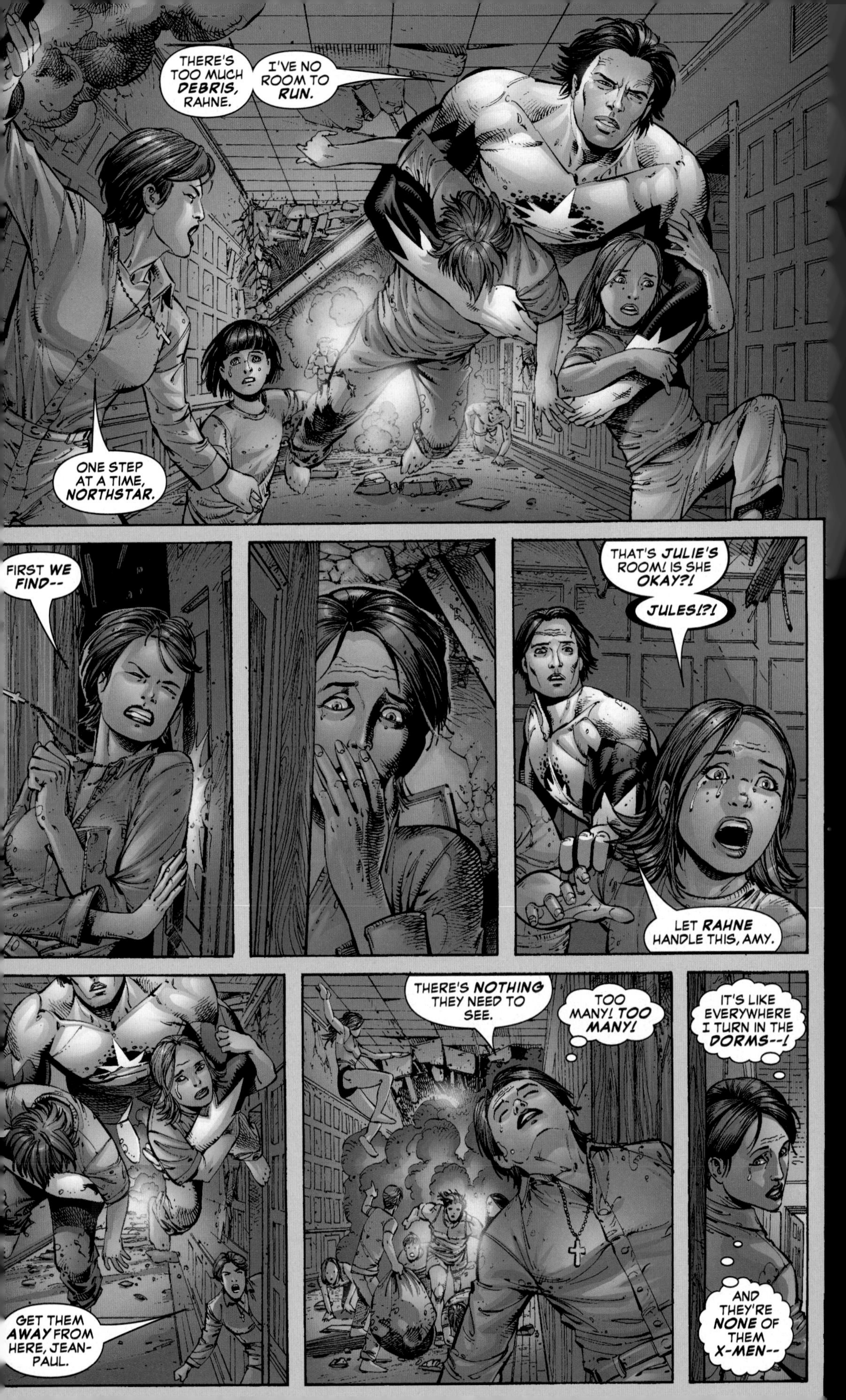
THERE'S TOO MUCH DEBRIS, RAHNE.
I'VE NO ROOM TO RUN.
ONE STEP AT A TIME, NORTHSTAR.
FIRST WE FIND--
THAT'S JULIE'S ROOM! IS SHE OKAY?!
JULES!?!
LET RAHNE HANDLE THIS, AMY.
GET THEM AWAY FROM HERE, JEAN-PAUL.
THERE'S NOTHING THEY NEED TO SEE.
TOO MANY! TOO MANY!
IT'S LIKE EVERYWHERE I TURN IN THE DORMS--!
AND THEY'RE NONE OF THEM X-MEN--

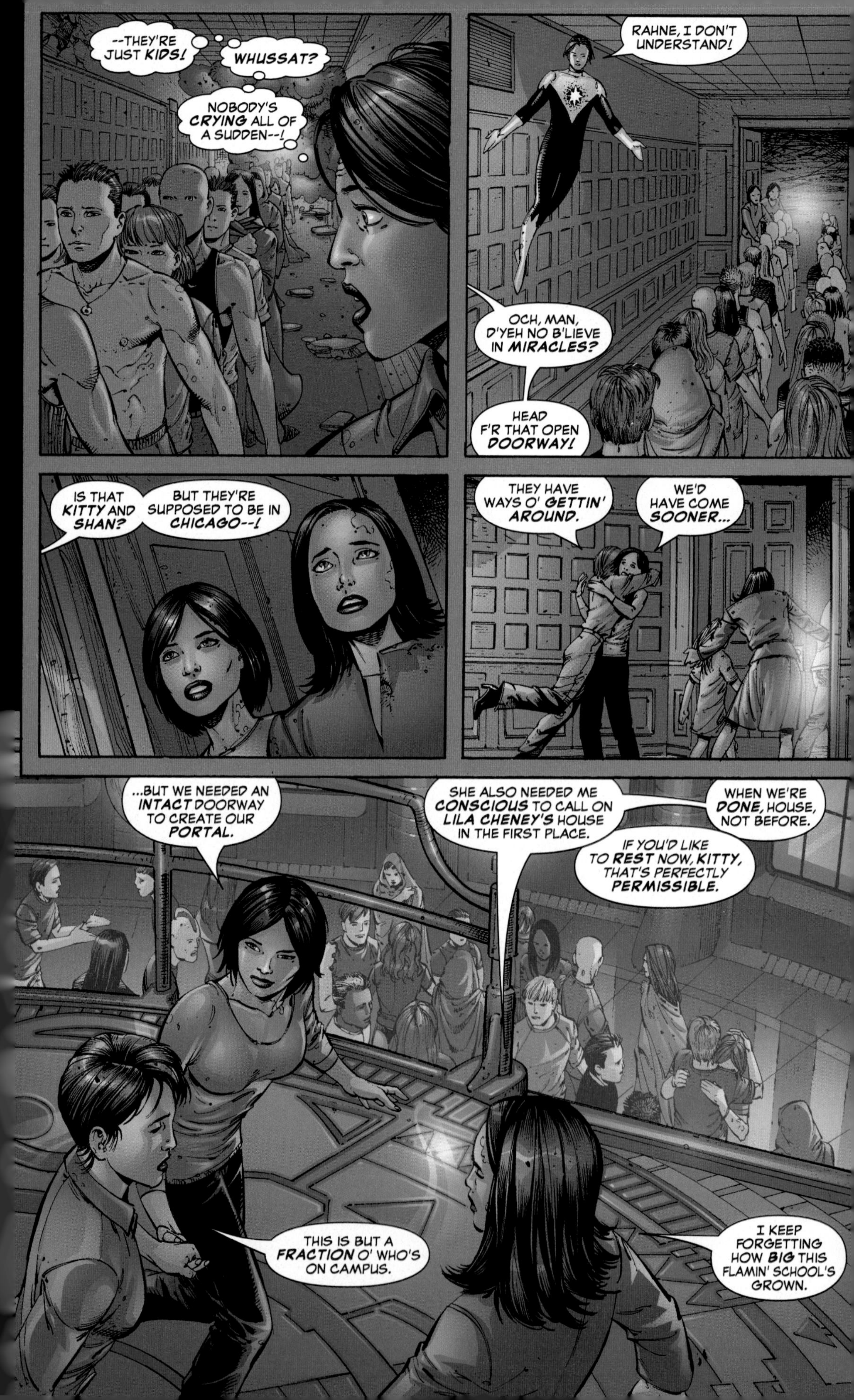

--THEY'RE JUST KIDS!
WHUSSAT?
NOBODY'S CRYING ALL OF A SUDDEN--!
RAHNE, I DON'T UNDERSTAND!
OCH, MAN, D'YEH NO B'LIEVE IN MIRACLES?
HEAD F'R THAT OPEN DOORWAY!
IS THAT KITTY AND SHAN?
BUT THEY'RE SUPPOSED TO BE IN CHICAGO--!
THEY HAVE WAYS O' GETTIN' AROUND.
WE'D HAVE COME SOONER...
...BUT WE NEEDED AN INTACT DOORWAY TO CREATE OUR PORTAL.
SHE ALSO NEEDED ME CONSCIOUS TO CALL ON LILA CHENEY'S HOUSE IN THE FIRST PLACE.
WHEN WE'RE DONE, HOUSE, NOT BEFORE.
IF YOU'D LIKE TO REST NOW, KITTY, THAT'S PERFECTLY PERMISSIBLE.
THIS IS BUT A FRACTION O' WHO'S ON CAMPUS.
I KEEP FORGETTING HOW BIG THIS FLAMIN' SCHOOL'S GROWN.

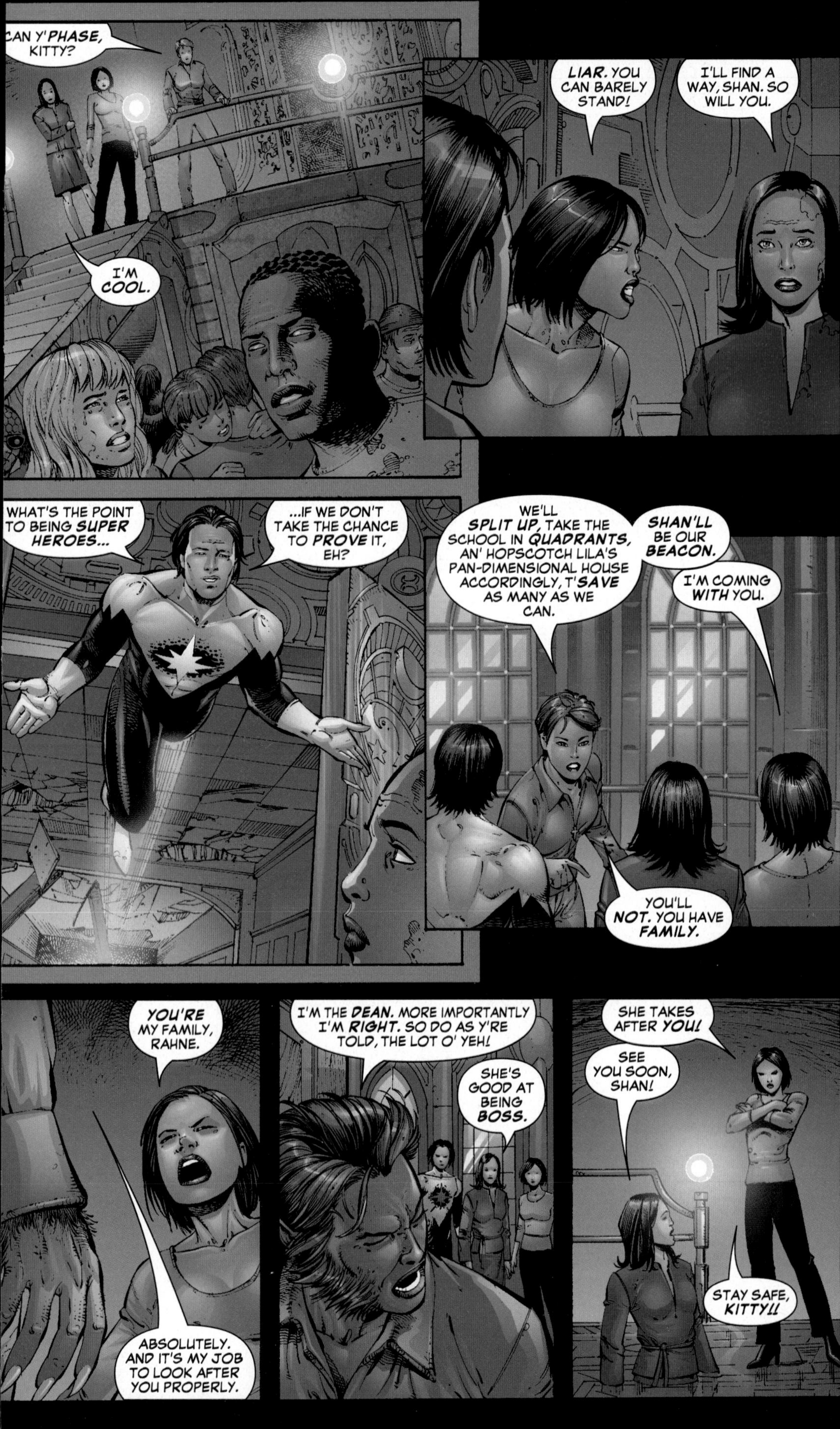
CAN Y'PHASE, KITTY?
I'M COOL.
LIAR. YOU CAN BARELY STAND!
I'LL FIND A WAY, SHAN. SO WILL YOU.
WHAT'S THE POINT TO BEING SUPER HEROES...
...IF WE DON'T TAKE THE CHANCE TO PROVE IT, EH?
WE'LL SPLIT UP, TAKE THE SCHOOL IN QUADRANTS, AN' HOPSCOTCH LILA'S PAN-DIMENSIONAL HOUSE ACCORDINGLY, T'SAVE AS MANY AS WE CAN.
SHAN'LL BE OUR BEACON.
I'M COMING WITH YOU.
YOU'LL NOT. YOU HAVE FAMILY.
YOU'RE MY FAMILY, RAHNE.
ABSOLUTELY. AND IT'S MY JOB TO LOOK AFTER YOU PROPERLY.
I'M THE DEAN. MORE IMPORTANTLY I'M RIGHT. SO DO AS Y'RE TOLD, THE LOT O' YEH!
SHE'S GOOD AT BEING BOSS.
SHE TAKES AFTER YOU!
SEE YOU SOON, SHAN!
STAY SAFE, KITTY!!

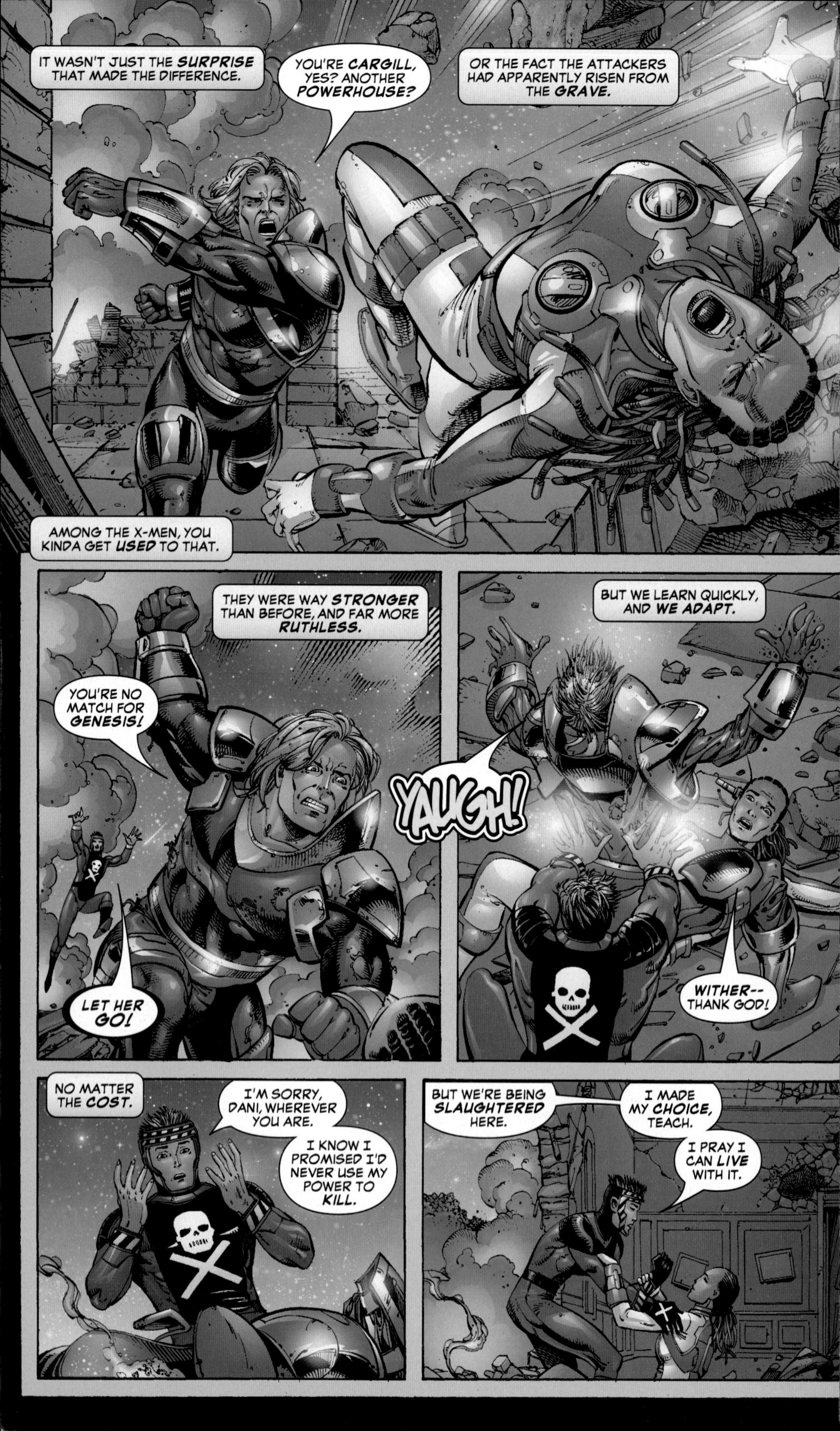
IT WASN'T JUST THE SURPRISE THAT MADE THE DIFFERENCE.
YOU'RE CARGILL, YES? ANOTHER POWERHOUSE?
OR THE FACT THE ATTACKERS HAD APPARENTLY RISEN FROM THE GRAVE.
AMONG THE X-MEN, YOU KINDA GET USED TO THAT.
THEY WERE WAY STRONGER THAN BEFORE, AND FAR MORE RUTHLESS.
YOU'RE NO MATCH FOR GENESIS!
LET HER GO!
BUT WE LEARN QUICKLY, AND WE ADAPT.
YAUGH!
WITHER-- THANK GOD!
NO MATTER THE COST.
I'M SORRY, DANI, WHEREVER YOU ARE.
I KNOW I PROMISED I'D NEVER USE MY POWER TO KILL.
BUT WE'RE BEING SLAUGHTERED HERE.
I MADE MY CHOICE, TEACH.
I PRAY I CAN LIVE WITH IT.

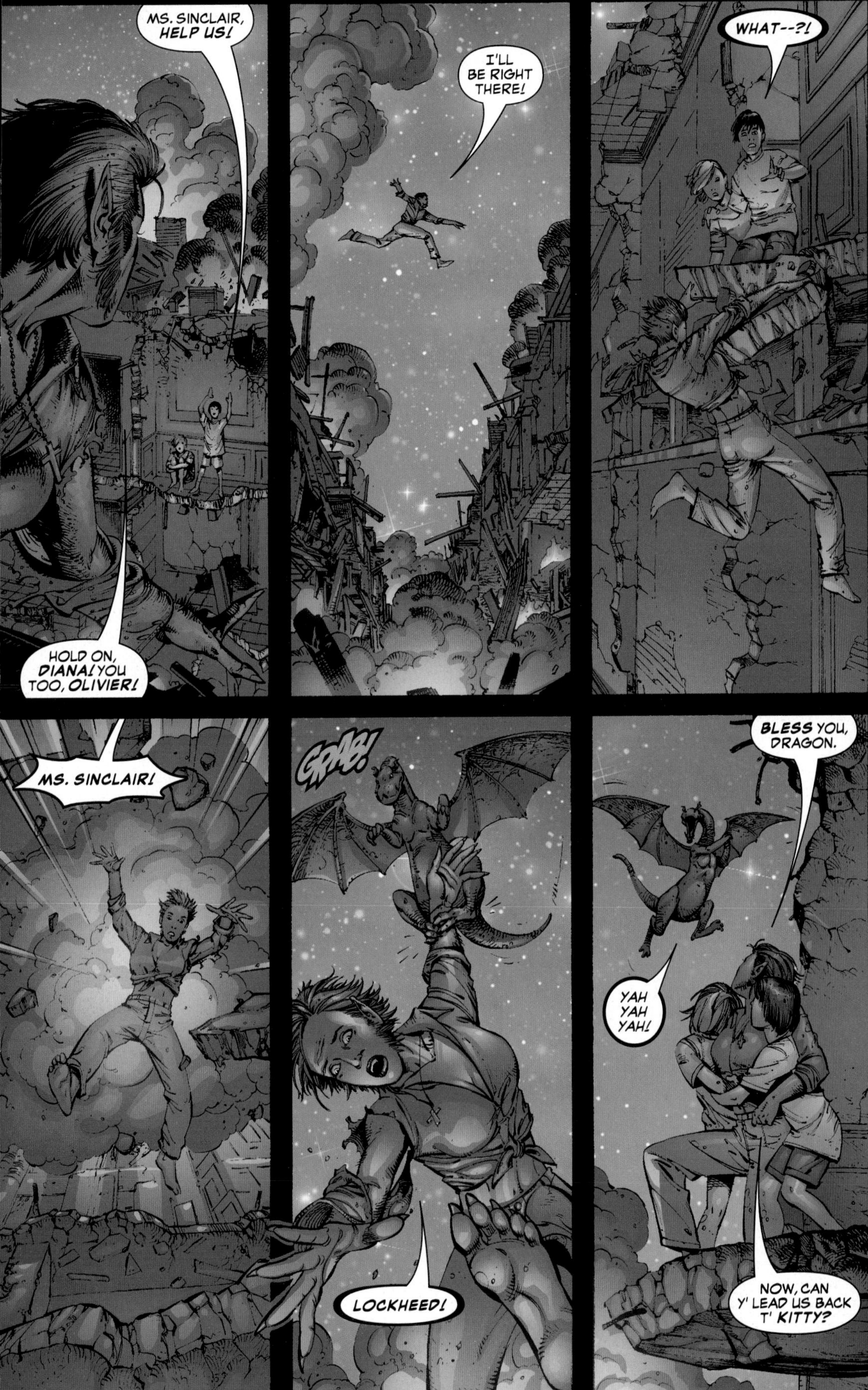
MS. SINCLAIR, HELP US!
HOLD ON, DIANA! YOU TOO, OLIVIER!
I'LL BE RIGHT THERE!
WHAT--?!
MS. SINCLAIR!
GRAB!
LOCKHEED!
BLESS YOU, DRAGON.
YAH YAH YAH!
NOW, CAN Y' LEAD US BACK T' KITTY?

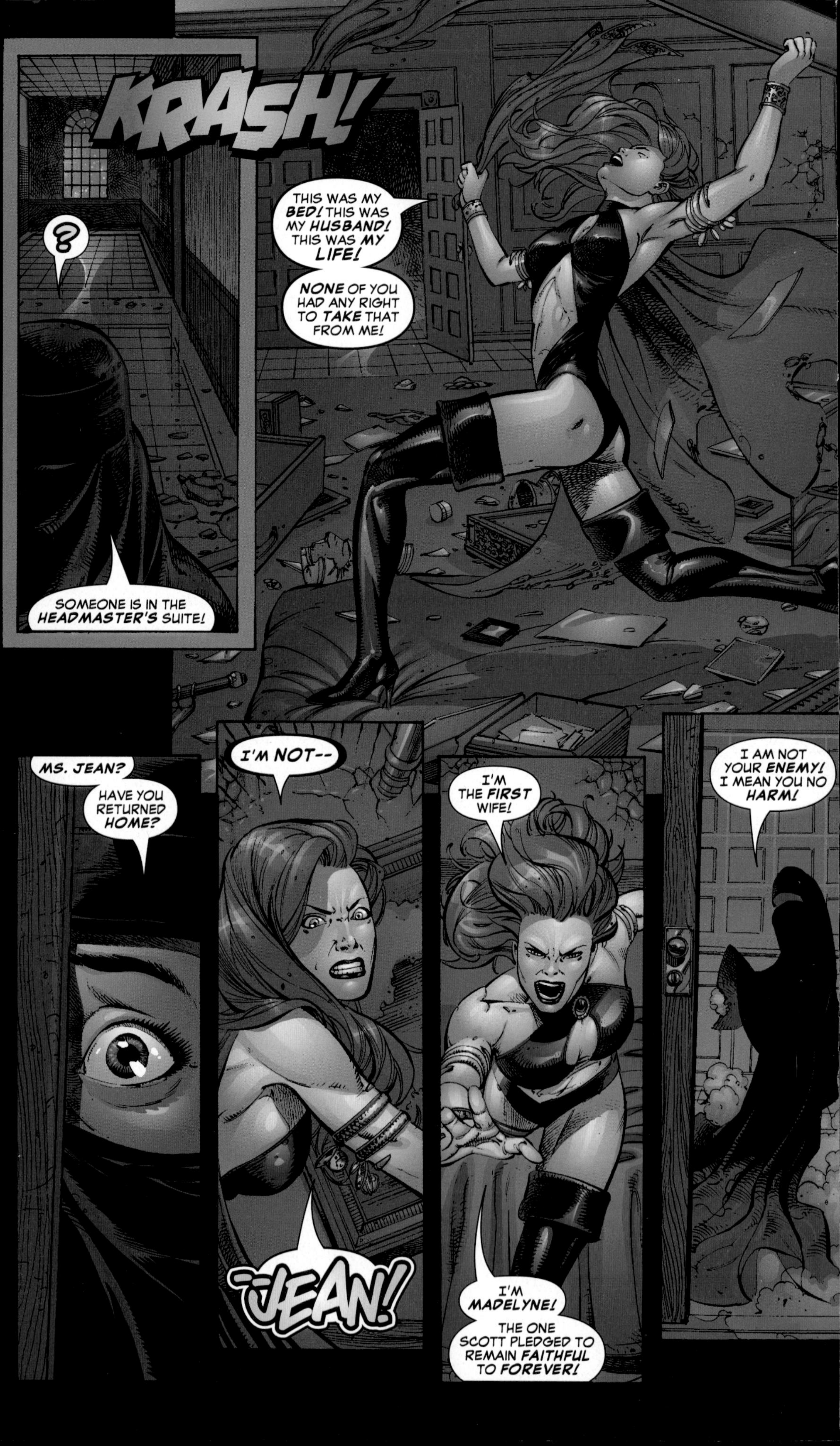
KRASH!
?
SOMEONE IS IN THE HEADMASTER'S SUITE!
THIS WAS MY BED! THIS WAS MY HUSBAND! THIS WAS MY LIFE!
NONE OF YOU HAD ANY RIGHT TO TAKE THAT FROM ME!
MS. JEAN?
HAVE YOU RETURNED HOME?
I'M NOT--
--JEAN!
I'M THE FIRST WIFE!
I'M MADELYNE!
THE ONE SCOTT PLEDGED TO REMAIN FAITHFUL TO FOREVER!
I AM NOT YOUR ENEMY! I MEAN YOU NO HARM!

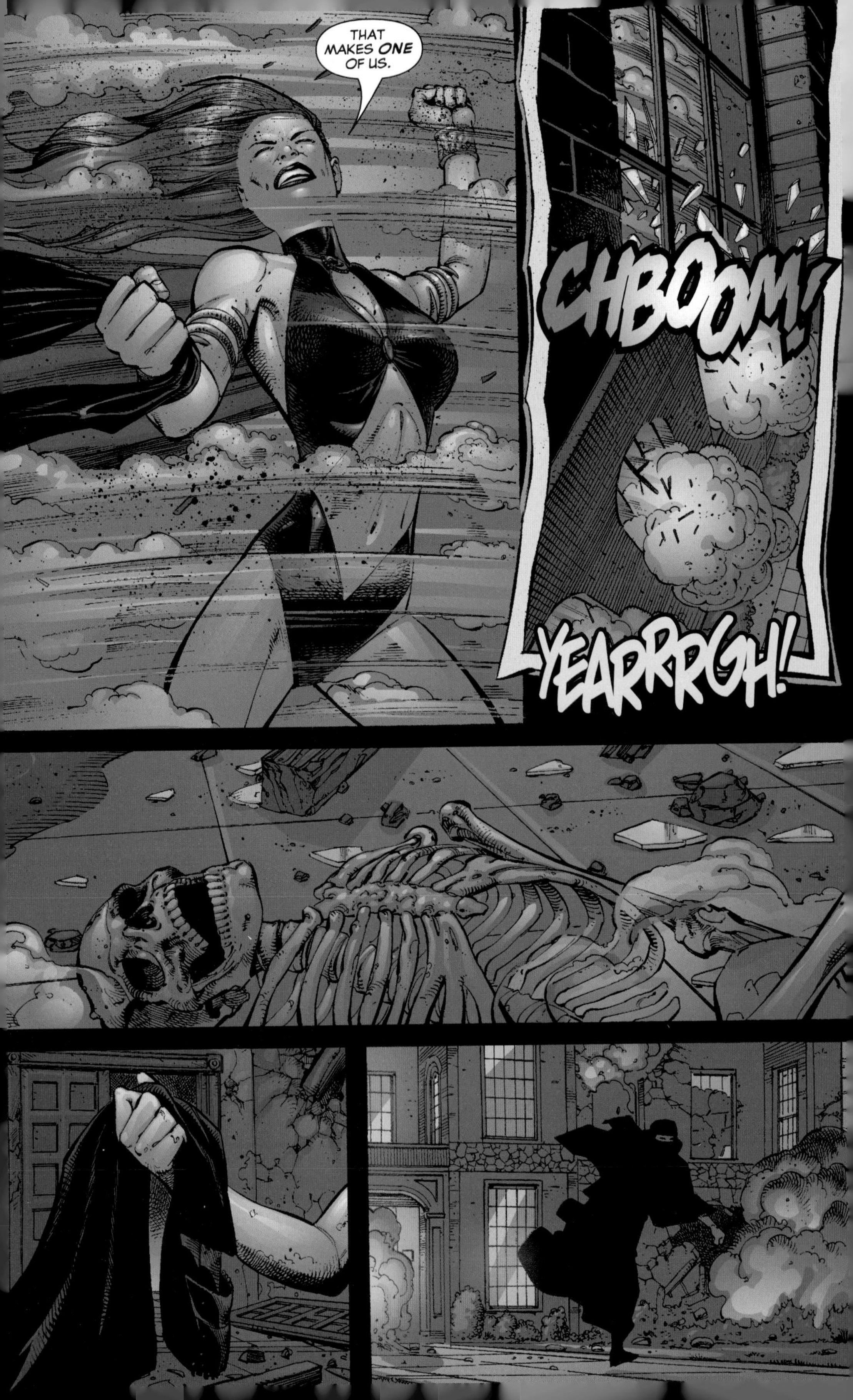
THAT MAKES ONE OF US.
CHBOOM!
YEARRRGH!

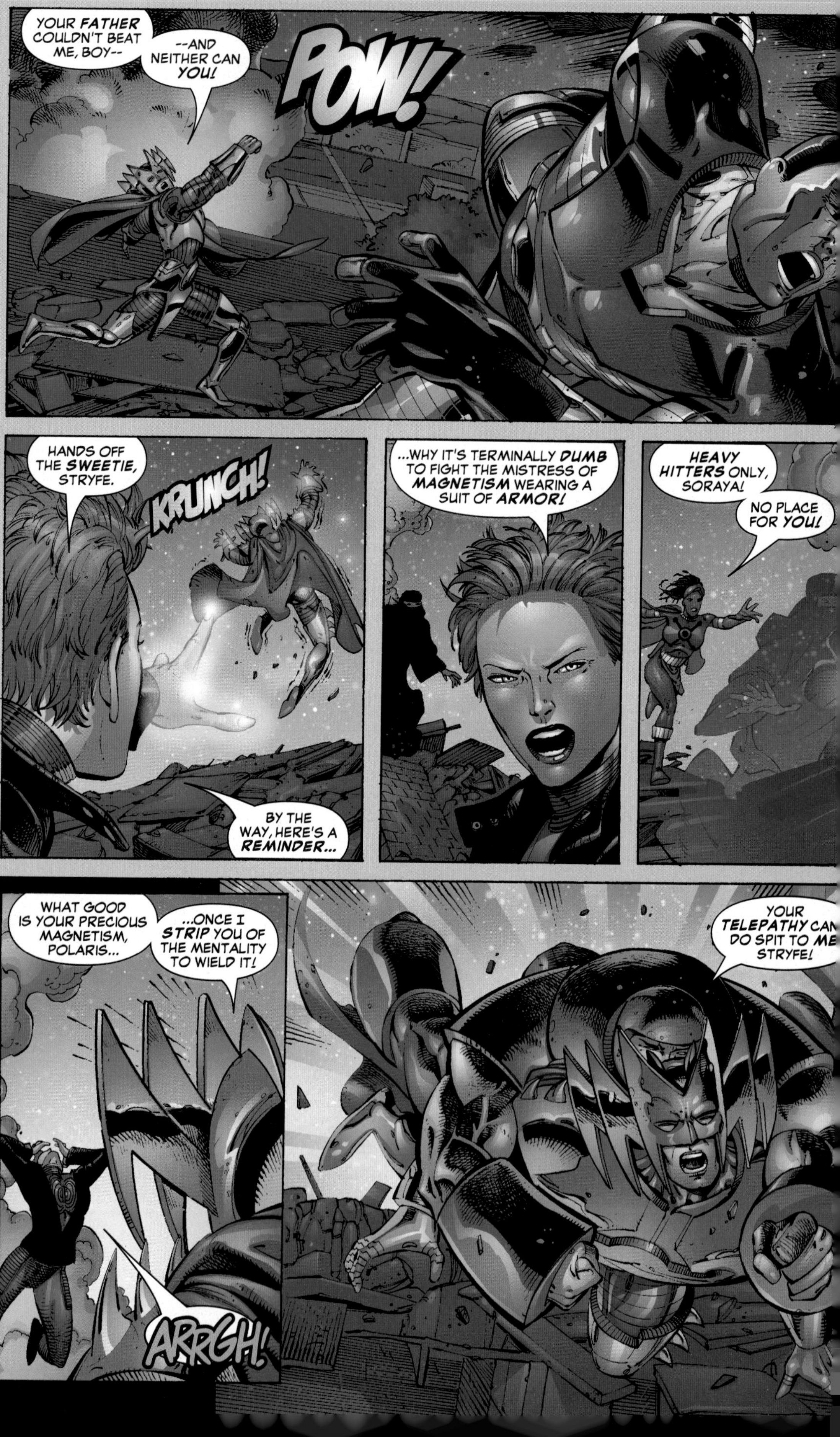
YOUR FATHER COULDN'T BEAT ME, BOY--
--AND NEITHER CAN YOU!
POW!
HANDS OFF THE SWEETIE, STRYFE.
KRUNCH!
BY THE WAY, HERE'S A REMINDER...
...WHY IT'S TERMINALLY DUMB TO FIGHT THE MISTRESS OF MAGNETISM WEARING A SUIT OF ARMOR!
HEAVY HITTERS ONLY, SORAYA!
NO PLACE FOR YOU!
WHAT GOOD IS YOUR PRECIOUS MAGNETISM, POLARIS...
...ONCE I STRIP YOU OF THE MENTALITY TO WIELD IT!
ARRGH!
YOUR TELEPATHY CAN DO SPIT TO ME STRYFE!

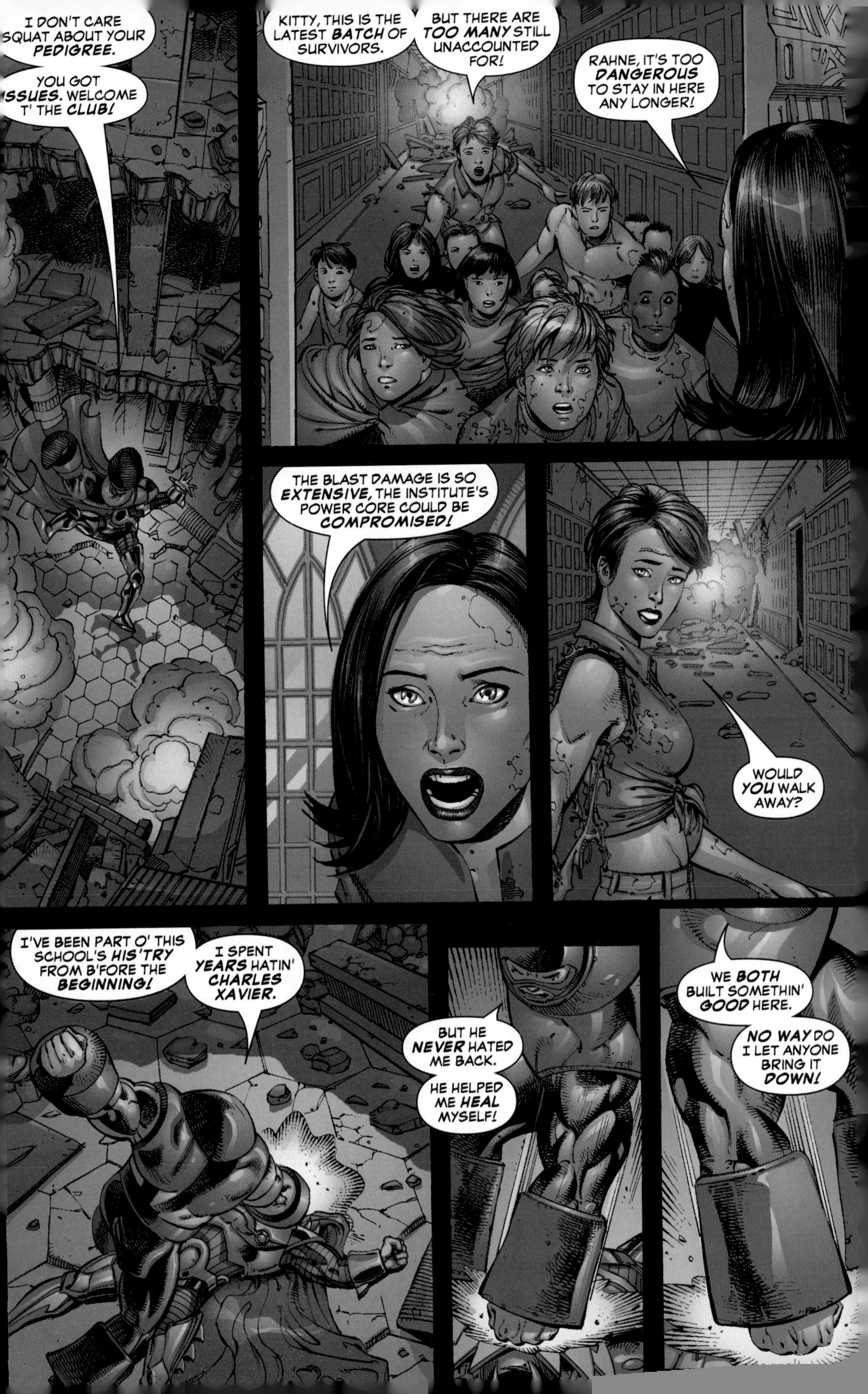
I DON'T CARE SQUAT ABOUT YOUR PEDIGREE.
YOU GOT SSUES. WELCOME T' THE CLUB!
KITTY, THIS IS THE LATEST BATCH OF SURVIVORS.
BUT THERE ARE TOO MANY STILL UNACCOUNTED FOR!
RAHNE, IT'S TOO DANGEROUS TO STAY IN HERE ANY LONGER!
THE BLAST DAMAGE IS SO EXTENSIVE, THE INSTITUTE'S POWER CORE COULD BE COMPROMISED!
WOULD YOU WALK AWAY?
I'VE BEEN PART O' THIS SCHOOL'S HIS'TRY FROM B'FORE THE BEGINNING!
I SPENT YEARS HATIN' CHARLES XAVIER.
BUT HE NEVER HATED ME BACK.
HE HELPED ME HEAL MYSELF!
WE BOTH BUILT SOMETHIN' GOOD HERE.
NO WAY DO I LET ANYONE BRING IT DOWN!

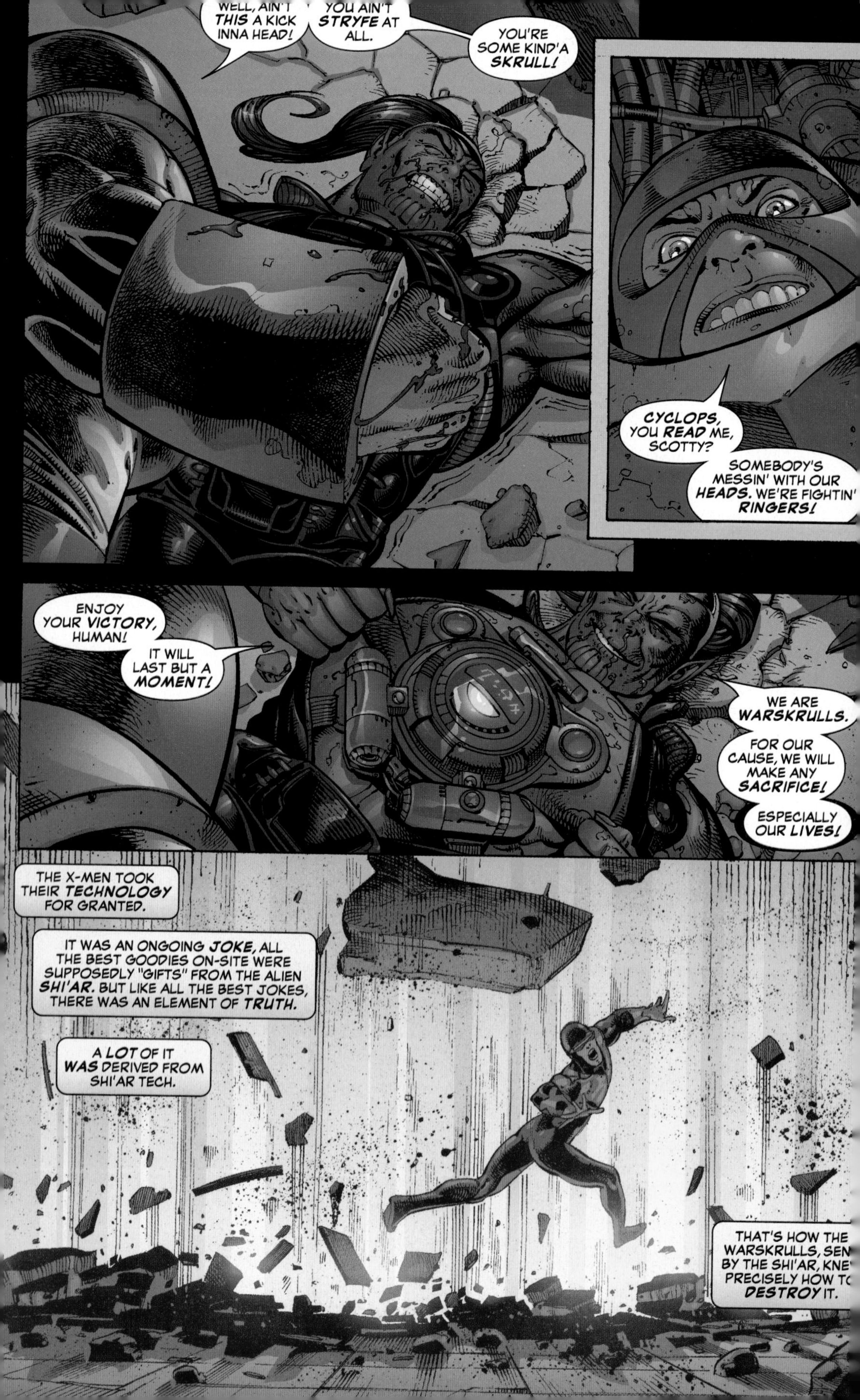

WELL, AIN'T THIS A KICK INNA HEAD!
YOU AIN'T STRYFE AT ALL.
YOU'RE SOME KIND'A SKRULL!
CYCLOPS, YOU READ ME, SCOTTY?
SOMEBODY'S MESSIN' WITH OUR HEADS. WE'RE FIGHTIN' RINGERS!
ENJOY YOUR VICTORY, HUMAN!
IT WILL LAST BUT A MOMENT!
WE ARE WARSKRULLS.
FOR OUR CAUSE, WE WILL MAKE ANY SACRIFICE!
ESPECIALLY OUR LIVES!
THE X-MEN TOOK THEIR TECHNOLOGY FOR GRANTED.
IT WAS AN ONGOING JOKE, ALL THE BEST GOODIES ON-SITE WERE SUPPOSEDLY "GIFTS" FROM THE ALIEN SHI'AR. BUT LIKE ALL THE BEST JOKES, THERE WAS AN ELEMENT OF TRUTH.
A LOT OF IT WAS DERIVED FROM SHI'AR TECH.
THAT'S HOW THE WARSKRULLS, SEN BY THE SHI'AR, KNE PRECISELY HOW TO DESTROY IT.

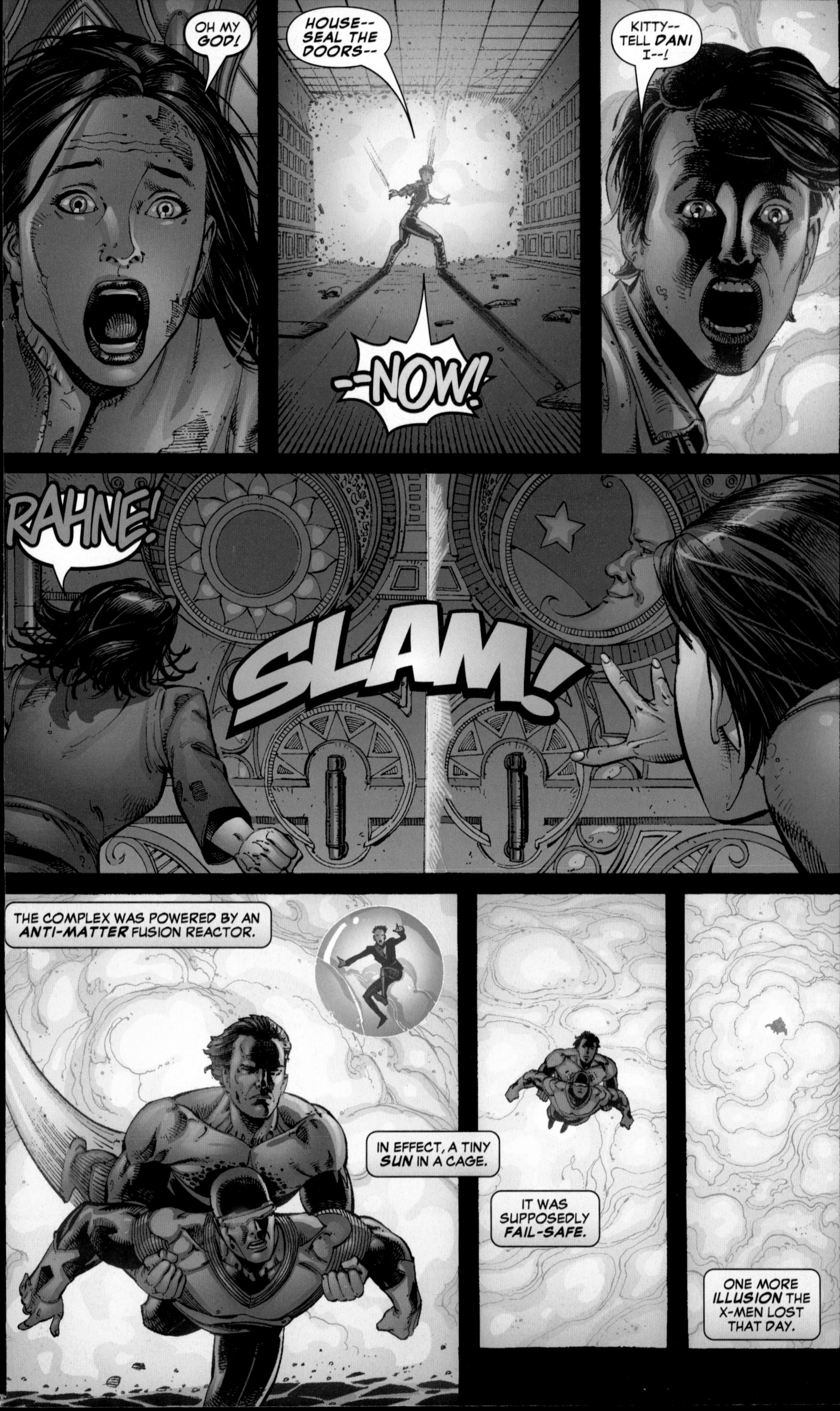
OH MY GOD!
HOUSE-- SEAL THE DOORS--
--NOW!
KITTY-- TELL DANI I--!
RAHNE!
SLAM!
THE COMPLEX WAS POWERED BY AN ANTI-MATTER FUSION REACTOR.
IN EFFECT, A TINY SUN IN A CAGE.
IT WAS SUPPOSEDLY FAIL-SAFE.
ONE MORE ILLUSION THE X-MEN LOST THAT DAY.

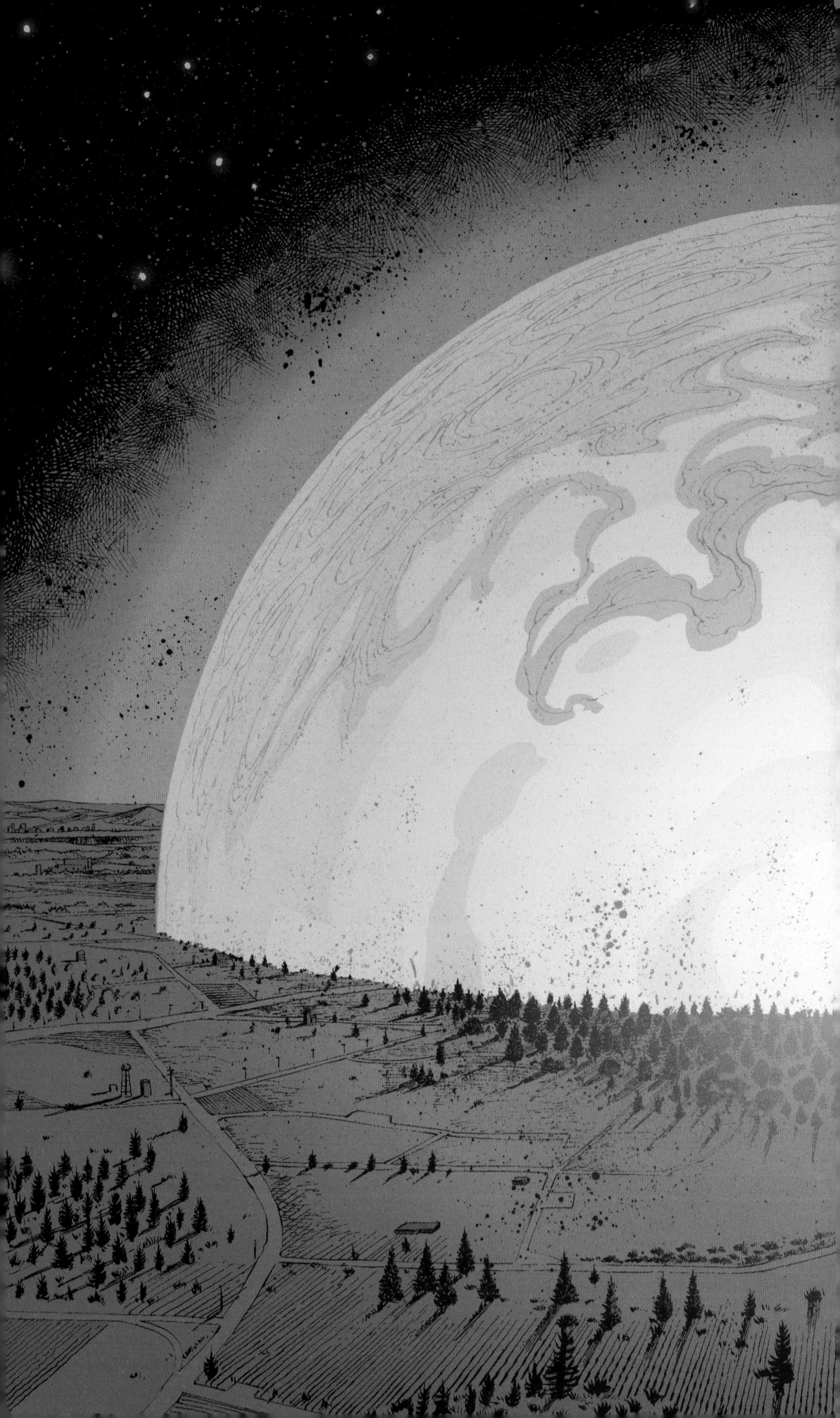

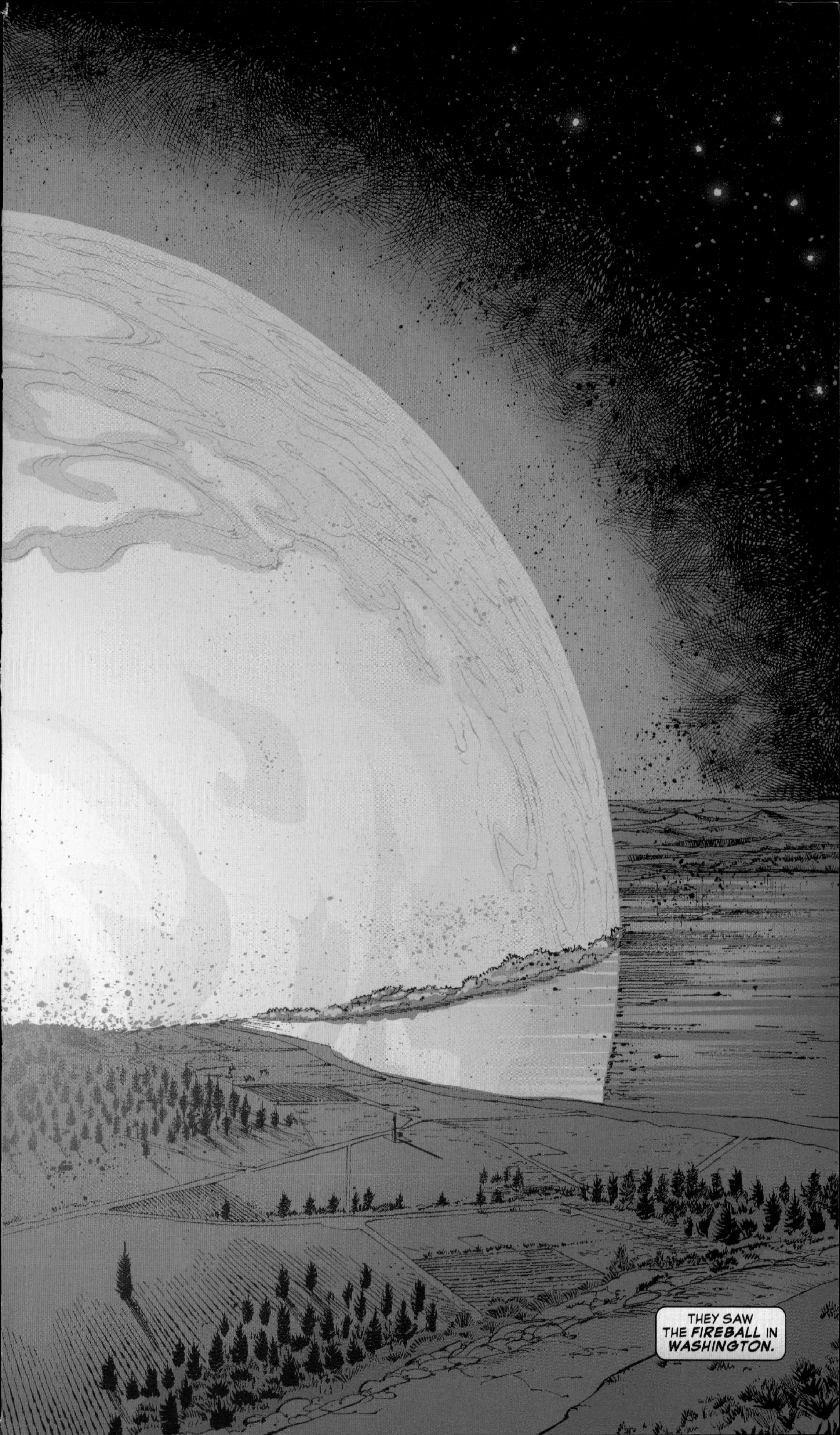
THEY SAW THE *FIREBALL* IN *WASHINGTON.*

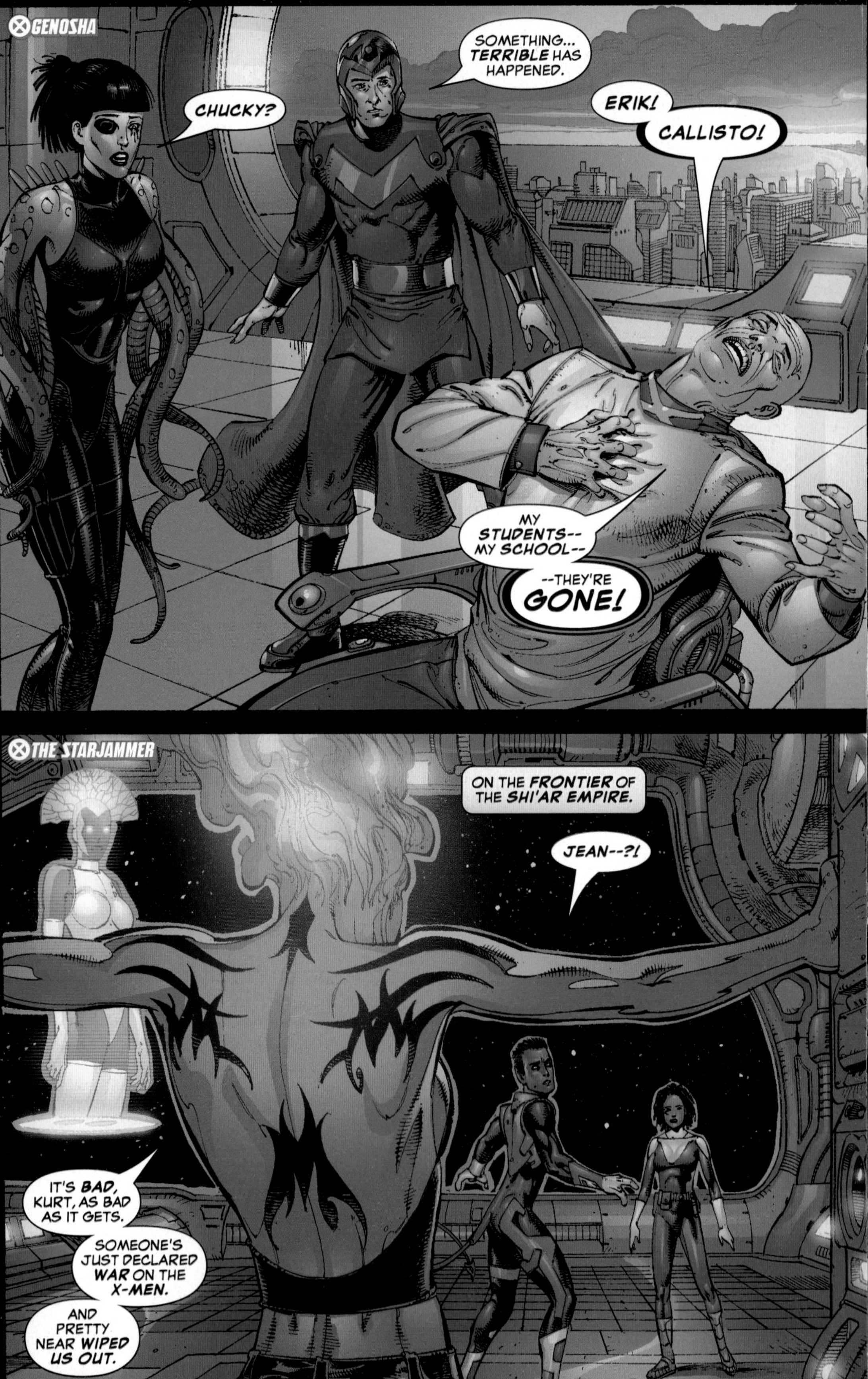
GENOSHA
CHUCKY?
SOMETHING... TERRIBLE HAS HAPPENED.
ERIK!
CALLISTO!
MY STUDENTS-- MY SCHOOL--
--THEY'RE GONE!
THE STARJAMMER
ON THE FRONTIER OF THE SHI'AR EMPIRE.
JEAN--?!
IT'S BAD, KURT, AS BAD AS IT GETS.
SOMEONE'S JUST DECLARED WAR ON THE X-MEN.
AND PRETTY NEAR WIPED US OUT.
END OF BOOK ONE
NEXT: HEROES & MARTYRS